Triumph
of the Heart

Triumph
of the Heart

Forgiveness in an Unforgiving World

MEGAN FELDMAN BETTENCOURT

HUDSON
STREET
PRESS

HUDSON STREET PRESS
Published by the Penguin Publishing Group
375 Hudson Street
New York, New York 10014   •

First published by Hudson Street Press, an imprint of Penguin Random House LLC, 2015

REGISTERED TRADEMARK—MARCA REGISTRADA

LIBRARY OF CONGRESS CATALOGING-IN-PUBLICATION DATA
Bettencourt, Megan Feldman.
Triumph of the heart : forgiveness in an unforgiving world / Megan Feldman Bettencourt.
pages cm
Includes bibliographical references and index.
978-1-59463-263-1
1. Forgiveness. I. Title.
BF637.F67.B475 2015
155.9'2—dc23
2014048570

Printed in the United States of America
1   3   5   7   9   10   8   6   4   2

Set in Warnock Pro
Designed by Alissa Rose Theodor

To my mother, Dr. Gail Carr Feldman, who taught me the transformative power of curiosity, deep listening, and compassion, and who helped me discover that storytelling is one of the most potent medicines at our disposal

The world breaks everyone, and afterwards many are strong in the broken places.
                                                    —ERNEST HEMINGWAY

As I walked out the door toward the gate that would lead to my freedom, I knew if I didn't leave my bitterness and hatred behind, I'd still be in prison.
                                                    —NELSON MANDELA

CONTENTS

INTRODUCTION

How I Reluctantly Discovered Forgiveness and Why I Set Out to Explore It

In early 2012, I found myself writing a magazine story about a remarkable man. Seventeen years earlier, Azim Khamisa was working as an international investment banker based in San Diego when his only son, a college student working a pizza delivery job, was shot to death by an aspiring teenaged gang member. Azim's response shocked everyone, from the prosecutor in the murder case to local crime reporters: He forgave the killer. He reached out to the killer's family. He befriended the killer's grandfather. And then, together, these two unlikely friends launched an organization that teaches nonviolence in public middle schools. I learned about Azim through a mutual friend who had attended one of his speaking engagements, and my interest was piqued.

I wanted to know why he forgave. I wanted to know how. And I wanted to know what it meant—for him, for me, for all of us. I was intrigued, if more than a little unsettled, for reasons I couldn't quite identify.

Forgiveness had never been my forte, nor my aspiration. If I thought of forgiveness at all, I did so with disdain, as something weak and almost pathetic. When I was two, my mother took me to the neighborhood pool. As she grabbed one of my chubby arms and led me toward the water, a middle-aged woman stopped us. "She is so *cute!*" the woman said to my mother, bending toward me with a smile. Before anyone could say or do anything, I kicked the unsuspecting stranger hard in the shin. The woman recoiled and rubbed her leg. My mother, horrified, apologized and ushered me away. When she demanded an explanation, I narrowed my eyes and stuck out my chin. "I'm not cute," I said. "I *hate* cute." Cute was for babies and docile animals. I wanted to be fierce. I wanted to be strong and smart, someone to be taken seriously. As I grew older, the idea of being forgiving seemed just as embarrassing to me as being cute did on the day I rewarded a stranger's compliment with a merciless kick.

Growing up, the more I learned about the world's injustices, the angrier I became. I was angry about the Holocaust (one of my favorite books was *I Never Saw Another Butterfly*, a compilation of art and poems by Jewish children interned at Terezin), I was angry about the U.S. genocide against the Native Americans, and I was angry that some people were reduced to sleeping on the streets and scrounging for food in dumpsters. My outrage over these injustices was linked to the fact that I seemed to feel everything—particularly the suffering I saw around me—so deeply. I remember learning about the gas chambers at Auschwitz in a middle school class. I was so devastated after the documentary we watched that I could barely speak at recess, and I was horrified—and yes, angry—to see my friends playing tag and telling stories, as if nothing had happened. I felt like I'd just discovered that the world was actually hell, and my friends were carrying on as if no one let them in on the secret. My mother, meanwhile, was a psychologist specializing in treating trauma, and I gleaned tidbits about her patients' lives. They'd been beaten by mothers, raped by fathers, stalked and nearly killed by strangers or colleagues. At one point, on the eve of middle school, misfortune struck even closer to home.

One afternoon, my best friend's father was late to pick her up from school. The next morning, my mother sat on my bed to wake me. A knockout who was normally perfectly put together, Mom's eyes were red and nearly hidden by great, swollen folds of skin. Through tears, she told me that my friend's father had killed himself, and her mother found his body. We jumped in our car and drove to their house. All I remember is the five of us—my mother and me, and my best friend, her older sister, and their mother— holding each other under a big elm in their backyard. Their family moved away that summer. I began sixth grade alone at a new school that my bestie and I had planned to attend together. At night, I filled my pink, heart-covered diary with sad, lonely entries.

When my English teacher assigned a personal essay, I wrote about what happened. I was amazed at how cathartic it was, how I felt I'd somehow made sense of something senseless, and in the process, purged some of the haunting feelings that kept me awake at night. My teacher read that essay aloud to every single one of his English classes. Peers I'd never even met approached me in the halls to say how the piece moved them. Some confided that they, too, had experienced puzzling tragedies in their young lives, and that they related to what I'd written. Unwittingly, I had stumbled upon something that helped me understand—or at least express my feelings about—pain and suffering, something that could perhaps also help others.

It was my outrage over injustice and pain, as well as my fascination with the ways in which people overcame tragedy, that led me to journalism. I focused on stories about suffering and triumph: addicts finding unique ways to recover, fathers fighting unjust paternity laws, war widows launching support groups for other grieving loved ones, and Central American migrants fleeing poverty and violence to ride freight trains fifteen hundred miles to the U.S. border. In my twenties, I spent almost two years living in Guatemala and reporting on the ways people were trying to remake their lives after a thirty-six-year civil war.

By the time I met Azim, my penchant for indignant anger and even blame hadn't faded. In fact, I was more pissed off than ever.

At thirty-three, I was trying to earn a living as a freelancer in Denver, Colorado. While my friends were buying houses and getting married, I was receiving rejections from editors and stocking my cupboards with beans and canned tuna fish. I'd arrived in Denver after working for several years for a newspaper in Dallas. While I enjoyed the job, I grew up in the Mountain West, a devotee of forests and ski trails and alpine streams, and I felt like a dying aspen tree amid Dallas's concrete and shopping malls. By 2010, most journalism jobs had dried up, which fueled my general bitterness. Unable to imagine staying in Texas any longer, I made the impulsive decision to move back to Colorado and try my luck freelancing. I published some well-received magazine feature articles, moonlighted as a part-time professor, and launched a new Web site with a professional head shot and a respectable portfolio. But I was also accruing credit card debt and borrowing money from my parents, which I considered a blazing sign of failure, and most of my story ideas were rejected with notes like, *This sounds like a powerful story, Megan, but we're going to pass.* If you want to find out just how angry and disillusioned you can get, try a career like acting or writing that has you squaring off against rejection at every turn. You'll quickly plumb the depths of your capacity for discomfort.

In the winter of 2011, after months of rejection notes, I was finally assigned a profile of an outdoorsy software engineer who created skiing apps, but the assignment evaporated when a larger company bought the engineer's firm and said they didn't want to be featured in a publication alongside ads for local head shops. Probably because it was a near-success after traversing what felt like a desert of failure, it undid me. I broke down on the floor of my apartment, sobbing into the carpet next to my bed.

I felt ridiculous. My father, a physician, and my mother, a psychologist, had worked their entire lives, doing what they loved and providing me and my sister with a comfortable life and myriad opportunities. They'd given me everything, and here I was, floundering. The shame. I blamed myself for choosing so fickle a profession and for not being great enough at it to make more money. I blamed editors for not assigning stories or for failing to hire me. I even blamed my parents, for "letting" me pursue such an unstable profession. Even as I told myself to get up and get over it, I became immobilized by the racked sobs of a hyperventilating toddler throwing a tantrum. I spotted a stack of magazines nearby and snatched one. Without thinking, I ripped it up. I did the same with the rest, tearing them up one by one. I found the methodical ripping somewhat comforting. When they were gone, I lay, quiet and spent, in the sea of shredded paper.

Since such moments always seem to come in twos or threes, my relationship with the man I was dating soon unraveled in spectacular—and dramatically public—fashion. Instead of the private fight that heralds most breakups, this death knell tolled in the form of an improv show called Blind Date.

We were there with two other couples. There was my longtime friend Lara, a tall strawberry blond attorney whose sunny disposition makes her seem an unlikely prosecutor; my friend Rachael, a pilot and former model; and their boyfriends. When we walked into the bar outside the theater, the improv star was working the crowd. She would choose a man from the audience to play her date onstage—for a whopping ninety minutes. Lara and Rachael's boyfriends defined their strategies quickly: They would be quiet and nonresponsive, rude even, to avoid getting picked. My boyfriend didn't take that route. No, when the actress turned to him, he continued to be his friendly, warm social self.

Her character name was Mimi, and her buxom figure was clothed in a tight red dress that emphasized her cleavage in a classic, decidedly non-trashy way. Speaking with a French accent, she introduced herself. Then she asked how long we'd been dating (ten months) and how we'd met (mutual friends). Mike returned her smile and shook her hand, and as the bar announced last call, the three of us chatted amiably. As we made our way into the darkened theater, Mimi asked if I would be okay with her choosing Mike as her date. "Sure," I said. Sure, as if she were asking me if I take sugar with my tea. If it was a strange situation in which to find myself, I didn't let on. I just flashed a steely smile and acted like it was the most normal thing in the world—just more amusing—for a sexy, flirtatious actress with a tight dress and a French accent to yank my boyfriend away for the evening.

Later, I would look back and wonder what the hell I had been thinking. Of course, I wasn't thinking at all. I was reacting. And when it came to foreign or threatening situations, for as long as I could remember my reaction was to cling at all costs to the role of the Cool Girl, rolling with the punches, going with the flow, acting as if I could take it all in stride. Growing up skiing in the mountains of New Mexico and Colorado, I knew that the moment you got scared and hesitated, you were liable to lose your balance and cartwheel into the air to land in a heap of wrecked bones and equipment. The way to traverse the rough patches was to grin and flex your muscles, to soldier through without letting on that that steep pitch was really freaking you out.

Of course, if I'd considered the analogy, I would have conceded that at a certain point, fear and the action it precipitates—say, roaring to a halt at the edge of a cliff—are lifesaving. But I didn't. I responded to discomfort with a stiff smile, a laugh, or the occasional sarcastic zinger. Lascivious comments hurled by men twice my age received a half smile that said, "I heard you but I'm in no way affected by your idiocy." The time my best friend and I rolled a car going eighty miles per hour and miraculously emerged with minor scrapes, I transformed into a congenial, plastic-faced talk show host on fast-forward, chirpily questioning the EMTs about their jobs and kids and hometowns as if I spent all of my days chatting with strangers while strapped to a gurney in the back of a speeding ambulance.

So on that clear October night in 2011, as I took my seat in the theater and waited for my boyfriend to walk onstage with another woman in front of several hundred people, I stared straight ahead as my friends, on either side of me, cast questioning glances my way. I laughed. *It's fine. Life's nothing if not an adventure, right?*

The set was simple: a red-cloth-covered table set for two with a chandelier overhead. Mimi, in her formfitting scarlet dress and bright red lipstick, sat waiting. Mike stepped onto the stage. He mumbled an introduction, shook her hand, and sat down. Normally pale, he was now the color of a fluorescent glow-in-the-dark skeleton. Gone was his usual gregarious personality, his smiles and jokes. When vivacious Mimi asked him a series of get-to-know-you questions, he nearly whispered the answers. A pained silence settled over the crowd.

And then she asked the question.

"So, do you want kids?"

I felt an involuntary intake of breath, as if a ghost had jabbed me hard below the sternum. This was a point of contention. I'd always thought I wanted children, but as I advanced into my thirties and a decade of being single or in long-term relationships that didn't stick stretched into fifteen years, I wondered if it was wise to want something that seemed so out of my control. Maybe I was mistaking the fear of running out of time for actual desire. And yet, his resistance deeply troubled me.

"I don't think so," he replied, still stiff and uneasy.

Every muscle in my body was suddenly on alert, coiled, tense. My jaw clamped as I gripped the sides of my chair.

Mimi looked surprised. "But how do you know for sure?" she asked.

"I don't, but I'm leaning toward no."

A tux-clad waiter appeared and took Mike's order: whiskey on the rocks. He gulped it down and ordered another. This time the waiter returned with an entire bottle of Jack Daniels. As Mike drank, that wooden board of a man none of those in our group recognized loosened up and morphed back into the jovial guy we thought we knew. He even scored a few jokes. You could almost feel the audience breathing a collective sigh of relief.

Mimi invited him to her "flat," and they mimed hopping into her car and driving across Paris, bouncing along in an imaginary vehicle rolling over imaginary cobblestones. Once they arrived—Mike taking large swigs from the bottle of liquor while seated in the imaginary car—they opened the pretend doors, climbed out, and sat down on an all-too-real velvet sofa on the edge of the stage. Mimi managed to extract from him the fact that he was a musician, and with the snap of the fingers she summoned her assistant. The actor who had played the waiter reappeared moments later, as if by magic, with a guitar. "Will you play me a song?" Mimi asked Mike, batting her eyelashes at him like a cartoon Bambi. He obliged, and as soon as he strummed the first few chords, my stomach churned. The guitar was badly out of tune, but I could hear well enough to identify the song as one he'd written after a breakup. Perfect. Now there were three people up there—him, a sultry French vamp, and an ex-girlfriend.

"Wow, you wrote that about a girl?" Mimi breathed, sidling closer to him on the sofa. Was it just me, or was the entire audience tense but pretending this was mildly entertaining? I could no longer tell where I ended and the rest of the crowd began. It felt like I was floating above the room, detached from my hammering heart, sliding up against the ceiling. Mimi leaned in for a kiss and Mike paused like a deer facing a pair of sun-sized headlights. Somewhere below me I heard my voice. "Bullshit!" I called, just as Mimi had instructed me to do if I felt overly uncomfortable. My voice rang through the darkened room, high and tinny, foreign, distorted.

Mimi addressed the audience and said she was pausing the skit. She looked out into the crowd and called to me from inside her spotlight bubble: "Megan, is it okay if we fast-forward to five years from now?" I nodded numbly.

The stage darkened and the lights came up to reveal a bedroom set. In this five-years-hence future, Mimi and Mike were married and shared a flat in Paris. Mike was a touring musician, and Mimi was . . . pregnant. *Oh, dear God.* She appeared on stage with a ball protruding from beneath her dress and waddled toward Mike. Wait a second. Wasn't the first rule of improv that you empower whatever your partner comes up with? As in, if he says he's a Purple People Eater or a pink elephant or a Maori warrior, you go right along with it and act as if he absolutely is that? And if he says he doesn't want kids, you don't emerge with a goddamned baby in your belly?

Mike, now dressed in a robe and clutching the half-empty bottle of Jack, wheeled to face her. He spotted the mound at her abdomen and his face turned to stone. "I told you on our first date that I didn't want kids," he said, his voice low, even, and cold as lead. "Remember?" The icy, razor-sharp resentment was as real as the bottle in his hand. *Holy shit. I knew stay-at-home-daddy wasn't on his bucket list, but where did Charles Manson come from?*

"Well, yes," Mimi stammered, taken aback but doing her best to remain the sweet, embattled French wife. "But then we got married, and, and now I'm pregnant . . ."

He cut her off, spitting out the words like bullets: "I'm gone all the time, the band isn't doing great, and money's tight. This is *not* good timing."

While the face of me-sitting-in-the-audience formed a frozen mask, me-on-the-ceiling noticed that sounds became muted, the lights and faces shimmering into a jumble of shapes. Far away on the stage, Mimi and Mike continued their argument, as Mimi tried to make it funny and save the show. Audience members booed and some called Mike a jerk—mostly men, it sounded like.

Mimi mimicked labor, her already-huge doe eyes growing wider and her red lips forming a circle. She lay on the bed, the waiter/assistant appeared in scrubs, and Mike crouched at the side of the bed to feign the reluctantly helpful husband. Finally, to the soundtrack of the audience's cries and strained laughter, a baby doll shot out from under Mimi's dress. Mike caught it. Then he stood up, stepped toward the edge of the stage, and hurled it into the crowd.

Afterward, at the bar next door, Mike looked at me, drunken sadness and fear etched into his features. His thirty-one-year-old face looked about twelve. "Are you okay?" he said. "Do we have to talk about anything?"

"We'll talk tomorrow," I replied, alcohol and digestive juices sloshing together in my stomach.

But the next day didn't improve matters. It just so happened that the *Denver Post* theater critic had chosen that evening to review the play. He described Mike as "a caveman who just kept blurting out creepy, date-killing kinds of remarks that, in 99 percent of cases, would result in slapped cheeks." The play served as a giant cosmic megaphone, announcing what I'd feared but resisted acknowledging—that Mike and I weren't compatible. And yet, in spite of the growing evidence and the radiating ball of anxiety in my chest, I tried to convince myself otherwise. That meant sticking around for a few more months, hoping something would change. Have you ever been craving something you can't quite identify, and even though there's nothing in the refrigerator that qualifies, you stand there, staring at the nearly empty shelves and waiting in vain for something delicious to materialize? It was like that. And then, the day before Valentine's Day, we took a walk in the park near my apartment.

The snow was white as a bone left out in the desert, so bright it hurt my eyes even though I wore sunglasses. The midday sun wrapped its harsh glare around us. "I'm just not life-partner material," he kept saying. Um, okay. But couldn't he have said that before? But of course, he had. In spite of insisting on numerous occasions that he was ready and committed, in spite of telling me he thought I had some sort of gift of enlightenment be-cause I made all of the people around me want to be better—including him—and calling me "Bee," because he said I was sweet like honey and always busy—in spite of all of that, he'd been giving lightning-bright sig-nals that he was, in fact, not at all committed to the future I wanted. (He basically resisted any discussion of the future.) The play was just the most recent and glaring of those signals. Yet I still refused to accept it.

I stopped. Turned to him in the snow that crunched under my run-ning shoes. Took off my sunglasses. "If that's true," I said, "then I want you to tell me you're not in love with me."

He turned. Slowly took off his shades. "I'm not in love with you."

"Then there's nothing left to say." I walked away, my shoes making tracks in the white dusting over the grass.

At first, I was angry and bitter because I felt misled. Later, though, I would realize that more than anything, I was angry at myself for ignoring what deep down I knew to be true and lying to myself about it. I once read that self-betrayal is the worst kind, and I would have to agree. The most humiliating part was that I'd done it so many times before—tried to force something to work when it just wasn't right. There was Ollie, the Norwe-gian tennis player who stood me up for the senior prom, Chris, my college boyfriend who called me selfish because I didn't pay for his cocktails, and Ricardo, a man I managed to fall in love with in my early twenties despite the fact that he was a decade my senior, with a pending divorce and two kids. There were guys whom I worked with and admired, generous, won-derful souls whom I tried to love in spite of scant physical attraction, and there was the one who drank too much and once became physically violent. Now, as I trudged through the snow back to my apartment, I felt as if I were accompanied by at least a dozen ghosts of boyfriends past, the infuriating reminders of failures and disappointments billowing around me like smoke.

There's a story about a baboon that Charles Darwin chronicled in 1871, after hearing about it from the zoologist who witnessed it:

At the Cape of Good Hope an officer had often plagued a certain baboon, and the animal, seeing him approaching one Sunday for parade, poured water into a hole and hastily made some thick mud, which he skillfully dashed over the officer as he passed by, to the amusement of many bystanders. For long afterwards the baboon rejoiced and triumphed whenever he saw his victim. (!)

By 2012, I may have been intrigued by forgiveness, but my tendencies still ran more in the direction of that baboon. I would have loved nothing more than to throw a bucket of shit in my ex-boyfriend's face, cackling with glee. I was angry at him. I was angry at myself. I was angry at the economy and the so-called death of journalism.

Sometimes it takes a powerful story to take you out of your own and set you on a new, better path. For me, that story was Azim Khamisa's. If forgiveness helped him, could it help me and others? Was there any scientific evidence that actually showed that it improved health and happiness? I did a few Internet searches and found that over the past twenty years, multiple studies have shown that forgiveness can indeed improve physical and emotional well-being, and that it may even be a crucial survival skill developed throughout human evolution. Wanting to learn more, I embarked on an inward and outward adventure.

I decided to travel throughout the United States and even to the heart of Africa to explore a series of questions: Is forgiveness merely altruistic and self-sacrificial, or is it also motivated by self-interest? Is forgiveness possible after the most extreme of offenses, such as genocide? Is forgiveness natural, and does it provide health benefits? What are the roles, and the importance, of apology and redemption? How does forgiveness help sustain interpersonal relationships? Is forgiveness a onetime event, or a habit? And, if individuals can practice forgiveness, what about communities and even nations?

These questions led me to a series of people, from a burn surgeon in Louisiana to a recovering alcoholic in Arizona. I talked to scientists, therapists, and trauma survivors; I interviewed people about forgiving parents and sought the wisdom of happy couples on the role of forgiveness in romance. I observed programs that facilitate forgiveness in schools, including one that's nearly eradicated fighting in a tough Baltimore neighborhood and another that mediates bullying in suburban New Jersey. In Rwanda, I met an extraordinary woman with one of the most moving tales of survival and triumph I have ever heard, and at a mountain summer camp in New Mexico, I watched as Israeli and Palestinian teens came together to confront the judgments they held of one another and the humanity they shared. I also attended a forgiveness ceremony, experimented with how forgiveness relates to mindfulness meditation, and mined my own past to make peace with a dark chapter.

This book is about the discoveries I made, the captivating people I met along the way, and how they changed my life. Throughout, I was constantly aware of the absurdity of comparing my own experiences to those of someone like Azim. How can you equate a breakup or professional struggle to the loss of a child? You can't. Yet ultimately, I would conclude that in light of how Azim and the other extraordinary people in this book responded to tragedy—and the possibilities their responses have created—the rest of us have a moral obligation to examine their choices, reflect upon our own, and give forgiveness a try. Because, as I would discover, through developing our innate ability to seek and grant forgiveness, we can bolster our health and happiness, improve our relationships, and maybe even make the world a more peaceful place.

It turns out that forgiveness isn't what I thought it was. Thank God.

Triumph
of the Heart

1

The Heart of Darkness: How Two Lives Were Taken and Two Friends Were Made

On the morning of January 22, 1995, Azim Khamisa was standing in the kitchen of his La Jolla, California, townhouse in his nightshirt when his phone rang. He'd returned from a business trip to Mexico the night before and was enjoying a relaxing Sunday morning, sipping tea and looking out the window at the fountain in his courtyard as he answered the phone. The words sounded jumbled and incomprehensible: "Your son . . . shot . . . dead . . ."

He was sure it was a mistake. He hurried the detective off the phone and dialed twenty-year-old Tariq's number, but there was no answer. He then called Tariq's fiancée, Jennifer, and when she picked up the phone, she was crying so hard that she could barely speak. As he listened to her choking out the words to confirm the news, the truth suddenly registered throughout his body. Azim's knees buckled. He fell backward, hitting his head on the refrigerator, and as the phone crashed to the floor, he was enveloped by a shattering, all-encompassing pain that he would forever describe as "a nuclear bomb detonating" in his heart.

Soon after, a close friend arrived to comfort him and they sat in a daze together at his dining room table. The artwork around them—a painting of an elephant called the Lone Tusker that reminded Azim of his native Kenya; another of a skier gliding down a snow-covered mountain that evoked memories of teaching Tariq to ski—suddenly seemed like artifacts from a past life. A detective came over and told him that witnesses reported four teens running from the car where Tariq, felled by a single bullet that tore through his heart and lungs, drowned in his own blood after a botched

robbery. The police were still searching for the teenagers. After the inves-
tigator left, Azim's friend shook his head. "I hope they find those bastards
and fry them," he said. He was thinking of his own son, who was twelve,
and how he would feel if anyone harmed him.

Azim was slow to respond, but what he said was startling.

"I don't feel that way," he said. "There were victims at both ends of
that gun."

The words rolled out of his mouth and when he heard them, the meaning rang true. He felt they came from God.

The next morning, Ples Felix sat in his car outside a modest apartment
building in the middle-class San Diego neighborhood of North Park, fifteen
miles southeast of La Jolla. Minutes earlier, he'd called the police to report
that his fourteen-year-old grandson, Tony Hicks, had run away and was
holed up here, inside the apartment where the boy's friend Hakeem lived
with his mother. Before watching the officers disappear through the front
door, Ples warned them that there were probably gang members inside. He
didn't know that the officers were pursuing his grandson for something
exponentially more serious than merely running away.

Tony had recently stopped doing his homework and started ditching
school. Ples, whom Tony called "Daddy," had tried to talk sense into his
grandson, but over the weekend he'd returned home to find the teenager
gone. A brief note read, "Daddy, I love you. But I've run away." By Monday,
Ples had been able to track him to this apartment complex.

Now, as he sat across the street, Ples prayed things would go smoothly.
Like many people from South Central Los Angeles, he'd grown up amid
unsettling violence and hardship, and at age sixteen, he had fathered a
child—his daughter, Loeta. When Loeta was sixteen, she gave birth to
Tony, who spent his first eight years living in gang-ridden chaos, which
included witnessing his favorite cousin being gunned down in a drive-by
shooting. Loeta thought Tony would stand a better chance under the wing
of his grandfather, so she shipped him off to the comparatively gentle en-

virons of San Diego. With Ples's guidance and structure, Tony went from well behind grade-level to earning Bs in school—until adolescence, when the rigid household rules began to grate and the approval of Tony's homies took precedence over grades and family.

Ples's prayers were interrupted when the San Diego PD reappeared. As an officer led Tony in cuffs to a police cruiser, Ples took one last look and drove to work.

That afternoon, he was sitting at his desk in downtown San Diego, where he worked as a city planner, when a homicide detective called. Tony wasn't merely being held as a runaway; he was a prime suspect in a murder investigation. A tipster had led police to Tony and his friends, who apparently had dubbed themselves "The Black Mob." The facts would soon fall into place: After fleeing his home on Saturday, Tony spent the day with Hakeem and the gang's ringleader, Antoine "Q-Tip" Pittman, playing video games and smoking weed. Later that evening, they called in an order to a nearby pizzeria, with the intent to rob the deliveryman.

Tony, who'd been bestowed the nickname "Bone" by the group, slipped a stolen nine-millimeter semiautomatic handgun into his waistband and walked with Q-Tip and two other teen gang members to a Louisiana Street apartment complex, where the pizza was being delivered. When they arrived, Tariq Khamisa—a college student who'd recently taken a part-time job at DiMille's Italian Restaurant to earn spending money—was leaving the building, still carrying the pizza. As the group demanded that Tariq hand over the pizza, Tony drew his gun. Tariq refused, and clambered into his white eighties-model Volkswagen.

"Bust him, Bone!" Q-Tip shouted, as Tariq attempted to pull away. Tony aimed and squeezed. The car rolled to a stop. The boys ran. As the blood drained from Tariq's body, a father and grandfather were unknowingly being drawn into a future that they never could have imagined.

Azim and Ples, both in their late forties at the time, were unlikely ever to cross paths. Azim was the son of educated Persian merchants who settled in Kenya and practiced Sufi Islam, while Ples was born to a blue-collar black family in Los Angeles and raised Baptist. Azim studied in London and became an international investment banker; Ples studied in New York and became an urban planner.

Yet their lives show striking similarities: as a young man, Azim fled feared persecution in Kenya at the hands of the Idi Amin regime in neighboring Uganda, eventually settling in the United States; Ples left South Central LA by joining the United States Army and served two tours in Vietnam before forgoing a military career to attend college and pursue a civilian profession. Both men turned their backs on violence. On separate continents, they both learned to meditate—Azim from a Sufi friend in Africa, Ples from a monk in Vietnam—each making it a lifelong daily practice.

These similarities would enable both men to respond in extraordinary ways after Ples's only grandson murdered Azim's only son.

The day Azim and his family buried Tariq in Vancouver, where both sets of Tariq's grandparents lived, it was cold and rainy. Azim chanted prayers in a mosque with hundreds of worshippers. In accordance with tradition, he climbed down into the grave, muddy from the rain, to receive his son's body. A group of men lowered Tariq down, and Azim, rain pouring over his head, held his son for the last time, saying goodbye again and again.

In the weeks that followed, Azim contemplated suicide. Just months before, he'd been going from one international business trip to the next and working hundred-hour weeks; now he could barely rise from bed. Things like showering and eating lunch felt like enormous tasks. He couldn't sleep, so he'd begun meditating for four hours a day instead of his usual one. On a chilly day three months after Tariq's death, Azim drove to a cabin near California's Mammoth Mountain. He hoped a few days away might help break the grief that seemed to be drowning him.

When he arrived he built a fire, and as he gazed into the flames memories began to surface: Tariq collecting stones at the beach; Tariq laughing at some clever joke, his joy contagious and in contrast with his father's serious mien; Tariq asking for help balancing his checkbook. Azim had always loved numbers, acing accounting and preparing to run his father's

Peugeot dealership in his twenties. But Tariq had little interest in business; his real loves were music and art. Their differences caused friction, but the last time they saw each other, over breakfast at a popular San Diego spot called the Hob Nob, less than two weeks before the murder, they amiably traded stories about their divergent interests. Tariq said his recent trip to Kenya to visit family had strengthened his resolve to become a National Geographic photographer, and that he and his fiancée, Jennifer—both art majors at San Diego State—were considering moving to New York.

Mostly, in the quiet of the cabin, Azim felt sadness, but anger, too— anger that he wasn't somehow able to protect Tariq; anger that his son had been killed over something as trivial as a pizza; anger, most pointedly, at his adopted country. How absurd that he'd left the chaos and violence of Africa only to see his son slain on the streets of America! While Azim had set the intention to forgive months earlier, merely setting that goal couldn't replace the natural process of grieving. The intention to forgive, he was learning, was only the beginning. Amid his feelings of anger and devastation, Azim considered how, before Tariq died, news of shootings seemed faraway and inconsequential, but now he applied his business mind to sociology, obsessively studying the dire statistics of America's street wars. His son and the boy who killed him were victims of something dark and sinister, a cycle of violence for which he felt every American—including himself—was responsible.

Maybe this was what that Sufi teacher had meant. Weeks before Azim undertook his mountain retreat, a family friend and spiritual guide had told him that a soul was earthbound for forty days before departing to a new level of consciousness. But the journey, he said, could be hindered by the unreconciled feelings of loved ones who remain behind.

"I recommend you break the paralysis of grief and find a good deed to do in Tariq's name," the teacher told him. "Compassionate acts undertaken in the name of the departed are spiritual currency, which will transfer to Tariq's soul and help speed his journey."

That was it. Azim wouldn't just study violence, he would return to San Diego, consult the best minds he knew, and devise a plan to change the status quo. Somehow, he also knew that if he didn't reach out to the killer's family and forgive them—maybe even invite them to join his crusade—he'd forever be a victim of his anguish. When, at the end of the weekend on Mammoth Mountain, he drove back toward the California coast, it was with a renewed sense of purpose.

While attorneys argued over whether Tony would be tried as an adult (a new state law subjected fourteen- and fifteen-year-olds to full adult felony charges), Ples prayed for a way to help Tariq's family. Then, one day he received a call from Tony's attorney, who said that Azim wanted to meet him. The invitation came at a particularly emotionally wrenching time. Many North Park residents wanted Tony to receive the maximum penalty, and some, upon learning that the accused killer's grandfather was managing a local redevelopment effort, demanded the city fire him from the project. The mayor refused, but the verbal attacks, coupled with a probable life sentence for Tony, had taken a toll.

Ples wore a suit and tie on the day he met Azim at Tony's attorney's office. Azim arrived with prosecutor Peter Deddeh, who made the initial introduction. Ples had anticipated this moment for months. As he shook Azim's hand he said, "If there's anything I can do to be a support to you and your family, please call on me." He added that Azim had been in his daily prayers and meditations.

Ples's mention of meditation struck Azim as fortuitous, and he immediately felt close to this man. "We both lost a child," he told Ples. Then he explained that he was launching the Tariq Khamisa Foundation, founded with the goal of preventing children from committing senseless violent crimes. He even invited Ples to attend upcoming meetings about the organization. Ples felt a weight start to lift.

A week later, Azim held one of the foundation's first meetings at his townhouse. His parents had come in from Vancouver for the occasion. Also there were his ex-wife, Almas, and their daughter, Tariq's sister, Tasreen.

Ples imagined the grief he would walk into at that meeting, and prepared with more meditation than usual.

Inside, some fifty people were gathered, and Azim introduced Ples to his parents. His father was frail, but fixed Ples with a clear, steady gaze, accepting his condolences and placing a hand on his arm in welcome. Azim's mother, a devout woman who for decades served tea daily during four a.m. prayers at her local mosque, said, "We're glad you are with us." Almas, Tariq's mother, took Ples's hand, and as he looked into her eyes he could feel her trembling. "I'm so sorry for your loss," Ples said, feeling deep, heavy sadness and the sense that any words he might say were about as impactful as a few minuscule water droplets flung onto a raging fire. "I've been praying for your family."

When he was invited to speak to the group en masse, Ples glanced at some notes he'd made, then folded and returned them to his pocket. Looking around, he saw people of all ages—Azim's friends, colleagues, neighbors. He began by expressing his condolences for the loss of Tariq. He was unspeakably sorry that his grandson had been involved, he said, and thanked Azim for reaching out to him and inviting him to this meeting. As those gathered in the living room listened in silence, Ples said he was determined to help prevent the type of violence that claimed Tariq's life and landed Tony in jail. He was committed, he told them, to "support anything that promotes the precious value of our future: our children."

Unlike most victims' families, who track a case's every twist in pursuit of justice, Azim told the prosecuting attorney that he preferred to leave the legal maneuvering to the state and focus on violence prevention. Today, the Tariq Khamisa Foundation teaches the virtues of nonviolence to middle-schoolers in San Diego and young people nationwide. TKF raises $1.5 million annually for educational, mentoring, and community service programs that target at-risk youth. The centerpiece of the program features Azim and his surprise ally, Ples, sharing their story at school assemblies. Educators who have opened their doors to the duo say gang activity and discipline problems have dipped as a result. TKF has reached nearly one million kids in San Diego County through live presentations, plus another eight million through Azim and Ples's visits to schools in Canada, Europe, and Australia, and broadcasts on Channel One News (broadcast in schools throughout the United States).

After launching TKF, Azim partnered with an Ohio-based nonprofit called the National Youth Advocate Program to create Constant and Never Ending Improvement, or CANEI, a program that teaches nonviolence and personal responsibility to young offenders and their families. As of this writing, it operates in seven cities. The concept of forgiveness is key to both programs, and in addition to lecturing on the topic in cities around the world, Azim leads two-day workshops for individuals, therapists, and community groups entitled "Forgiveness: The Crown Jewel of Personal Freedom."

While Azim was laying the foundations for those programs, Tony's case plodded forward. In May 1995, a judge ruled that Tony, then fifteen, would be tried as an adult. Tony's attorney notified Ples and asked if he would talk to his grandson. While in custody, Tony was still posturing as street tough (during interrogations he'd referred to Tariq as a "stupid pizza man" who should have just handed over the food), which wouldn't serve him well in court. He faced twenty-five years to life if, in advance of a trial, he pled guilty to first-degree murder, or forty-five years to life if he chose the trial route.

At juvenile hall, Tony sat sullenly, silent in a blue jumpsuit while his attorney laid out his options. The lawyer then left grandson and grandfather alone, and Tony's hard exterior softened as Ples began to talk to him. He reminded the teenager of the pain Azim and his family endured as they faced this unforeseen world that no longer included their beloved son. He reminded Tony that in spite of this pain, Azim had managed to forgive him. He emphasized that just as Azim's life would never be the same since Tariq died, so Tony's life was also forever changed, and Azim felt sad about that. As Tony listened in silence, Ples handed him an orange.

The boy soon began to cry—maybe because this reminded him of his grandfather's ritual of talking while they shared some fruit, or perhaps because the gravity of his predicament had finally hit him. As if he were suddenly five again, he jumped into Ples's lap. "Daddy, I'm so sorry for what I did," he sobbed. "I never wanted to hurt anybody, I was just angry, stupid." He grew quiet after a moment and returned to his seat. He took the orange, peeled it, and gave half to his grandfather. Then, his body trembling, he seemed to momentarily shrug off his childlike personality and calmly spoke like a man twice his age: "I have to take responsibility for what I did."

Tony, the first juvenile to be prosecuted as an adult in California, took a plea bargain and was sentenced to twenty-five years to life. He won't be eligible for parole until at least 2020.

The Sufi poet Rumi is one of Azim's favorite writers, and in those first years after Tariq's death, one line often thundered through his mind: "The cure for the pain is the pain." Even as he spent his days meditating and building the foundation's programs with his daughter, Tasreen, who became TKF's executive director, he operated under a shroud of profound sadness. It permeated every waking moment, and most sleeping ones. How could he feel joy when Tariq was dead? It was impossible. And yet, one evening while out with friends, nearly four years after the murder, someone told a joke and he found himself laughing—for the first time since Tariq's death.

In the spring of 2000, five years after the crime, Azim traveled to California State Prison near Sacramento for his first one-on-one encounter with Tony. He had spent countless hours meditating in preparation, but as he made his way through the prison's maze of dim hallways and high walls topped with barbed wire, his heart pounded. He wondered how he would react to meeting his son's killer, and thought about how cold and inhuman the prison felt. When he reached the visiting area, Ples was there to greet him, with Tony by his side. Azim shook the young man's hand and looked into his eyes. The three of them made small talk about prison life and shared some candy, then Ples left them alone.

Tony was fidgety at first but grew more composed as they began to talk. He struck Azim as much more polite and well-spoken than he had expected. Tony told him that he was sorry for shooting Tariq and for causing Azim and his family so much pain. He said he had a lot of problems in his life, but that was no excuse for what he did. He said he should have listened to his grandfather, and he was sorry he didn't. Could Azim ever forgive him? Azim replied that he forgave him with his whole heart. Then he told Tony that he wanted to hear about Tariq's last moments. Tony said he didn't recall Tariq saying anything. He described the scene and Q-Tip's order to shoot. And then he said something strange. He said that as he squeezed the trigger, he saw a bright white light that came from the sky and illuminated only him and Tariq. He described it like a massive spotlight. Combined with the coroner's description of the unlikely "perfect path" the single bullet took through Tariq's vitals, this luminous vision reinforced Azim's conviction that his son's death was destiny and should serve a larger purpose.

Azim told Tony that he looked forward to his release from prison, expressed his hope that he would join Ples and him at the foundation, and hugged him goodbye.

Within a few months, Azim and Tony began writing to each other. Azim keeps their letters in a thick folder in his home office, where the walls are covered with framed photos (Tasreen's wedding, Tariq on the African savannah) and award certificates, including the California Peace Prize and the National Crime Victims Special Community Service Award, presented to him by President Bill Clinton.

Azim's letters are typed on his computer; Tony's are written in looping cursive. Their correspondence touches on books, health, and family, with Azim commending Tony for completing his GED and starting college courses, and Tony wishing Azim a happy Father's Day and congratulating him on becoming a grandfather. In one letter, Tony thanks Azim for keeping him informed about "the great work that you and my grandfather have turned this around to be." In another, he describes Azim's forgiveness as "a shock" that goes "against what I believed to be the natural order of things."

In 2002, Tony got in trouble again and pled guilty to battery on a prison guard and weapons possession—a lapse that added ten years to his sentence and got him transferred to Salinas Valley State Prison, a level-four maximum-security facility.

Azim was saddened by the news of Tony's backsliding, but he continued to correspond with him, and even lobby for his freedom. In 2005, he wrote to then-governor Arnold Schwarzenegger to request that Tony's sentence be commuted. "With Tony outside the prison walls and helping the foundation," Azim wrote, "the world will be safer than it is now." He also proposed that fourteen- and fifteen-year-olds convicted of violent crimes in adult court be eligible for an earned gubernatorial commutation after ten years, arguing that lengthy prison terms for juveniles only increase their odds of continuing a life of crime if and when they're released. The governor's office responded with a form letter that acknowledged the plea without making any commitment to take action.

Azim remains unshakeable in his commitment to forgiveness as a way to heal and serve others. His foundation hires AmeriCorps volunteers to mentor high-risk middle school students in order to reduce misbehavior, since kids with attendance and discipline problems are more likely to be expelled for acting out in violence. A yearlong study of San Diego middle school students involved in TKF programs found that their number of disciplinary actions was cut by more than half.

While TKF's staffers embrace Azim's message of forgiveness and discuss it as part of their mentoring curriculum, they admit that living it can be challenging—simple but not easy, as Ples often says. TKF's mentorship supervisor, a thirty-three-year-old named Mayra Nunez, lost her older brother in a drive-by shooting when she was twelve. The shooter was never apprehended. When a guidance counselor took Nunez to see Azim speak a decade ago, she couldn't understand his message. "This man's nuts," she said to herself. Yet she was curious, and she chatted with Azim afterward and wound up speaking at his Violence Impact Forums. "It took me ten years of working at TKF, but I can honestly say I forgive that person," she says. "Part of that was being tired of living with hatred, anger, and [a desire for] revenge." She echoes what Azim says—forgiveness doesn't condone an act; it isn't for the offender, but is "a gift you give yourself."

Even Almas, Tariq's mother, has found solace in participating in these school assemblies, though it took six years before she was willing to do it. At first, she couldn't understand the way Azim was dealing with the loss of Tariq, mostly because it was so different from the way she was dealing with it. He was handling the worst event of their lives so publicly, and for her, it was so private. While Azim was in the process of launching TKF, Almas walked outside one morning to get her mail and a neighbor asked when Tariq was coming to visit. She could barely utter the words, "My son is dead." Yet by 2005, she began participating in TKF's events and talking about Tariq. "It was painful to talk about losing my son," she told me over the phone. "But the reaction I got was healing. Students would come up and hug me, write letters, and say, 'I promise I will never hold a gun or join a gang.' That meant a lot to me."

Contribution is integral to both TKF, where students participate in projects such as serving the homeless, and to CANEI, the program for juvenile offenders that Azim created with the National Youth Advocate Program. CANEI is based on restorative justice, an approach that strives to heal victims, rehabilitate offenders, and repair crime's damage to communities. Participants are required to apologize to and ask forgiveness of their victims, then to repay their debt in some way, often through service. Rehabilitating prisoners—a task that the U.S. prison system fails to do in more than 80 percent of cases—is one of Azim's greatest passions, one he often spoke about during our conversations in San Diego while I was profiling him for a magazine.

Instead of staying in a hotel while I interviewed Azim and attended his presentations at local schools, I opted to stay with my aunt, a restaurateur with a beautiful home in La Jolla, overlooking the ocean. I was thrilled to escape my lonely apartment with its stacks of bills and reminders of my breakup, including a pair of earrings, some photos, and a pile of notes and cards that I was considering throwing away.

I first met Azim on a mild April evening, at the restaurant at the La Jolla Sheraton, where he's a regular. I walked into the dining room, set with glassware and crisp white tablecloths, and spotted Azim at a small table in the corner. Wearing a suit and tie, he rose to shake my hand. A warm smile crinkled the corners of his eyes, which were clear brown under thick arched brows. We made small talk and ordered wine and entrées.

Soon, he was sipping red wine and telling me about his son, the murder, and the work that he did now. He was the first person I'd met who referred to himself as lucky after having befallen such a painful misfortune. "I met a man the other day who said it took him twenty years to acknowledge that his son had died, to come out of denial," he said. "I'm lucky that I made the choice that I did." The choice to forgive and start TKF came not from his intellect or rational mind, he told me, but from his soul. "I went to good schools, but my degrees were useless when Tariq died," he said. "The intellect can only solve so many things. But there are no problems that the soul cannot solve."

One moment, Azim was speaking passionately about the U.S. justice system's soaring recidivism rates ("Our system is lock 'em up and throw away the key, but you can't, because most criminals are paroled after an average of three years and eight months, and eighty-five percent re-offend!"), and the next, he was describing his work as a spiritual mission. "I wasn't trained in this work, I was an investment banker," he told me, speaking slowly and deliberately as he finished his last bite of fish. "But this is more meaningful to me. Investment banking was all about making money. This is about saving children's lives. What could be more important or fulfilling? That was a gift from my son. I like to say I had a soul-ular shift. I'm not the same person as when my son was alive. I led from the intellect then. I had a spiritual side, but I never brought it into my work. Now I do all the time, and I think that's why it has gone so well."

I asked if he thought people had to be religious in order to lead "from the soul," as he put it. "Not necessarily," he said. "It's about connecting with your spirit, with your heart." He often speaks to groups of parents who have lost children, and after one recent presentation, a man came up to talk to him. Like Azim, this man was a Sufi Muslim and a Rumi fan. "I was really moved by your talk," the man told him. "It reminded me of a Rumi quote: 'God will break your heart over and over and over and over again until it stays open.'"

Azim nodded as he recalled the moment. "It's true. And that's what this work is about. What life would I have if I was just angry and resentful? I wanted my life back. And I knew that the decision I made after Tariq's death would determine the quality of the rest of my life. Unless I forgave, I would remain a victim—and there's no quality of life being a victim. I have a very full life now, Megan. I kind of like this life better. Not that I don't want my son back—I'd give my eyetooth for that. But I wouldn't be doing this had he not died. So is this a tragedy or is it mysteriously meaningful? It's a bit of both."

The next morning, I sat in the back row of the Correia Middle School auditorium and watched as hundreds of students took their seats. The musty-smelling room filled with the sounds of feet shuffling and kids whispering, but the noises ceased when Azim stepped onto the stage. He began with a video about Tariq's murder. "Tariq is already dead and gone forever, and Tony is in prison for a very long time, so we're not here just to share their story," he told the children. "We're here for you. Because every one of you is a very important person, and it would break my heart if any of you ended up dead like my son, or in prison like Tony."

While the students remained still and quiet, I sat behind them and wept, wiping away my tears with the back of my sleeve. There was such pregnant possibility in the silence that had settled over these children. It seemed to me that this rare, awed focus was an acknowledgment that something they heard next might just have the power to reach out into the future and dismantle whatever crimes or mishaps or booby traps they might be unknowingly building right now, here on the precarious brink of adulthood.

"How many of you have lost a brother or sister as a result of violence?" Azim asked. Nearly a quarter of the few hundred students raised their hands. "And how many of you would want revenge if a brother or sister was killed?" Almost every hand shot up.

He said he understood. But then he countered, "Let me ask you this: Would revenge bring Tariq back?" Silence. A few heads shaking no.

Several students wanted to know what happened to Q-Tip, the eighteen-year-old who ordered Tony to pull the trigger. Azim told them he was serving two life sentences (in the weeks before Tariq's murder, Q-Tip had gunned down a homeless man outside a liquor store).

And Tariq's fiancée, the children wanted to know, how is she? Sadly, Jennifer never recovered from Tariq's death, Azim explained, and she began abusing heroin. She overdosed and died at twenty-seven. "See," he said, "that's the ripple effect of violence. . . . And do you think Tony's homeboys visit him in prison?"

"No," the children murmured.

"That's right. I visit him, his grandfather visits him, his mother visits him." Azim paused and gazed out at the sea of young faces. "I look forward to the day Tony can join us. Maybe he'll be speaking to *your* children."

I knew, as I sat there, that Azim's vision for Tony may be unrealistic. He might never get out of prison, and even if he does, there is no way to predict what he will do. Regardless, what I found mesmerizing was how Azim's hope for these children, for the chance to prevent even one of them from becoming another Tony, drives him to rise each morning, day after day, and retell the story of his son's death. How he prays that his suffering and his story might be able to change a school, a city, a community, and maybe even the world.

On my final day in La Jolla, Azim insisted on giving me a meditation lesson. "I could talk about it all day," he said, "but in order to understand you have to do it." I'd learned to meditate once in a yoga class and wanted to maintain a regular practice, but I never seemed to be able to stick to a routine for more than a few days. I arrived at his townhouse at lunchtime with a couple of sandwiches, and after we ate, he showed me into the living room. I sat down in an upholstered chair and scanned the family photographs atop the bookshelves. Many showed Tariq smiling at the camera with his round dark eyes and dimples, his whole life stretched out ahead of him.

"Take a long, deep breath," Azim said. He sat opposite me on a velvet cushion by the fireplace and beamed the sort of radiant peacefulness I associated with Buddhist monks.

I closed my eyes and did my best to follow his instructions: "The purpose of meditation is to be in your body or in your consciousness but not in your mind. What we want is to switch off the mind." Earlier, he had explained that while it's impossible to actually stop thinking, you can notice the thoughts and let them pass, instead of following each one down a tunnel into a thicket of frenzied thinking. *Right.* I'd tried that before, only to succeed for a fraction of a second—if at all. I generally lived from one to-do list item to the next, barely relishing the satisfaction of scratching one out before leaping in my mind to the next task, the next project, the next thing to be figured out or assessed or planned.

"Breath is very important," Azim continued. "It's like the reins on a horse. Breath is the reins of the mind."

As I slowed and lengthened my breaths, I began to feel heavier and more relaxed, as if my body were filled with mud. Even my eyes felt calm, softening and sinking into the sockets like snails retreating into their shells. As I listened to Azim's voice, I became aware of smaller, less prominent sounds: birds chirping in the trees outside, a truck rumbling past, water trickling through the fountain in the courtyard. Azim's voice sounded far away now, as if he were speaking through a long tube from a block away. He told me to visualize a fountain of light emanating from my third eye, the radiance cascading out around me like a halo-turned-cocoon. Somehow I felt euphoric and deeply peaceful at the same time. *Sold. I could do this every day. In fact, maybe I will.* And then the meditation, all unicorns and rainbows and butterflies, took a different turn. I had mentioned my breakup to him over dinner, when he asked me if there was anyone whom I had yet to forgive. Now, to my horror, he brought it up.

"Bring in the image of your ex-boyfriend who just broke up with you. The mind thinks in pictures better than it thinks in words, so visualization is a good way to go. Make the image large in your mind's eye . . ."

Why had I told him about that?

I breathed more deeply, willing my inner peanut gallery to shut up. And there was Mike, with his moss-colored eyes and square jaw and that ridiculous T-shirt he refused to throw away, the faded blue one that was too short and rode up to show his doughy gut.

"Set the intention that you want to release and forgive him," Azim said. "To wish him well in his life. To set him free and to also set you free."

Suddenly, I felt this raw sadness sitting in the pit of my stomach, and along with it, a bone-deep weariness spreading throughout my entire body, heavy as lead.

"Bless him and send him a prayer of gratitude for the time you had together and the lessons you learned."

As Azim spoke, I imagined that ex-boyfriend and me solemnly shaking hands, like warring colleagues who finally decided to bury the hatchet and maybe even write each other recommendation letters. *Maybe I'm better at this than I thought.*

But wait.

I didn't wish him well. He'd allowed me to believe that at least one part of my life was going well, and then pulled the rug out from under my feet. Nope. In the same way I'd desperately longed for a Cabbage Patch Kid doll when I was seven, or a goldfish named Gil when I was ten, I deeply and ardently wanted to take that imaginary ray of angelic light shooting from the center of my forehead, transform it into an iron fire poker, and wield it like a maniac, ripping that heinous old blue T-shirt to shreds.

Alrighty, then. My attempt at forgiveness, or what a friend recently referred to as "Zenny peace," was off to a grand start.

In spite of my failure at forgiveness, that trip to San Diego was like a refreshing glass of lemonade after a long hike in dry heat. As much as Azim's ability to forgive—and the topic of forgiveness itself—vexed me, it also inspired me. Even after hearing his entire story and watching him in action, I couldn't imagine how he did what he did, and I doubted I could do the same if it ever came to that. And yet, just witnessing it touched me deeply and opened the door to a world of burning questions. When I returned to Denver, it was with an expanded view of what is possible in this world.

I felt renewed and grateful to be alive, aglow from the ocean air, the visit with my aunt, and the inspiring time I spent with Azim, Ples, and TKF. I was happy to be back in my neighborhood, a bustling area near downtown Denver. It was almost as if I was seeing it all for the first time: the restaurants with outdoor patios filled with young professionals, the tapas bars and brewpubs I could walk to, the vast flagship REI store housed in a nineteenth-century brick train station. I love to wander through that store, watching people try out climbing shoes on the floor-to-ceiling faux rock wall, and admiring the rows of skis and snowboards, jackets and hiking boots, tents and kayaks. Next door to that is my favorite burger joint, My Brother's Bar, the oldest bar in Denver and the favored watering hole of Jack Kerouac and his ragtag army of beat poets immortalized in *On the Road*.

Nearby is the whimsical Little Man Ice Cream, housed in a giant metal milk jug that's nearly as tall as the surrounding buildings, which has always reminded me of my favorite children's book, *James and the Giant Peach*, or the nursery rhyme "There Was an Old Woman Who Lived in a Shoe." And down the hill is my favorite part of the neighborhood and the reason I lived there: the convergence of the Platte River and Cherry Creek. They meet in a T, with the creek spilling into the river in a series of rapids often dotted with kayakers. Miles of bike paths and running trails extend from this T and its surrounding grassy parkland; I would take a break from work every day to walk or run along the river, admiring the mallard families that swam on the surface, the red-tailed hawks that soared above and perched in the huge catalpa tree that dropped its white flowers over the rapids, and the view of the snow-capped Rocky Mountains where I loved to ski.

That blissful exuberance upon my return from San Diego lasted about three days. After that, the colors faded once more and my irritability and self-pity, like a pair of dark glasses, slid back into my life. Two close friends were recently engaged, and while we were planning engagement celebrations and bachelorette parties, I landed a magazine story about women in their thirties who were spending thousands of dollars to flash-freeze their eggs in an effort to outsmart the biological clock. It turned out that one of the most famous clinics that utilized this new egg-freezing technology was located in Denver, and women were coming from around the United States and even the world for the procedure.

With each interview, my anxiety grew. A restaurant owner from Telluride named Jennifer told me how, at her thirty-fourth birthday in 2009, she was unmarried, childless, and spending long hours battling to keep her restaurant business afloat amid the recession. "I had a baby shower to go to every other weekend, and I felt like the only person in my world who wasn't married," she said. "I was really, really tired of worrying about my biological clock." Soon after, she traveled from Telluride to the Colorado Center for Reproductive Medicine, and after enduring hormone injections and harvesting procedures—not to mention spending some $10,000—within six weeks, she had nineteen eggs cradled in a cryogenic tank, suspended in time.

One patient, a Denverite named Renee who works in financial reporting, was my age. Recently divorced, the thirty-three-year-old had elected to freeze her eggs to eliminate "the pressure of having to find somebody and immediately have a baby." When clinic physicians tested her hormone levels, they found they were similar to those of a woman in her midforties. They also discovered that she had a lower-than-normal resting follicle count (number of eggs) for someone her age. Neither problem had been detected during her annual gynecologic exams, as those visits don't typically include such tests. Six months and $20,000 later, Renée had twenty-one eggs frozen in storage.

I toyed with the idea of asking my parents for a loan to freeze my eggs, but it seemed rash. Did I even care that much about being a mother? I always assumed I would be, but it wasn't as all-encompassing a dream as being a writer was. A friend who'd recently had her first child said, "I wouldn't think about it unless you find yourself tempted to kidnap babies on the street." Sage advice. I decided to put the cryogenics on hold, realizing it was more the loneliness that bothered me, and the nagging feeling that I was far behind the universally acceptable level of achievement that I should have reached by my age.

I'm embarrassed to admit that I sometimes allowed myself to fall into what a friend calls "Facelurk mode." Intending to briefly log on to Facebook, I'd instead get sucked into poring over friends' pages and comparing myself to them, with woeful results. Those who triggered the most self-loathing were wildly different from one another, but they all provoked my insecurities like poison ivy starts a rash. There was Diane, who earned a PhD and ran a consulting business while raising three children (in truth, that sounded exhausting, but who needs truth when you're collecting convincing evidence to prove your hunch that you are an utter loser?), and Damian, who used to park the Volkswagen bus in which he lived outside the house I rented with three college roommates in order to use our bathroom and kitchen, and was now a contributing photographer for National Geographic. He seemed to be on a new adventure every week, scaling rock faces in the Himalayas, building a tree house for his son, and documenting life on the Pine Ridge Reservation in excruciatingly beautiful images that made me weep. Eventually, disgusted with my succumbing to envy instead of feeling happiness for the people I loved, I would shut off the computer.

One night, I awoke feeling nauseous. I'd dreamed that Paris Hilton had written a bestselling book and that I, broke and needing a gig, any gig, had agreed to be her publicist, trotting along behind her at book signings and juggling her purses and makeup bags. During the book tour, she refused to spend money on my lodging, and so I was forced—of course—to stay with a different ex-boyfriend in each city. All of them were happily married and most had children. In the dream, one ex and his wife tried to set me up with a man three times my age. Another ex served me breakfast while feeding his tot in a high chair, asking with pity in his eyes how my writing and love lives were going.

It was around this time that I flew into a rage over a pedicab. I was walking back from the gym one night when I started across a bridge that goes over the Platte River. Alongside the road is a raised sidewalk. I looked up to see a pedicab rolling toward me, the young man pedaling with a laughing couple in tow. It is illegal for people to ride bikes on the sidewalk, not that most people follow the law, but this was a different sort of sidewalk: If you stepped off to one side, you were in traffic, and if you stepped off to the other, you were in the river more than thirty feet below. When I spotted them barreling toward me in the murky darkness, I started and said, "Whoa—what are we going to do here?" Continuing to pedal hard, he glanced up and said, rudely, "You're gonna move unless you want to get hit." Shocked, I glanced at the oncoming traffic roaring past me to my right.

The pedicab was about fifteen feet away. The oncoming cars wouldn't stop, as the light at the next intersection was green. Just as the pedicab came within a bicycle wheel's width of me, I spotted a small break in traffic and leapt off the curb into the street. After they passed and I jumped safely back onto the sidewalk, I turned and yelled at his back, "Fuck you, you fucking asshole!" I was shaking. My face felt hot, my heart was hammering, and in my ears I heard a sound like a rushing river—much louder than the small rapids beneath me. I fired off some more expletives and briefly considered trying to chase the pedicab down so I could identify it to police. For a moment, the yelling was gratifying. But then I immediately felt foolish.

As I neared my apartment, I thought about Azim. I remembered watching him talk at the restaurant, his face flushed with passion, his hands drawing forceful shapes in the air to emphasize his points. I seriously doubted he ever shouted obscenities at people. Not only that, he had one thousand times the right to be miserable as I did, and yet he was not. He was huge, and suddenly I felt so small. When had I become this way? I used to travel frequently and live abroad, but I hadn't left the country in three years. Instead of doggedly searching for stories that I thought could create positive change and waking up in the middle of the night with new ideas like I used to, I spent my evenings ruminating about money and complaining to my mother over the phone. Entering my building under the twinkling stars, I felt about the size of a grain of sand. Sure, I'd been subsisting on Kraft between measly freelance checks and had recently walked away from yet another failed relationship, but what right did that unoriginal collection of mediocre complaints give me to rail at God like Job?

I was ashamed. But I also felt that growing sense of curiosity and inspiration. Azim and Ples had taken the most horrific experience of their lives and fashioned it into a battle cry for a better world. They took the thing that made them want to die, and used forgiveness to make it their reason to live. They seemed to have reached a sort of pinnacle of humanity. What exactly was this mystical and mysterious thing called forgiveness, anyway? And, was there scientific proof that it actually helped people?

I decided to find out.

2

The Science: Is Forgiveness Natural, and Does It Provide Health Benefits?

Being the skeptical journalist that I was, I immediately wanted to know two things: First, is there scientific evidence showing that forgiveness improves our physical and psychological health? And second, what exactly is forgiveness and how is it defined?

I discovered by searching a few scholarly databases online that over the past twenty-five years, a growing number of scientists pulled forgiveness from the realm of preaching and prophesy into the terrain of academic research. It began in the eighties with a few Christian psychologists who wondered if clinical studies would bear out the Bible's teachings on the virtue of forgiveness. Then it grew into a larger, more diverse group of researchers that included social scientists and cardiologists, neuroscientists and molecular biologists. They conducted their studies at institutions throughout the United States and around the world. I homed in on two bodies of research: The first examines the detrimental physical and psychological effects of stress and anger; the second explores the physical and psychological effects of forgiveness. My preliminary searches yielded studies showing that forgiving can help alleviate everything from high blood pressure and heart problems to pain and mood disorders.

Generally, these researchers define forgiveness as replacing negative feelings about an offender with more positive or neutral ones. (Often, this process is accompanied by replacing aggressive behavior toward the person with more neutral behavior.) This means that forgiveness doesn't rule out justice, nor does it require reconciliation. In the collective mind, forgiveness is often confused with related words like "pardon," "excuse," or "condone." *The Oxford English Dictionary* traces the roots of the word "forgive" to the words "give" and "grant." *Merriam-Webster's* defines "forgive" as giving up resentment or remitting a debt. Though in certain cases it has been used to imply the pardon of an offender, most psychologists and researchers distinguish forgiveness from pardon or excuse. As I heard more stories and did more research, my working definition became closest to *Merriam-Webster's*: giving up resentment.

This was radically different from the moralistic platitudes and religious pressures I'd long associated with forgiveness. From this vantage point, forgiveness becomes not something we *should* do to be "good," but a crucial skill in the pursuit of a healthy, fulfilling life. As I explored the fascinating history of the science of forgiveness, I came across the surprising contributions of two unlikely men, an eccentric burn surgeon and a famed investor. I read studies on the physical effects of forgiving, and I examined the role of anger, which, as it turns out, can be both productive and destructive. One of the most surprising discoveries I made was that forgiveness may be just as inherent, just as evolutionarily hardwired into human nature, as aggression and revenge. If that's true, if that duality is within us all and is triggered by certain factors, then we may ultimately have the power to choose which one we express and nurture. And choosing forgiveness, and the factors that make it more likely, could have enormous implications for our individual well-being, interpersonal relationships and wider societies.

Anger as Fuel for Progress

As I learned about the dangers of anger to our physical health, and in turn the potential of forgiveness to neutralize it and alleviate a range of physical and emotional problems, something within me balked. I couldn't stop thinking about that baboon that Darwin described at the Cape of Good Hope. The one that punished the guard who bothered him by tossing a bucket of mud on the man's head. I loved that story. I found it hilarious. I thought it a great illustration of how anger—and even its cousin, revenge—are natural mainstays of not only human history and culture, but also primate history and culture. As moviegoers, we love to see the villain drubbed in humiliating fashion, and as citizens, we relish the sight of a politician we dislike getting crushed during a debate.

The truth is, I happen to like anger. I think it's one of the most productive emotions at our disposal. What revolutionary hasn't been angry? What leader who challenged the status quo and created some leap of progress wasn't pissed off? The list of historical events that never would have happened but for anger is long: the French Revolution, the American Revolution, the Haitian slave revolt, the suffragist movement, and the civil rights movement, just to name a few. Mahatma Gandhi, who most people think of now as a peaceful saint, launched his lifelong crusade for freedom because he was angry. Outraged by the way he and his compatriots were treated as subhumans in South Africa—thrown off trains for riding first class, ridiculed for wearing turbans, and barred from hotels reserved for Europeans—he began the nonviolent resistance activities that would make him famous. It was indignant anger that drove him to overcome a stutter, become involved in politics, and launch the independence movement that freed his home country from British rule. While Malcolm X advocated violent retaliation and Martin Luther King Jr. repudiated it just as Gandhi did, both men were angry. Also angry were the legions of activists and muckraking journalists who exposed public corruption and workplace abuse in early twentieth-century America, ushering in the workplace safety regulations that we enjoy today.

Just as I had always admired these productive examples of righteous anger in action, I often privately savored the emotion. I enjoyed the memory of the newspaper reviewer calling my ex a "caveman." It gave me a sweet, sickly joy. For some people, vengeful feelings have even yielded popular works of fiction or hit songs. Take the gossip speculating that musician John Mayer's single "Paper Doll" was a revenge ballad about ex-girlfriend Taylor Swift, who accused him of breaking her heart in the song "Dear John." Still, in spite of my love of anger and my appreciation for revenge, I had to concede that while perhaps there is an upside, these emotions also wreak havoc, from intergenerational wars and gang violence to provincial family feuds like the one that famously claimed more than a dozen members of the Hatfield and McCoy clans in Kentucky and West Virginia in the late 1800s. More personally, anger and its various permutations had hampered my own life.

Several months after my breakup, I found myself at a music festival with friends. Near one of the entrances, I spotted a handsome bearded guy wearing a hat and leading an enormous brindle mastiff on a leash. His eyes were the color of a turquoise glacial lake I once saw while backpacking in Patagonia. Entranced, I watched him for a few minutes but refused to approach. What would I say? Besides, I was still bitter and raw. I was taking a hiatus from men. About six weeks later, I attended a comedy event organized by a journalist friend. I wound up sitting at a table with some friends of the journalist, including a man named Anthony. For reasons I'll never know but suspect have something to do with anger and fear and denial, I didn't recognize this guy as the same one I'd spotted at the festival, the one with the blue-lake eyes and the mastiff. Feeling antisocial and rushed, I scarfed down a couple of tacos and left to attend my writing group, barely speaking to him even though he was seated right next to me.

As I left, I asked if anyone wanted my raffle tickets. Anthony said he'd take them. A few days later, he sent me a message via Facebook (we had mutual friends, after all), to say that he had won tickets to a concert with my raffle number—would I like to go? I told myself that even if I didn't feel like it, I should. I'd been indulging my bitterness for months now, and the research I'd been doing made it clear that that wasn't exactly the most productive way of coping. Maybe I should try something different, I told myself, so I agreed to go on the date. However, I listened to the band online and determined that they were "kind of a downer." In classic judgmental fashion, I told him so, ostensibly so that if the show wasn't good, we could go somewhere else. Anthony would later tell me that this reminded him of a particularly picky and ever-complaining ex-girlfriend. When we spoke via phone to confirm our meeting place, his monotone suggested that he was even less thrilled than I was. Yet once we met and began talking at a Mexican restaurant near the concert venue, the time flew. We talked about jobs and magazines and politics and camping, and before I could think too much about it, I was having a great time.

After he walked me to my car, I thought, "Wow. That was so . . . natural." It wasn't until the next date, while I watched him order drinks at the bar and caught his face from a certain angle, that I remembered the man from the festival. The resemblance was striking. Could it be the same person? On the way out of the restaurant, I caught a glimpse of his brindle mastiff, Stella, sitting in the backseat of his black Honda. That confirmed it—this was the same guy, with the same dog, whom I'd admired at the music festival more than a month earlier. Later, as we began to date more seriously, we laughed about how it took multiple coincidences to throw us together in order for us to see each other clearly through our bitterness. In our midthirties and jaded after years of breakups, we were both so cynical that it's a miracle we got together at all.

As I researched this chapter, I came to understand that there are important distinctions between anger and bitterness and between anger and resentment. Maya Angelou described this beautifully. In a video conversation with comedian Dave Chappelle, they're discussing the friends she lost to assassinations, including MLK Jr. and Malcolm X, when Chappelle says, "I think, if it were me, I would be angry." Angelou looks at him in her silent, thoughtful way, and says, "If you're not angry, you're either a stone or you're too sick to be angry. You *should* be angry. You must *not* be bitter. Bitterness is a cancer that feeds upon the host and does nothing to the object at which it's directed. So, what do you do about anger? You write it. You paint it. You dance it. You march it. You vote it. You do everything about it. You talk it. Never stop talking it." Gandhi described—and demonstrated—the same thing: "As heat conserved is transmitted into energy, even so our anger controlled can be transmitted into a power that can move the world."

When I talked to my mother about this, she put it in psychological terms. Anger is an important drive to action, she said, as well as an integral phase of grief. It's when people get stuck in anger that it turns into bitterness and long-standing resentment. And resentment—bitter indignation at being treated unfairly—can destroy you from the inside out. Nelson Mandela, after spending twenty-seven years in prison in South Africa, said, "As I walked out the door toward the gate that would lead to my freedom, I knew if I didn't leave my bitterness and hatred behind, I'd still be in prison." It was also Mandela who popularized one of Azim's favorite quotes: "Resentment is like swallowing poison and waiting for your enemy to die." Eppie Lederer, writing as Ann Landers, put it this way: "Hate is like acid. It can damage the vessel in which it is stored as well as destroy the object on which it is poured."

Anger as Poison

Equating resentment with poison isn't a stretch. Anger triggers the body's fight-or-flight response, which increases pulse, blood pressure, and respiration, while constricting blood vessels. This has been hardwired through evolution to help us react when we find ourselves face-to-face with a charging grizzly or an armed robber. Yet when the body fails to return to normal after a stressor—when one remains angry, nursing a grudge and stuck in the fight-or-flight response—there are physiological consequences. Merely thinking about someone against whom you're holding a grudge spikes heart rate, lowers immune response, and floods the brain with neurotransmitters like cortisol and adrenaline, which over time impede problem-solving and increase depression.

A study of thousands of heart attack patients found that those who recalled flying into a rage during the past year were more than twice as likely to have had their heart attack within two hours of the angry episode as opposed to at other times. The study, conducted by the Cardiovascular Epidemiology Research Unit at Harvard Medical School and published in *The American Journal of Cardiology* in 2013, found that the more explosive the fury, the greater the risk of heart attack. The most intense tantrums—usually about family conflicts, job stresses, or commuting—were linked to a more than fourfold higher risk, while milder expressions of anger were tied to less than half that risk level. The researchers found that with each increasing level of anger, the risk of heart attack in the next two hours rose: It was 1.7 times greater after feeling "so hassled it shows in your voice," 2.3 times greater after "body tense, clenching fists or teeth," and 4.5 times greater after feeling, "enraged, loss of control, throwing objects or hurting yourself or others."

In 2007, a different study found that older adults with explosive tempers were more likely than calmer peers to have calcium deposit buildup in their coronary arteries, a key sign of heart disease. Washington State University researchers had 185 participants fill out questionnaires on how they dealt with anger, and used an X-ray to measure the calcium deposits in their arteries. In the 40 adults aged fifty or older at the start, those more prone to angry outbursts had higher calcium buildup at the outset and nine years later. The link between high temper and calcium deposits, a precursor to blocked blood flow and, by extension, oxygen to the heart, held up even after accounting for other risk factors such as blood pressure and cholesterol.

Since it's unhealthy to erupt like Homer Simpson when he's infuriated by Bart, what about holding the rage inside? That's no solution, either. Studies show that repressing negative feelings can be detrimental, as revealed by a team of researchers at the University of Jena in Germany who found that bottled-up rage is tantamount to poison. Published in the journal *Health Psychology* in 2013, their analysis of six thousand patients showed that people who internalized their anxiety, or "repressors," had higher pulse rates and higher risk of high blood pressure, heart disease, and other illnesses. The researchers even theorized that their findings may help to explain why the more passionate, expressive Italians and Spaniards tend to live an average of two years longer than their more staid English neighbors.

Since both flying off the handle and repressing rage are dangerous, the goal is to express anger constructively, either to fix a problem, release the emotion, or both. After all, anger serves a purpose, alerting us to injustice, power imbalances, and moral transgressions. A 2010 study by the Columbia University Medical Center showed that discussing anger in order to solve a problem is associated with a lower rate of cardiovascular disease, while destructive expression of anger or blaming was linked to higher risk. A 2006 study published in the *Annals of Behavioral Medicine* found that while both explosive and suppressed rage play a role in heart disease, moderate anger expression can lead to better heart health. In his book *Nonviolent Communication*, Dr. Marshall Rosenberg argues that at the core of anger lies an unfilled need, and the most productive response is to identify that need and work to fulfill it.

The Burn Surgeon: How Anger Can Impede Healing

In 1978, Dr. Dabney Ewin, a surgeon specializing in burns, was on duty in a New Orleans emergency room when a man was brought in on a gurney. A worker at the Kaiser Aluminum plant, the patient had slipped and fallen into a vat of 950-degree molten aluminum up to his knees. Ewin did something that most would consider strange at best or the work of a charlatan at worst: He hypnotized the burned man. Without a swinging pocket watch or any other theatrical antics, the surgeon did what's now known in the field of medical hypnosis as an "induction," instructing the man to relax, breathe deeply, and close his eyes. He told him to imagine that his legs—scorched to the knees and now packed in ice—did not feel hot or painful but "cool and comfortable." Ewin had found that doing this—in addition to standard treatments—improved his patients' outcomes. And that's what happened with the Kaiser Aluminum worker. While such severe burns would normally require months to heal, multiple skin grafts, and maybe even lead to amputation if excessive swelling cut off the blood supply, the man healed in just eighteen days—without a single skin graft.

As Ewin continued using hypnosis to expedite his burn patients' recoveries, he added another unorthodox practice to his regimen: He talked to his patients about anger and forgiveness. He noticed that people coming into the ER with burns were often very angry, and not without reason. They were, as he put it, "all burned up," both literally and figuratively. Hurt and in severe pain due to their own reckless mistake or someone else's, as they described the accident that left them burned, their words were tinged with angry guilt or blame. He concluded that their anger may have been interfering with their ability to heal by preventing them from relaxing and focusing on getting better. "I was listening to my patients and feeling what they were feeling," Ewin told me. "It became obvious that this had to be dealt with. Their attitude affected the healing of their burns, and this was particularly true of skin grafts. With someone who's real angry, we'd put three or four skin grafts on, but his body would reject them." Whenever a patient seemed angry, Ewin would help them forgive themselves or the person who hurt them, either through a simple conversation or through hypnosis.

Ewin, now eighty-eight and semiretired after practicing surgery and teaching medical hypnosis at the Tulane University School of Medicine for more than thirty years, became interested in hypnosis while he was a young doctor training under the legendary Dr. Champ Lyons, who pioneered the use of penicillin and treated survivors of the famous Cocoanut Grove nightclub fire in Boston in 1943. As Ewin learned to stabilize patients and conduct skin grafts, he wondered about an intriguing practice that he'd learned of from his great uncle. As an independently wealthy "man of leisure" in Nashville, this uncle had dabbled in hypnosis. He even held séances, which had become so popular in the late 1800s that First Lady Mary Todd Lincoln held them in the White House to attempt to reach the spirit of her dead son. (President Abraham Lincoln reportedly attended.) Many of the most popular séance leaders were eventually exposed as frauds exploiting the grief-stricken, but Ewin's uncle found another forum for hypnosis that was less controversial than hypnotizing an audience into believing that dead friends were speaking to them. He hypnotized the patients of surgeon friends before they went under the knife in order to minimize their pain. (This was before anesthesia was widely used.)

Ewin took a few hypnosis courses to find out more. "I figured it couldn't hurt," he told me in his friendly New Orleans drawl when I reached him at home by phone. Once he started trying hypnosis on his burn patients, he noticed a difference immediately. If he could reach them within half an hour of the injury, the hypnotic suggestions of "coolness and calm" seemed to halt the continued burning response of the skin that usually occurs for twelve to twenty-four hours, leading to speedier recoveries. (While there are no empirical studies of hypnosis on burn patients and Ewin's data is anecdotal, multiple studies do show that hypnosis can alleviate symptoms and improve medical outcomes in various scenarios, from asthma and warts to childbirth and post-traumatic stress disorder.)

Once Ewin began helping his patients forgive, he noticed even more improvement. "What you're thinking and feeling affects your body," he would explain to his patients, using the analogy of something embarrassing causing someone to blush. "What you're feeling will affect the healing of your skin, and we want you to put all your energy into healing." At this point, he would learn how the victim had unthinkingly opened a blast furnace without turning it off, or how the workmen at a construction site had repeatedly told the boss about a dangerously placed can of gasoline, to no avail.

"I'd do hypnosis with them and help them forgive themselves or the other person," Ewin said. "I'd say, 'You can still pursue damages through an attorney. You're entitled to be angry, but for now I'm asking you to abandon your entitlement and let it go, to direct your energy toward healing, and turn this over to God or nature or whoever you worship. It's not up to you to get revenge on yourself or someone else. When you know at a feeling level that you're letting it go, raise your hand.' Then I'd shut up, they'd raise their hand, and I'd know that skin graft was gonna take." Ewin taught other burn doctors what he discovered, and has received letters from colleagues in burn units around the world thanking him for helping them achieve faster recovery times for their patients.

The Investor Turned Research Patron: How Forgiveness Hit Mainstream Science

Like Dabney Ewin, John Templeton was a son of the South, a man of letters who came of age during the Depression and combined his success with less mainstream pursuits. Born to a middle-class family in Winchester, Tennessee, in 1912, Templeton managed to put himself through Yale after the 1929 stock market crash and became a Rhodes Scholar at Oxford. He launched his career on Wall Street by taking the "buy low, sell high" mantra to the extreme, borrowing money at the onset of World War II to buy one hundred shares each in 104 companies selling at one dollar per share or less, including 34 companies that were in bankruptcy. He reaped a healthy profit on all but four. Templeton entered the mutual funds business in the fifties, eventually selling his Templeton Funds to the Franklin Group in 1992. *Money* magazine called him "arguably the greatest global stock picker of the century."

Yet Templeton was equally passionate about spirituality, morality, and science, and how the scientific method could increase our understanding of life's "Big Questions"—questions about the nature of consciousness and the role that love and creativity, compassion and forgiveness, play in all areas of human life. In 1987, Templeton founded the John Templeton Foundation, dedicated to funding scientific research "on subjects ranging from complexity, evolution, and infinity, to creativity, forgiveness, love, and free will." With the motto "How little we know, how eager to learn," Templeton sought research grantees who were "innovative, creative, and open to competition and new ideas."

Templeton announced the Campaign for Forgiveness Research in 1997, a funding initiative for scientists in multiple disciplines who were interested in taking forgiveness out of the purview of religion and using rigorous scientific protocol to determine its effects on the body and mind. Spearheading the campaign was Dr. Everett Worthington, a psychology professor at Virginia Commonwealth University. One of the first psychologists to create therapeutic tools using forgiveness, he came to the topic through personal tragedy: His elderly mother was bludgeoned to death by an intruder, and, in part because of her death, his brother committed suicide. Struggling with rage and grief, Worthington switched his focus from marriage counseling to forgiveness. He designed a research framework for the Campaign for Forgiveness Research, Archbishop Desmond Tutu became a cochair for the campaign, and the Templeton Foundation provided a $5 million grant.

Between 1998 and 2005, the foundation, along with thirteen partners including the Fetzer Institute, a Michigan-based nonprofit that funds research and educational projects focused on love and forgiveness, dedicated $9.4 million to 43 scientific studies on the health impacts of forgiveness. Whereas before, Worthington and a few other researchers were alone in their pursuits (and most of their research was aimed at affirming their own therapeutic models), the Campaign for Forgiveness Research took a traditionally religious concept and placed it firmly on the scientific landscape. In addition to funding researchers directly, the campaign sparked dialogue and interest in the broader scientific community. While in 1998 there were 58 empirical studies on forgiveness in the research literature, by 2005, when the campaign concluded, there were 950.

Throughout the process, Templeton was highly engaged. Even into his eighties, he was known to walk waist-deep in the surf for an hour near his Bahamas home each morning before sitting down to read grant proposals. When he died at ninety-five, he was lauded by both the business and scientific communities. *The Wall Street Journal* called him the "maximum optimist," whose confidence in rising stocks paid off and whose philanthropy left an enduring legacy. The leading scientific journal *Nature* wrote, "His love of science and his God led him to form his foundation in 1987 on the basis that mutual dialogue might enrich the understanding of both."

While it's up for debate whether the research Templeton funded has enriched our understanding of God, it certainly has enriched our understanding of forgiveness, demonstrating that what was traditionally seen as a religious ideal is actually an important skill for anyone, whether atheist, agnostic, or believer, who seeks to live a healthy, happy life.

The Science of Forgiveness

One of the researchers who participated in the Campaign for Forgiveness Research was Dr. Robert Enright, a developmental psychologist at the University of Wisconsin–Madison. Enright began contemplating forgiveness back in the mideighties. As a Christian, he'd been raised on Jesus' teachings about tolerance and forgiveness. He asked himself: Could forgiveness help patients in a clinical setting? In spite of skeptical colleagues who ridiculed him for applying science to something so "mushy" and "religious," he designed forgiveness interventions for therapy and studied their psychological and physiological impacts.

He began by developing therapies aimed at helping elderly women to forgive those who had wronged them in the past, and to help victims of abuse and incest to understand their tormentors without justifying the abusers' actions. His initial findings were encouraging. His first study, which compared women undergoing forgiveness therapy with a control group who underwent therapy for emotional wounds without a forgiveness focus, found that the experimental group improved more in emotional and psychological health measures than the control group. It was published in the journal *Psychotherapy* in 1993. Afterward, Enright honed his therapeutic forgiveness tools, from helping people develop empathy—the ability to understand and share the feelings of another—toward aggressors, to learning to forgive and accept themselves, and tested them on a range of groups. Among battered women and "parental love–deprived college students," for instance, those subject to forgiveness therapy showed more improvement in emotional and psychological health than control groups who received therapy without a forgiveness focus.

Enright's forgiveness model has four parts: *uncovering your anger, deciding to forgive, working on forgiveness*, and *discovery and release from emotional prison*. All take place through therapist-patient dialogue. Uncovering anger means examining how you've both avoided and dealt with it, and exploring how the offense and resulting anger has changed your health, worldview, and life in general. The phase involves learning about what forgiveness is and what it's not, acknowledging that the ways you've dealt with your anger up until now haven't worked, and setting the intention to forgive. Next, working on forgiveness entails confronting the pain the offense has caused and allowing yourself to experience it fully, then working toward developing some level of understanding and compassion for the offender.

The final phase includes acknowledging that others have suffered as you have and that you're not alone (for some, this means connecting with a support group of people who have endured a similar experience), examining what possible meaning your suffering could have for your life (learning a particular life lesson, perhaps contributing to one's strength or character, or prompting one to help others), and taking action on whatever you determine to be your life purpose.

Since developing that therapy model and pioneering the first studies, Enright and his colleagues have found positive results in drug rehabilitation participants (less anger, depression, and need for drugs compared to the control group receiving standard therapy), victims of domestic violence (decreased anxiety, depression, and post-traumatic stress disorder relative to the control group), and terminally ill cancer patients (more hope for the future and less anger than the control group).

When it comes to determining the existence of a causal relationship between forgiveness and physical health, Enright says the most definitive study he has done was conducted with a team of researchers on cardiac patients. Published in 2009 in the journal *Psychology & Health*, their analysis found that when cardiac patients with coronary heart disease underwent forgiveness therapy, the rate of blood flow to their hearts improved more than that of the control group, which received only standard medical treatment and counseling about diet and exercise. "It wasn't that they were cured—these were patients with serious heart problems," Enright says. "But they were at less risk of pain and sudden death." Those results echo studies by another Templeton grantee, Charlotte Witvliet, a psychology professor at Hope College; and Sonja Lyubomirsky, a psychology professor at the University of California, Riverside, and author of numerous books on happiness, which found that people who forgive more readily have fewer coronary heart problems than those who hold grudges.

Perhaps the most comprehensive body of evidence showing links between forgiveness and health focuses on mood, says Dr. Frederic Luskin, the cofounder of the Stanford Forgiveness Project, an ongoing series of workshops and research studies at Stanford University. Researchers who measure emotional and psychological health outcomes following therapy that includes forgiveness are quantifying patients' levels of anger, anxiety, and depression, concluding in multiple studies that forgiveness elevates mood and increases optimism, while not forgiving is positively correlated with depression, anxiety, and hostility. Like Enright, Luskin has developed ways to teach forgiveness in various places and with various groups, including war-ravaged populations in countries such as Northern Ireland and Sierra Leone, and he asserts that anyone—from jilted spouses to widows who have lost husbands to terrorism—can heal.

Luskin developed a weeklong "forgiveness training" delivered in a group setting. In it, he leads participants through a series of discussions and exercises. The first steps involve teasing apart what he calls "your grievance story," which is usually formed by taking something personally that wasn't necessarily personal, and then blaming someone for your feelings. His argument is that when you blame someone for how you feel instead of holding them to account for their actions, you keep yourself stuck in victimhood and inaction (resenting your ex for her drinking and destructive behavior, for instance, instead of just seeking a restraining order). Luskin has participants "find the impersonal in the hurt" by realizing how many other people have experienced a similar offense or disappointment and how common it is, as well as acknowledging that most offenses are committed without the intention of hurting anyone personally. (If your mother yelled at you, for example, she likely did so not because her goal was to hurt your feelings and forever damage your self-confidence, but because she was stressed or afraid.) This doesn't negate that often there is a personal aspect to an offense, Luskin says, but it can lessen the pain and blame.

"When you don't forgive you release all the chemicals of the stress response," Luskin says. "Each time you react, adrenaline, cortisol, and norepinephrine enter the body. When it's a chronic grudge, you could think about it twenty times a day, and those chemicals limit creativity, they limit problem-solving. Cortisol and norepinephrine cause your brain to enter what we call 'the no-thinking zone,' and over time, they lead you to feel helpless and like a victim. When you forgive, you wipe all of that clean."

One of the main areas funded by the Templeton grant was the neuro-science of forgiveness. Around the time of the award, functional MRI, or fMRI, scanners were becoming increasingly common and sparking new discoveries in a variety of areas. The machines enable neuroscientists to capture X-ray images of people's brains in action to observe blood flow and see which brain components are activated in which situations. In 2001, Dr. Tom Farrow of the University of Sheffield in the United Kingdom used fMRI scanners to conduct the first scientific study of the "functional anat-omy" of forgiveness. Using ten subjects, he had each person climb into his laboratory's fMRI scanner and asked them to answer a series of questions designed to evoke empathy and forgiveness. The empathy-related questions asked participants to consider potential explanations for someone's emo-tional state (if your boss is unusually quiet or withdrawn, for instance, is it more likely that her child was expelled from school or that her child was caught shoplifting?), while the forgiveness-related questions asked people to evaluate which crimes they considered more forgivable (a neighbor who recently lost his job getting arrested for assaulting his girlfriend or for as-saulting his boss?).

Farrow and his team found that empathy and "forgivability judg-ments," basically contemplating whether a certain action deserves forgive-ness, activate various parts of the frontal lobe, which is associated with problem-solving and reason. In contrast, a researcher named Dr. Pietro Pietrini at the University of Pisa in Italy showed in a 2000 fMRI study that anger and vengeance inhibited rational thinking and caused high activity in the amygdala, which is involved in the fight-or-flight response. Anger and rage, then, impede reason, but the tasks involved in the complex pro-cess of forgiveness activate the more recently evolved parts of our brain, such as the prefrontal cortex and posterior cingulate, which are concerned with problem-solving, morality, understanding the mental states of others, and cognitive control of emotions.

Having cognitive control means inhibiting impulsive reactions fueled by rage and hatred toward a wrongdoer. This can be done through thought, such as by devising a new, less upsetting interpretation of a painful event.

When it comes to being hurt, this can mean viewing an infraction as less personal than you thought, or developing an understanding of someone's actions by considering his point of view. Psychologists call this "reframing" a painful memory. It's a key part of both Enright's forgiveness therapy and Luskin's forgiveness training. Taking things less personally is something I realized would benefit me and reduce a lot of my suffering. In my new relationship with Anthony, for instance, I would sometimes feel hurt when he teased me about something, whether my penchant for driving under the speed limit or the time I left a steak to thaw on the counter and his hundred-pound dog easily ate it. When I realized that he didn't mean to hurt my feelings and was just making a good-natured joke, I was less likely to take offense and get upset.

Another way to reframe is to consider a range of possible points of view that led someone to act a certain way. This makes it more difficult to blame and demonize that person and continue generating the same level of resentment as you did before. I once spent days feeling resentful about a former editor's criticism about a story—which I thought was harsh and took personally. When a colleague suggested that what he said likely came from a deep commitment to accuracy and excellence, I let it go and felt a lot better. A third way to reframe is to consider what constructive learning, meaning, or opportunity may have resulted from an offense and the suffering it caused. For Azim, that was the opportunity to work with youth and prevent violence, and for my more mundane example about editorial feedback, it was a lesson about being more diligent in checking my facts and considering my approach to a story.

Thanks to fMRI scanners, we can now identify the parts of the brain that make this sort of reframing practice possible. In one study, Farrow focused on two groups of people who struggle with empathy and, by extension, forgiveness: schizophrenics and people suffering from post-traumatic stress disorder. Both showed inhibited activity in the areas of the brain involved in forgiveness processes such as empathy and viewing another person's perspective. But after ten weeks of therapy that included the discussion and practice of forgiveness (and antipsychotic drugs for the schizophrenics), those brain areas' functions improved. While Farrow didn't use a control group to isolate and test the therapeutic forgiveness intervention specifically, the findings confirm the earlier evidence of so-called forgiveness areas in the brain, and show that psychological treatments such as cognitive behavioral therapy can improve this aspect of brain function.

In a separate experiment, Pietrini asked ten participants to lie in the scanner and consider a fictional scenario in which they were wronged and then forgave. As with the prior studies, both the dorsal prefrontal cortex (involved in cognitive control) and the posterior cingulate (involved in understanding the mental states of others) lit up on the screen. But a third part was also involved: the anterior cingulate cortex, which mediates the perception and the suppression of moral pain (such as the feeling of being wronged). Pietrini's interpretation? Forgiveness could be viewed as a sort of painkiller for moral distress.

When Pietrini presented his findings at a 2009 conference, he described them as evidence that forgiveness likely evolved as a way to overcome pain and alleviate suffering, and that even though it involves parts of the brain responsible for reason, it also requires a counterintuitive, and some would argue, irrational, choice: "You wronged me, but I forgive you, anyway."

"A great deal of evidence converges suggesting that forgiveness is a positive, healthy strategy for the individual to overcome a situation that otherwise would be a major source of stress from a psychological and neurobiological point of view," he wrote to me in an e-mail. "The fact that forgiving is a healthy resolution of the problems caused by injuries suggests that this process may have evolved as a favorable response that promotes human survival."

Is Forgiveness as Natural as Revenge?

Just how natural or unnatural is forgiveness? Is it, as Pietrini suggests, a response hardwired through evolution for some purpose? Or is revenge more inherent, dooming humanity to conflict and violence? It turns out that the impulse to forgive—along with being kind, compassionate, and peaceful—does not run as counter to human nature as we might think. The idea that human beings are inherently aggressive has persisted since Sigmund Freud talked about the so-called natural reservoir of aggression that lies within us and must be periodically drained lest it explode. But that theory—that aggressive human behavior, from revenge to war, is inevitable and dominant in our nature—has been discounted by modern sociologists, anthropologists, and psychologists.

Back in 1988, *Psychology Today* published a feature story called "Are Humans Innately Aggressive?" in which the author reviewed research and questioned the era's leading social scientists to conclude that the answer to whether humans are doomed to aggression was an emphatic no. From animal behaviorist John Paul Scott to psychologists Leonard Berkowitz and Erich Fromm, the experts rejected the argument that aggression for aggression's sake is a ruling human instinct, attributing its causes more to nurture—including culture, societal structure, and politics—than to nature. And while popular culture and common wisdom may insist on arguing otherwise, nothing has changed to suggest that humans are biologically predetermined to choose aggression and, by extension, revenge.

According to evolutionary psychologists, we evolved with adaptive tendencies toward *both* vengeance and forgiveness, and our environments determine which impulse gets expressed. To prove that any trait became "hardwired" as adaptive, or survival-enhancing, throughout evolution, scientists must show that the trait is universal—which several have done regarding both revenge and forgiveness. Primatologists have documented among chimps and macaques the sort of intergroup violence and generational blood feuds associated with medieval Scotland or the nineteenth-century Hatfield-McCoy feud. The evolutionary psychologist Michael McCullough, a professor at the University of Miami, has written about a chimpanzee community in Tanzania studied by Jane Goodall in the early sixties. When the number of adult males surpassed fifteen and prompted squabbles over females and food, the group split. Relations between the two

groups became increasingly tense, and soon one group began to systematically attack the other. After several years of raids and murders, the group
that left the original clan had been annihilated. In turn, a group of primatologists discovered that Japanese macaques that were attacked by a
higher-up would leave the aggressor alone but attack one of the offender's
younger family members in retaliation. Apparently, the vengeance-fueled
family feud predates our species.

In answer to the question of whether revenge is an adapted trait in
humans, developed and refined in order to survive—and thus, universal—
cue a 1998 study by the evolutionary biologists Martin Daly and Margo
Wilson. Searching a database called the Human Relations Area Files Prob-
ability Sample, which features high-quality ethnographic information on
sixty cultures selected to represent each of the world's geographies and
language groups, the husband-wife duo looked for references to blood
feuds, capital punishment, or the desire for revenge. They concluded that
fifty-seven of the sixty cultures showed that evidence, either in the form of
customs to implement revenge or indications of the desire for revenge.
That's 95 percent. (In some groups, the desire for revenge was not acted
upon, but those cultures also happened to have specific customs such as
judicial procedures designed expressly to punish killers and prevent vigilante justice.)

Having established the universality of vengeance, McCullough details
the precise problems that ancestral humans most likely used revenge to
solve. (Adapted traits develop to accomplish something specific that enables a species to thrive and propagate future generations.) Revenge would
have been useful for deterring and punishing aggression. Since ancestral
humans lived in close-knit clan groups and depended on collaboration to
hunt and gather food, banishment meant almost-certain death, so you
couldn't just walk away from someone who hurt or stole from you. If, however, the members of your group knew that if they slept with your mate or
stole your meat you would rip their face off, well, those who tried it wouldn't
do it again, and anyone else contemplating it would back off.

Two of the more fascinating bits of evidence for this revenge raison d'être: Social psychologists have shown in lab studies that a victim of a provocation or attack is likely to retaliate more strongly when an audience has witnessed the provocation. This explains why teachers at rough schools make the rest of the class leave the room when a fight erupts. It also explains why, in communities such as inner cities and developing countries where chaos and violence are rampant and residents can't necessarily rely on law enforcement, justice, or general order, codes that employ revenge to defend one's honor and deter further transgressions by third parties are so common.

After deterring aggression, the next goal revenge evolved to accomplish was to compel cooperation, McCullough argues. Since early humans depended on teamwork to hunt, and their descendants created agriculture and architecture, they inevitably encountered what evolutionary biologists call "the free-rider problem." Why spend countless hours hiking and stalking and sharpening and aiming in order to bring down a woolly mammoth if you can just pretend you were doing so and still get a full meal? If members of the group could benefit from the cooperation without actually cooperating, that would mean the eventual demise of cooperation, and the rewarding and propagating of free riders.

The most logical solution: Primates, and humans, developed ways to punish free riders so that such behavior was less profitable. If a rhesus macaque finds a food source but fails to alert other group members, for example, he's likely to be viciously attacked when his cohorts discover he failed to share. Modern research on humans shows that people go out of their way, even at substantial cost to themselves, to punish free riders through humiliation, pain, or revoking a resource in order to make it less profitable for the transgressor to benefit from being parasitic.

The fact that humans have evolved an impulse for revenge as a solution to certain problems probably doesn't come as a shock. Yet forgiveness is just as evolutionarily adaptive, and in highly complex, interdependent modern societies such as the ones in which most of us live, it's even more adaptive than revenge.

Just as ancestral humans encountered problems that could be solved by revenge (aggressors and free riders), they also encountered problems for which forgiveness emerged as a solution. First, since the main goal of survival from an evolutionary standpoint is to propagate one's genes, annihilating your kin wouldn't win you the genetic lottery. As a result, ancestral humans were more likely to maintain good relations with family members, as we are today. (While people do kill relatives on occasion, such incidents are statistically uncommon, and research shows people are more likely to forgive close family members than strangers.) The seventeenth-century French writer François de La Rochefoucauld wrote mostly about morality, but this famous quote jives just as much with evolutionary psychology: "We forgive to the extent that we love."

As humans developed larger and increasingly complex groups, they depended on cooperation and reciprocity to hunt and gather, and to build homes and, later, cities, farms, and architecture. That meant they needed a reliable mechanism for promoting reconciliation among nonrelatives, not only family members. They needed, in a sense, to love—or at least be able to work with—a larger number of individuals. Forgiveness seems to be exactly that mechanism. As McCullough puts it, "forgiveness is the bridesmaid; cooperation is the bride."

While as humans we distinguish between "forgiveness" (giving up resentment) and "reconciliation" (renewing relationship after conflict), the two seem to share evolutionary roots. Forgiveness, McCullough argues, appears to have evolved as a way for people to continue to cooperate and gain value from relationships. In the late seventies, the Dutch primatologist Frans de Waal began studying one of the largest colonies of chimpanzees in the world at the Burgers' Zoo in the Netherlands. He noticed one day in 1975 that a male and female kissed right after the male attacked the female. Did chimps kiss and make up just like humans do? he wondered. The study he did to find out drew a definitive conclusion: Kissing, touching, and embracing were chimps' most common behaviors after an aggressive conflict. Of 350 aggressive encounters, just 50, or 14 percent, were preceded by friendly contact. Yet 179, 51 percent, of aggressive encounters were followed by conciliatory contact—friendly contact was far more common after a fight than after peaceful periods. So, even though chimps can be violent, especially with different clan groups, within their own colonies they are also well-versed in reconciliation.

Following de Waal's study, primatologists developed what they call a conciliatory tendency, or CT index, to measure the extent to which conflict is followed by friendly behavior. Gorillas, bonobos, and some species of macaques have conciliatory tendencies as high as that of chimps. Of the thirty or so primate species that have been studied, only a few lack a pattern of conciliatory behavior, ranging from kisses, hugs, and grunting to sex. Even nonprimates use such practices to reconcile. Goats and sheep rub horns, dolphins rub flippers, and hyenas rub fur. Most animals that show highly conciliatory behavior live in tight-knit social networks that depend on cooperation. Apes and monkeys help each other find food, alert each other to predators, and raise young, while male dolphins collaborate to isolate females for sex, and sheep depend on each other for refuge from predators.

While there are few numerical studies that measure the conciliatory tendency of humans, several studies on children show they have a conciliatory tendency of around .40 on a scale of 0 to 1, which is similar to chimpanzees. The ways preschool children reconcile after conflict vary depending on culture, but most use some combination of apologies, hugs, invitations to share, and holding hands.

To see if forgiveness, like revenge, is cross-culturally universal, McCullough reviewed the ethnographic data on those sixty societies studied by Daly and Wilson, the ones in which they found evidence for blood revenge in 95 percent of cultures. He found that displays of forgiveness, reconciliation, or both were documented in fifty-six, or 93 percent, of them (nearly the 95 percent considered the threshold for a universal trait). Strategies for smoothing rifts have included public apologies, formal gift exchanges, and compensation for victims, as well as third-party mediation and religious rituals. In parts of Macedonia, some Orthodox Christians still observe a traditional holiday called Forgiveness Day, or Prochka. Leading up to Lent, young people ask their elders for forgiveness for any wrongs they've committed over the past year, presenting the older relatives with gifts such as citrus fruit or sweets. In the Jewish tradition, Yom Kippur, the day of atonement, requires seeking forgiveness from God after ringing in the Jewish New Year. The Dogon tribe of Mali used a ritual in which a perpetrator takes three bites of coal and spits it out in the presence of his or her victim, and many native peoples, from the Dogon to the Maori to the tribes of North America, used third-party mediation to settle disputes.

The scientific reality that our biology is predisposed to both aggression and peacemaking because both impulses come in handy sheds an illuminating spotlight on the moral debate over human nature. This inherent duality is just as evident in our stories and mythology as it is in science. In Egyptian, Greek, and Roman mythology, the gods—described as men and women with superpowers—were just as capable of violent horrors as they were of miracles. The stories of the Old Testament show the same dichotomy. While Cain kills his brother, Abel, and lies to God about it, Jacob apologizes to his brother, Esau, for tricking their dying father into giving him the inheritance due to his brother, and Esau forgives him. Then there's Joseph, sold into slavery by his own brothers. Not only does he forgive them when years later they arrive in Egypt seeking refuge from famine, he takes them in and feeds them.

What Determines Which Response Is Expressed, Revenge or Forgiveness?

According to McCullough, what tips the scales are the specific circumstances in which we find ourselves. Because of the way we've evolved, we are most likely to forgive when we view an opponent or transgressor as "worthy of care," valuable, and safe. The closer someone is to you, the more you judge them to be "care-worthy." Empathy plays a big role in this. The more empathy you have for someone, either because he's suffering or because you know him well or because you can imagine yourself in his shoes, the more you care about that person—and as a result, the more readily you forgive him. McCullough found in a 1997 study that the more empathy someone experiences toward a transgressor, the more difficult it is to remain vengeful toward that person.

The next factor, value, is straightforward: People who collaborate or depend on one another are more likely to forgive each other. In a famous social science study done on male campers at Robbers Cave State Park in Oklahoma in the fifties, a psychologist named Muzafer Sherif divided the boys into two groups. When they were given separate team names and made to play games against each other, they developed a growing rivalry. But when they were assigned projects to do together, especially to accomplish something that was important to all of them, such as fixing a break in the drinking water delivery system or raising money to see a movie, their rivalry dissolved. More recent research in classrooms has gone further, showing that children of different ethnicities and social classes are less likely to argue or shun one another when engaged in cooperative projects at school.

The last factor that makes forgiveness more likely from an evolutionary standpoint, safety, means that if victims feel a perpetrator is unwilling or unable to harm them again in the future, they're less inclined to seek revenge or remain resentful. This is one reason why studies show that it's easier to forgive a criminal offender who has been convicted and served justice, and that remorse shown by an offender often leads to forgiveness in a victim. In a 2014 study, McCullough and a team of researchers at the University of Miami found that peacemaking efforts such as apologies, offers of compensation, and owning up to one's responsibility increase forgiveness—and reduce anger—by making the aggressor seem more valuable and by causing the victim to feel less at risk of getting hurt again.

This sheds light on the fact that people who live in inner cities or countries rife with crime, chaos, and injustice are more likely to use revenge as a survival tool, while people who live in communities with more reliable law enforcement and justice are more likely to forgive and even reconcile. One evocative piece of evidence for this is what happened in

Europe when nation-states decided to monitor blood feuds by taking punishment out of vigilante hands and making it a state responsibility. Starting
in 1350, according to data assembled by the Cambridge University crimi-
nologist Manuel Eisner, homicide rates plummeted in Europe through
1975. Using coroners' inquests and local records, he found that the annual
homicide rate in England went from between 4 and 100 homicides per
100,000 people in the Middle Ages to around 0.8 per 100,000 people in the
1950s. His explanation is that, along with increased economic cooperation
between towns and regions, consolidation of justice in state hands made
people feel safer and less inclined to seek revenge on their own. (His explanation for the uptick in homicides after the seventies is that once globaliza-
tion loosened borders for trade, intrastate organized crime and contraband
also surpassed borders, and kingpins don't tend to call 911.)

The discovery that both vengeance and forgiveness are natural, not
good or evil, was a revelation to me. It meant that in those moments when
I feel like a resentful bitch who just can't let something go, I'm not alone
or crazy. And yet, while the impulse for bitterness may be natural, it's not
the only choice I have. The brain research of the past decade shows that
our brains are malleable, and that the more we choose to think, feel, and
act in certain ways, the easier and more automatic it becomes to think,
feel, and act in those same ways. The less we take things personally, for
example, or the more we generate empathy for offenders without excusing
their actions, or hold someone accountable instead of just complaining,
the less prone our brains, and lives, will be to the corrosive effects of resentment. Hence the phrase "rewire your brain." I would eventually come
to discover that we can also "rewire" our societies. If our hardwired impulses for revenge and aggression, and forgiveness and reconciliation, are
triggered by our environments, then it must be possible to practice habits
and design families, schools, and justice systems to bring out our more
peaceful instincts. It requires revamping the forces that shape our individual and collective lives, and as I would find out, it's already happening in
some places.

If Forgiveness Is So Natural, How Do You Do It?

If we have a choice between vengeance and forgiveness, and science shows that forgiveness provides health benefits, how do you actually go about it? And doesn't the ability to do it vary depending on the person and the situation? Luskin and other psychologists who study and teach forgiveness say that no matter what's being forgiven, the process involves two main steps: grieving and letting go. How that plays out and how long it takes depends on both circumstance and personality. Research shows it's easier to forgive an offender who has been caught than one who remains at-large, for example, and even when the offense is not a crime it's still easier to forgive someone who has apologized. People naturally prone to anger or depression may take longer than others to forgive, while optimists tend to forgive more readily. Of course, all of these tendencies—toward being pessimistic or optimistic, forgiving or unforgiving—can be altered and "retrained." The many books that have recently explored the concept of neuroplasticity—how by repeating new thoughts, feelings, and habits over time, we can rewire our brains and alter our behavior and experience of life—include *Positivity*, by Barbara Fredrickson, *Flourish*, by Martin Seligman, *Mindset*, by Carol Dweck, and *The Power of Habit*, by Charles Duhigg.

When it comes to one's ability to forgive, I assumed the scale of an offense would make as much of a difference as optimism or pessimism, but according to Luskin that's not necessarily true. It may take someone who has lost a loved one longer to forgive than someone betrayed by a spouse, but when asked to rate their suffering on a scale of 1 to 10, both often rate it the same. "An 8.8 makes sense for a murder but not as much sense when someone left you," Luskin says. "On one hand, that indicates people going through lesser problems lack perspective on what horrors others may be experiencing, but on the other hand it means that when people are struggling, they're struggling."

Struggling continuously over time, remaining stuck in one of the phases of grief like depression or anger, and feeling like a victim all rob you of freedom and power, Azim and Ples say. When I watched them address college students at San Diego State University, Ples told the audience that he chose to support the Tariq Khamisa Foundation in order to be responsible and not hide in his misery over what his grandson had done—and that doing so gave him a sense of having a say over his own destiny. The pair's goal has a lot to do with directing their own lives and helping others do the same, which is essentially what Dr. Luskin and other therapists teach. "I'm not going to let nobody disturb my peace no time of day," Ples told the crowd that April day, pacing the auditorium stage like a preacher. "My peace belongs to me. I have rule over it. I'm a free man."

Reviewing the scientific evidence for the usefulness and health benefits of forgiveness, I felt increasingly hopeful. It shifted my largely negative view of the world, which held that it was a place dominated by violence and war, suffering and struggle. I wanted to learn more about how I could choose to nurture the more forgiving side of my nature, and how we might be able to make forgiveness a more common choice as a society.

I devised a plan: I would profile people who have forgiven in a range of places and circumstances, around the country and the world. I would explore everything from forgiveness in families and couples, to forgiveness as a daily individual practice and the habits and structures that are being implemented to make forgiveness more likely in collective institutions such as schools and prisons across the United States. I would even travel to Rwanda, the site of the most dramatic and brutal genocide in recent history, to see if and how forgiveness was possible after such extreme violence. But first, I wanted to explore the flipside of forgiveness, the phenomenon that has the power to set the stage for forgiveness and yet remains just as rare: redemption.

3

Making Amends:
The Role of Redemption

Long ago, on a dull gray afternoon, I huddled with my friends outside our sixth-grade building, talking about a sleepover we were planning for the weekend.

I looked up to see Liz walking toward us. She was slim and a little boyish, with cropped hair and blunt bangs that grazed her dark eyebrows. I'd known her since the first grade, when I admired her skill on the violin at summer camp.

She moved closer—sixty, fifty, forty feet away. She walked with her head down, hands shoved into her pockets, and treaded with caution, as if the ground might swallow her. Something about this disgusted me.

I turned to the circle of girls around me. "Here comes Liz," I said, pointing thirty, twenty, ten feet away. "Let's ditch her!"

As I turned to run, I glanced at Liz. Her little half smile had vanished, and she formed an *o* with her mouth. Her brown eyes registered hurt and confusion. The image of her face stayed with me as I ran with my friends, laughing, past brick buildings and brown lawns and spindly trees with bare branches. Whenever I saw her after that, in gym class or at the pizza parlor after school, I avoided her gaze.

Over the years, I revisited that scene a lot in my mind. It haunted me. I wondered what drove me to be so cruel and what it meant. Why, I wondered, when from a young age I'd been outraged by injustice and saddened by other people's pain, did I hurt someone like that? Even when I wasn't thinking about it, that moment shaped my curiosities. In graduate school, I wrote a story about anti-bullying programs in suburban New Jersey. Several years after that, I wrote an article for *Glamour* titled "Why are nice, normal girls getting bullied online?" I talked to experts who explained how online anonymity made harassment and bullying easier and much more common. I quoted young women who—on public gossip sites—were called "psychotic lying whore skank" and "thunder thighs."

In researching forgiveness and the role apology plays in it, my mind again turned back to those days when I excluded Liz from our group. I thought about how I'd once, in high school, made a bungled and wholly ineffective attempt to apologize to Liz. As I talked to people like Azim about granting forgiveness, I became increasingly curious about the process of seeking it. Social science research—not to mention personal experience—suggests that it's easier to forgive someone who has apologized and made an effort to repair the damage he or she caused. Yet while this seems obvious, what are the right and wrong ways to apologize? What precisely is redemption? And how do we rebuild trust once it's been violated?

Because I'd written about addiction before, I knew that most recovery programs included formal ways of seeking forgiveness, with the goal of changing destructive behavior instead of merely saying, "Sorry." I also knew that twelve-step programs use the term "amend" instead of apology, because most addicts have spent much of their lives violating apologies— among other promises—and the meaning of the word amend is "to repair damage." I wanted to find out more about how recovering addicts do this, and what the rest of us might learn from it. I should note here that I don't see twelve-step programs as the silver bullet of addiction treatment. After all, peer-reviewed studies estimate the programs' value at between 5 and 10 percent. That said, I'd known dozens of people who swore by the value of the twelve steps in helping them recover, and I was specifically intrigued by the concept and process of making amends.

Perusing a recovery Web site, I came across an advice column on amends by someone named Karen L. When I reached out to her via e-mail, she responded enthusiastically and said she was happy to share her experience as a recovering alcoholic with nearly a decade of sobriety. A few long phone conversations later, I was so intrigued by her tale of despair and re-demption that I booked a flight to Phoenix to visit her.

I drove my rental through a sea of Scottsdale subdivisions in the late summer heat, past the green mesquite that lined the boulevards and large, brown stucco homes designed by Frank Lloyd Wright to blend into the sandy foothills. It was unseasonably rainy in spite of the heat, and Karen answered her large wooden door wearing jeans and a long-sleeved shirt. She was petite and rail-thin at fifty-three, her hazel eyes and fine features framed by a brunette bob that curled under at the bottom and grazed her slender shoulders. She greeted me warmly and invited me inside. We sat down in her living room on caramel leather couches, and she told me her story.

Almost a decade before I met her, Karen sat down in that same room and took a deep breath. Her hands trembled, this time not from alcohol with-drawal but from nerves. Her husband, Jack, sat across from her, waiting. It seemed like everything around them hung suspended—the view through the wide window of Phoenix's Camelback Mountain, the sofa where they often sat to watch movies, the dining room table where they ate. The life they had spent more than two decades building together, working multiple jobs and raising two daughters, all seemed to hang on this moment, teetering over a deep crevasse. If this didn't go well, she knew she would probably lose it all.

Three months earlier, at the plummeting end of a long downward spiral featuring frequent blackouts and near daily mood swings, one night she got so drunk she fell face-first on their iron bed frame and got a black eye. No one believed her lie that she'd tripped over the family dog, and worse, some even thought maybe her husband, Jack, had hit her. Then Jack discovered she'd had an affair and threatened to leave her. He packed her suitcases and told her she'd better finally face the fact that she had a drinking problem. It was then that she called the Alcoholics Anonymous hotline, not because she actually intended to give up booze but because she wanted to make him stay. A few AA meetings later, though, after listening to stories of people losing spouses, children, and jobs to alcohol, she felt a real and growing desire to remain sober. She wanted to do her best to repair her life and her relationships, even if it might be too late.

When she sat down with Jack in the family room, she hadn't had a drink in more than ten weeks and had been attending three AA meetings a day. "I was wrong for lying," she started, her voice wavering as she began the amends process that is AA's ninth step, the one in which you acknowledge the ways you've hurt people and tell them you've changed. "I was wrong for cheating and for thinking anyone was more important to me than you are. I was wrong for being selfish. . . ." Karen collected the most painful memories—rekindling an old flame and then lying about it, making such a loud scene at a restaurant during a Hawaiian vacation that her college-aged daughter abruptly flew home alone the next day—and bundled them into categories: lying, cheating, yelling, blaming. She was wrong for all of it, she said, and she wouldn't do it again. She didn't explicitly ask her husband if he would forgive her, not yet, mostly because she was scared to get a definitive no, and because she felt there was no way she could ever make it up to him.

Her husband asked a few questions. He didn't say, "That's okay, honey." He didn't say, "I forgive you." He listened with hands clasped, watching his wife's expressions. When she finished, the air felt charged and heavy, filled with grief, sadness, hope, and the fear of daring to hope. They had been together for more than twenty years. The painful constellation of feelings that seemed to float in Jack's chest was complicated and deep and difficult to explain. He loved his wife more than anyone, no matter what. And yet she had hurt him more than anyone else ever had, too.

Watching Karen now, he saw a new agony etched into her face. She seemed to have aged, looking exhausted and hollowed out. And yet, she also seemed real. Accessible. Present. The "I have it together and it's fine" mask was gone. The pert smile was gone. The pleading puppy-dog look was gone, too, and so was any illusion of control. He felt closer to her than he had in a long time. She'd said sorry so often over the years, but never with this degree of genuine emotion. Seeing her suffer this way moved him. It was also heartbreaking. Part of him wanted to go to her and comfort her, but he remained on the couch, because he was still hurt and angry, and he knew there was no making it better with a hug or a word of absolution. Was this change real? Would she make it real? And was everything that had happened his own fault? Was there something he could have done to intervene, to prevent them from winding up here? He didn't know. He had no idea what would happen now. They would just have to wait and see.

Months earlier, before she realized she was ruining her marriage and wanted to save it, Karen sat poolside at a plush golf course, sipping a Bloody Mary with a man who was not her husband. He was a former crush from graduate school whom she'd invited to visit while Jack was away on business. Weeks earlier, while drunk in the middle of the afternoon, she had thought of this man on a whim, looked him up online, and picked up the phone. Despite the fact that he was also married, he said he wanted to come. During his whirlwind stay, this debonair attorney stayed at her and Jack's home, grilled meat and vegetables in their backyard, and shopped with her at their local grocery store. Karen didn't know that one of her husband's colleagues had seen her with this strange man at the store. Months later, she would look back on this period, a time during which she couldn't go an hour without a drink, and feel as if she were watching disjointed outtakes from a film she could barely remember—a film about someone else.

It makes sense, given the neurology of the addicted brain. Thanks to the advent of scanning technologies such as fMRI, researchers have discovered how substance abuse affects different parts of the organ and why addicts' neurology may be unique to begin with. They've identified the flood of neurotransmitters that lulls users into ever-deeper levels of dependency, and discovered that alcoholics eventually lose the ability to produce normal levels of cortisol, the steroid that helps the body cope with stress.

This explains why Karen needed a drink every time she felt anxious. Addicts have trouble "reversing their response" to pleasure, even when the consequences outweigh the benefits, because of a problem with their orbital frontal cortex—the part of the brain just behind the forehead that's responsible for reasoning and logical decisions. That part, whether because of substance abuse or the genetic factors that preceded it, tends to suffer from low blood flow in addicts, and therefore lacks the energy it needs to inhibit impulsive behavior. The more Karen drank, the less effective her orbital frontal cortex became at driving logical decision making such as acting based on the reasons *not* to pour a drink or have an affair, while her amygdala and insula, which record emotional and experiential memory and stoke cravings, were increasingly activated. The scenario is a biological version of the devil and angel over the shoulder, with the devil becoming increasingly influential.

Jack didn't know anything about the neurobiology of addiction, but he knew that something was going terribly wrong in his marriage. When he returned home and a coworker told him he'd seen his wife with another man, Jack's suspicions were confirmed. He immediately recalled the moment, weeks earlier, when he spotted an unfamiliar number on their phone bill. St. Louis. Who the hell lived there? Karen said it must have been a misdial, but something seemed strange in her voice, so he pushed her on it. She'd admitted the truth, but said she wouldn't contact the man again.

The day his coworker told him that his wife had invited the man to stay in their home, the doubts Jack had been having transformed into a molten ball of fiery rage in the center of his chest. "How dare you!" he shouted when he got home. "That's it. We're done." She started to cry. He threw her cell phone across the room, where it hit the wall and broke into pieces. The days that followed were filled with the silent treatment, punctuated by him either yelling or asking her why she did it. She said she was sorry again and again, but she couldn't explain why she'd cheated—nor could she explain what it was like to wake up trembling and look at the clock and think, "Today, I won't drink," and then immediately pour a cocktail.

As many addictions do, Karen's started out innocently enough. In college, she was president of her sorority and earned high grades, but she was often the last to linger at a party or close a bar. After she married, she would enjoy a glass of wine after work, or several at a dinner party. Over time, she began to monitor the liquor store hours and strategize about how much she could buy without looking like a lush. When their eldest daughter was in college and their youngest, Annie, was thirteen, Jack got a promotion and they moved to Arizona. Karen quickly found a job running a vocational school and kept their new house immaculately clean, but she also began drinking more and more. Her relationship with her daughter became tense; Annie resented the move and began to notice her mother's escalating drinking.

When a colleague who had no family nearby was diagnosed with terminal cancer, Karen offered to care for the woman and took a leave of absence from work. She moved the woman into hospice, cared for her until she passed away months later, and settled the estate, all the while drinking wine throughout the day. Soon she was waking up with bourbon instead of coffee. Unmotivated to return to work, she spent her mornings cleaning the house while nursing a glass of Maker's Mark, which she hid behind the microwave when anyone stopped by. In the afternoons, she sat in their living room, and sank into the leather couch to watch television while swilling whatever booze was left in the cupboard.

Jack, consumed with his demanding corporate job, had begun to notice her mood swings and the occasional hidden glass. Later, he would regret not doing or saying something about it, but it's not surprising that he didn't. He was a hardworking businessman from a family of Italian New Yorkers, and denial and avoidance were common traits among his male relatives. By the time he threatened to throw his wife's packed suitcases into the street in a frenzy of rage, she wept and stopped eating, in the hope that he would feel sorry for her. Finally, faced with losing her entire life as she knew it, this was when Karen told him, "I'm going to call AA." Jack, unmoved, didn't say anything. Once he left, she called the Alcoholics Anonymous hotline number she found in the phone book. A man named Ray answered. He asked if she'd had a drink that day. She had. "If you don't drink for the rest of the day, or tomorrow, meet me at noon and I'll take you to a meeting," he said. The amygdala-driven voice in her head said that was ridiculous. She didn't really need to stop drinking altogether, she just needed to monitor it. And yet, something deep within her must have agreed with Ray.

She somehow managed to avoid alcohol for twenty-four hours, in spite of the shaking and her pounding heart and the voice in her head telling her to have just one glass, and drove to meet Ray at a local McDonald's the next day. A thirtysomething with twenty sobriety chips on a round key chain, Ray led the way to the nearby North Scottsdale Fellowship, where twelve-step meetings are held seven days a week. They walked into a large room filled with tables, where a huge banner listed the twelve steps. Karen glanced at the group. Most were men, and she didn't see anyone she could imagine being friends with. *What am I doing here?* But when someone pressed a gold-colored token into her palm to commemorate her first twenty-four hours of sobriety, she felt a pang of pride.

The next day, Karen arrived for a women's-only meeting to find that many of those introducing themselves as alcoholics looked like her—well-dressed wives, lawyers, nurses, and pilots. She instantly felt more comfortable. As she continued to avoid drinking, her shaking increased and she noticed aches and pains she wasn't aware of before. She was also engulfed by waves of emotion, mostly anger and shame. She saw those frag-mented movie scenes flicker across the landscape of her mind—shouting at her daughter in a fancy Hawaiian restaurant, drinking Bloody Marys with the old crush and allowing him into her and Jack's home, wasting days on the couch with a glass in hand. The humiliation that accompanied these memories, no longer dulled by merlot or bourbon, made her want to disap-pear. *I'm from a family who loved me, I'm educated and well-off, with a loving husband. How did this happen?* Amid this ocean of self-loathing, the women she met at meetings became her life rafts, and she threw herself onto them with everything she had.

I'm not an alcoholic, but as I listened to Karen's story in Scottsdale over sparkling water and salad, and attended meetings with her, I could relate to the shame that she described. I'd always been a perfectionist, dogged by the sneaking suspicion that no matter what, my best work, my best self even, failed to measure up. I had the sneaking suspicion that that insecurity was what drove me to betray my friend Liz so long ago. After visiting Karen at her desert home, I researched shame and discovered that it's one of the most destructive emotions we can have. While most of us might not reach for a cocktail or a crack pipe when shame envelops us, it still tends to drive us to think and act in harmful ways. While guilt reflects an opinion that you *did* something bad, social science researcher Brene Brown writes in her bestselling book, *Daring Greatly*, that shame means you think you *are* bad. Shame triggers the fight-or-flight part of the brain that's wired for survival, not connection, and it leads us to run, hide, or attack. Whether that means insulting a colleague, yelling at your three-year-old, or refusing to return phone calls, dwelling in shame usually leads down a dead-end road.

The antidote? Brown lists four ways to develop "shame resilience": recognizing shame and its triggers, practicing critical awareness (looking at the expectations driving your shame and asking whether they're realistic, attainable, or fueled by others' needs or wants and not your own), reaching out to trusted loved ones, and talking about how you feel and what you need. Interestingly, these guidelines have a lot in common with the twelve steps. They feature honesty, connection, and compassion—concern for and understanding of suffering. One potential pitfall of participating in a twelve-step program is interpreting the idea that you need to redeem yourself as confirmation that you are deeply and irrevocably flawed and deserving of shame. The crucial distinction to make is between being accountable and taking responsibility for your actions (which includes treating your disease), versus collapsing in self-loathing and helplessness. To forgive addicts for the damage they've caused, it's helpful for the rest of us to distinguish between the person and the disease; likewise, addicts themselves must make the same distinction when it comes to their self-image. As a friend who has studied and dealt personally with mental illness and addiction says, "blame the disease, not the person—but hold the person accountable." Holding oneself or others accountable without placing personal blame starts with understanding.

As Karen talked with others in recovery, she began to understand herself better. She read the Big Book, the twelve-step bible, which explained that alcoholism is a disease, not a character flaw. She attended three meetings per day, at seven a.m., noon, and four p.m. She noticed certain things about her upbringing that drove insecurity, such as her mother's criticism and a perfectionistic need to win her parents' approval. She told her worst stories and was met with compassion. As the recovery community likes to say, "The group exists to love you until you can love yourself."

As the months passed, Karen attended 120 meetings in ninety days (the standard goal is 90 meetings in ninety days), and she grew stronger. But she still felt like she was walking on eggshells at home around Jack, while he regarded her from a distance, uncertain, as if waiting for the worst. He'd done some research on addiction and the twelve steps, and once he asked, "Isn't there some amends thing you're supposed to do?" Karen explained that yes, there was, but first she had to make her way through the first eight steps. She had to reach a certain level of self-acceptance, while at the same time taking responsibility for her mistakes and preparing to make amends for them. "If you don't love yourself," she would tell me, "you'll keep destroying yourself."

Considering the things she'd done, sometimes self-love seemed like a glistening castle reachable only by boat, when all she had was one puny oar. And yet, she felt more confident each day that she awoke without a drink and recited the Serenity Prayer at the seven a.m. meeting. "God," the group would start, holding hands in a circle as they addressed the higher power that some viewed as a deity and others saw as their own soul or higher self, "grant me the serenity to accept the things I cannot change, the courage to change the things I can, and the wisdom to know the difference."

Making Amends and Effective Apology

In the months after Karen made her amends to Jack, she began to accept that their marriage might never fully recover. And for the first time, she knew that while she didn't want that, she would be okay if they separated. Jack, meanwhile, listened thoughtfully to the insights Karen shared as she progressed in her recovery. As the months passed, he found that his love for her remained and even grew, and that he admired her for her tenacity and commitment. When Karen earned her celebratory coin for six months of sobriety, she requested four so she could give one to each member of her family. Jack told me later that as he watched her progress, he marveled at her resolve. "I honestly don't know if I would have had the courage to say, 'I failed and I'm trying to find my way back,'" he said. "I'm very proud of her for doing that." The more he understood and witnessed her struggle to recover, the more he was able to forgive. His forgiveness came not as a declaration, but as a series of small actions: handing her a cup of coffee in the morning, kissing her for no reason, bringing leftover pastries home from the office.

Next on Karen's list for amends was her youngest daughter, who was in her early twenties by then. Their relationship had long been tumultuous, and Karen felt nervous when she arrived in Virginia, where Annie was stationed with the navy. As Karen had expected, Annie was cold and distant. She avoided conversations by saying she had a headache or was going out with friends. Once, she left after dinner and didn't return until two a.m. Then, one afternoon, she agreed to talk. She listened, stone-faced, as Karen listed the things she was wrong for having done and her declaration that she had changed. Then, without conviction, Annie said, "Okay." That was it. Karen's stomach sank.

She hoped it would be easier with her eldest daughter. Ciri was already out of the house during the low point of her drinking, though she and her husband had moved away because they didn't want their child to be around Karen's drunken outbursts. During her visit, Ciri listened to Karen's list and grabbed her hands. "It's okay, Mom," she said, tears streaking her face. "I love you. You can do this." As Karen wept and held her daughter's hands, she felt like she could finally breathe again.

Several years after that first amends conversation, Annie called. She sounded less guarded. She had a new baby, and she cried into the phone and said that looking into her infant's face, she couldn't understand how Karen had lied to her and treated her the way she did while drinking. That was the first of many conversations that helped Annie to understand what her mother went through. Annie says she still sometimes gets angry at her mother, and often thinks about the embarrassment and pain of feeling like Karen was choosing alcohol over her. Even so, a decade and many coins later, Karen and Annie talk almost daily. Karen has nine grandchildren between the ages of one and ten, and sees them whenever she can.

On a recent summer day, as I sat with Karen on her back patio, Annie called to ask how long she should cook a casserole from a family recipe. She had also asked Karen to talk to a friend with a drinking problem, and was considering moving back to the Phoenix area to be closer to her parents. "This is the kid who couldn't get far enough away from me," Karen told me. "And asking me to talk to her friend—that's the highest form of flattery."

Her daughters aren't the only ones who seek input from Karen. Jack told me that their marriage is even better now than it was before Karen's drinking escalated. "She began to behave differently," he said, "and I've responded in kind." When she gets upset, for example, she shares her feelings instead of yelling or storming away, and Jack has learned to do the same. "She's much more open and accepting now, more willing to talk and consider. It's a whole different level of consciousness," he told me. "Things that we would have fought about twenty years ago, we don't. Her recovery has helped so many other people, including me. I love that about her."

The more time I spent with Karen and the more I studied the literature on apology, it became clear that seeking forgiveness from others and oneself is a crucial part of successful recoveries from substance abuse. After all, the most frequent causes of relapse are resentment, blame, and shame.

As I studied effective apology, I learned that seeking forgiveness is just as much about renewing our ability to trust ourselves as it is about restoring trust with others. Trust is defined as the firm belief in the reliability, truth, ability, or strength of someone or something. While many people think of trust as a mysterious currency that either exists or does not, or a solid substance that once shattered can never be rebuilt, that perspective doesn't leave much hope for repairing damaged relationships. In their book *Building Trust*, Robert Solomon, a business and philosophy professor at the

University of Texas at Austin, and Fernando Flores, a business consultant, describe trust as an ongoing emotional skill. That skill takes the form of choosing to trust others and making commitments ourselves: "We come to have expectations of others, and we respond to the fulfillment or frustration of those expectations. Trust isn't something we 'have.' . . . Trust is something we do, something we make."

Repairing trust requires awareness and effort, starting with acknowledging the truth. When I was four, for instance, I carved my initials in our family's wooden coffee table. When confronted, I denied it. "It was Scott!" I said, earnestly explaining to my father that my imaginary friend, a naughty apparition who wore a stained orange T-shirt and loved to break rules, carved my initials into the table in order to frame me. That may be part of a normal developmental phase at four, but how many of us have done the same as adults, insisting, in spite of plain evidence to the contrary, that "It wasn't me! I didn't do it!"? And yet, for those of us who aren't sociopaths—more than 95 percent of the population, by most calculations—hiding mistakes and failing to make them right not only erodes the trust we've built with others, it also lands us in a sinking pit of shame. The way to start the climb up and out is through truth and accountability.

Being accountable is more than saying sorry. An effective apology—one with the power to restore trust—has four parts, according to Dr. Aaron Lazare, dean of psychiatry at the University of Massachusetts Medical School and author of the book *On Apology*. They include acknowledging the offense, giving an authentic explanation (not an excuse), expressing remorse, and providing some sort of reparation. The most common mistakes people make when they apologize are avoiding responsibility for the blunder ("mistakes were made"), or minimizing the damage and blaming the victim ("sorry you were upset" or "sorry you found that offensive").

In legal settings, apologies can help resolve litigation, giving wounded parties a sense of justice that makes a settlement more likely. Jennifer Robbennolt, a professor of law and psychology at the University of Illinois at Urbana–Champaign, has researched apology for more than a decade. In one study, she asked 550 people to imagine that they were the injured party in a civil dispute. She gave half of them a version of the facts in which the defendant apologized, and she gave the other half a version in which there was no apology, or only an incomplete one. Those who received an apology expressed willingness to accept a lower settlement than those who did not. In scenarios where the settlement amount was fixed, participants who received a complete apology were more likely to accept the deal than those who didn't. Furthermore, Robbennolt found that incomplete apologies aren't just less effective—they often make things worse. Remarks such as "I'm sorry you were hurt" made people less inclined to settle than if they received no apology at all.

These findings dovetail with University of Miami researcher Mc-Cullough's argument that humans have evolved to grant forgiveness under specific conditions (when safety is assured and an offender presents value). A solid apology also restores a victim's sense of dignity, making her less intent on resorting to revenge to defend her honor; it signals that the victim will be safe from further harm, and it indicates that the victim and offender share similar values, which makes the offender seem more worthy of care. Lastly, the remorse in a complete apology satisfies the wronged party's desire to see a transgressor suffer. What drives revenge is not the brain's "rage circuit," but the pursuit of desire and pleasure housed in the brain's "seeking system." Seeing an offender suffering the pain of remorse just might satisfy that desire, McCullough says, making victims more likely to empathize with a transgressor, and thus, more likely to forgive. This is one reason apologies offered by politicians or business leaders on behalf of a large group are rarely effective—they tend to come off as remorseless and impersonal. Even group apologies that seem authentically remorseful—such as former Australian prime minister Kevin Rudd's apology to the "stolen generations" of Aborigines forcibly taken from their families and sent to white boarding schools—fall short when the apology isn't followed by some sort of reparation.

Another explanation for why apology and restitution make forgiveness more likely comes from Dr. Everett Worthington, one of the so-called fathers of forgiveness research, who recently published a book about self-forgiveness. Just as we expect people who make mistakes to apologize and make them right, he says we tend to expect the same of ourselves. "Forgiving ourselves is not simply a matter of letting ourselves off the hook," he writes in *Moving Forward*. "Imagine how you would react if Hitler had been tried at Nuremberg and, on the witness stand, said, 'I admit that I killed a lot of innocent people. But I have decided to forgive myself.'" We want others to face justice and to repair the harm they've caused, and we're no different when it comes to ourselves.

Apology and Self-Forgiveness

In addition to its other benefits, seeking forgiveness and repairing harm helps us to forgive ourselves, research shows, and forgiving oneself results in similar benefits to forgiving others. In a 2014 study, researchers at Baylor University surveyed 269 people who felt guilty about gossiping, cheating, and inflicting physical pain, among other things. When asked how much they had forgiven themselves, a stark difference emerged: Those who had admitted their mistakes and sought forgiveness from the wronged party were more likely to feel they had the right to forgive themselves, while those who hadn't taken those actions did not.

While blaming others is linked to anger and hostility, chronic self-blame is correlated with high anxiety, depression, and negative self-esteem. People who are better at forgiving themselves—meaning that they're able to cut themselves some slack and don't often engage in highly critical self-talk—are better at coping with stress and its potential health hazards. In a 2014 study, researchers from Brandeis University evaluated a group of forty-one healthy young adults, assessing their capacity for self-forgiveness through statements such as "I try to be understanding and patient toward aspects of my personality I do not like" and "I'm disapproving and judgmental about my own flaws and inadequacies."

Next, the scientists exposed the participants to a stressor. When they tested the participants' stress levels by measuring concentrations of an inflammatory agent called interleukin, those with higher self-compassion showed a lower stress response, even when controlling for self-esteem, depressive symptoms, demographic factors, and distress. The following day, the stress response in those with lower self-compassion was even stronger, indicating that those lacking in self-forgiveness are less able to cope with stress over time. That means that without self-forgiveness, you're at a higher risk of diseases linked to stress-related inflammation, such as cardiovascular disease and Alzheimer's.

When I discussed this with Karen, she raised an important point: One of the risks in all of this is making your own self-forgiveness contingent upon someone else's willingness or ability to forgive you. It keeps you stuck in the same way that refusing to forgive until someone apologizes keeps you stuck, a victim yet again of someone else's emotions or choices or abilities. So often, shame and an obsessive drive to be accepted are what drive us to commit harmful acts in the first place, so trying to repair the harm merely as another way to seek approval or drown our shame is not only manipulative and selfish, it also just doesn't work. In addition, being overly concerned about whether you actually receive forgiveness when seeking it can place undue pressure on the person who has been wronged. I'm guessing most of us can recall a time when someone apologized, yet their focus seemed more directed at absolving their own guilt than caring for our well-being. It's a delicate balance.

When Karen made her amends, she worked hard to ensure that her self-regard was not totally dependent upon whether her family forgave her. This is easier said than done, of course, and some days she failed, unable to imagine how she could ever forgive herself if they couldn't do it first. Nonetheless, she persevered, reminding herself that their forgiveness was up to them. Over time, her dedication to cleaning up the messes she had made strengthened her self-confidence and increased her self-respect. As she told the truth and began to repair the damage, she began to see herself in a more positive light, and she began to trust herself again. She realized that without shaming herself, she could see her own role in succumbing to her disease, and she could take responsibility for it. "I had to free myself," she told me. "To some extent, whether or not they forgave me was beside the point."

In Pursuit of Redemption

On a sunny afternoon, I accompanied Karen to the North Scottsdale Fellowship for the eleven a.m. meeting. She wore a white blouse and beige slacks, her shoulder-length dark hair neatly combed and curled. We sat against the wall, under a poster that read, *Alcoholism in a family is like a tornado; it can leave your life in ruins.* Some fifty women took their seats, a wide range of ages, styles, and ethnicities.

A fortyish woman with long, glistening black hair and a pink suit that matched her rosy cheeks introduced herself as Devorah. She kicked off the meeting by sharing her approach to Step 10, "Maintenance," which means practicing the first nine steps consistently, from self-love to consistently making amends.

Each night, she said, she does the "Personal Inventory" to determine if she did anything selfish, dishonest, or hurtful that day, and then makes a note to make an amend. Just that week, she'd apologized to a coworker for making a sharp comment. "Even if part of it is the other person's fault, I can take responsibility for my part," she said. "And I can forgive them and keep my side of the street clean. That makes me feel good about myself. When I was drinking I never even knew I hurt people, much less apologized. Now I can do the spot-check inventory and get a good night's sleep."

Across the table, a fifty-something woman with short bleach-blond hair said, "When I hurt someone's feelings I know it immediately—I get a sick feeling in my gut. So I check before I say something: Is it true? Is it kind? Is it necessary? If not, I don't say it."

Beside me, Karen sat with a copy of the Big Book open in her lap, the pages covered in orange highlighter. When her turn came to speak, she started with a joke. "I did a version of the Step 10 inventory [of wrongs] every night my whole life. . . . It just wasn't mine!" she said, triggering knowing laughter throughout the room. "Back then, it was about what everyone else did to me. Now, if I feel wronged, I can usually find my part in it, take responsibility, and let it go. I wake up every morning and feel like it truly is a new day."

As I sat there listening, I did my own "personal inventory." Scanning the past few weeks in my mind, I made a mental note to apologize to my mother for snapping at her about something silly, like plans for an upcoming family trip. I thought about how, so often, I spoke harshly to those closest to me when I was stressed. But then my mind drifted further back, to ditching Liz in the sixth grade. Just thinking about it made me feel queasy. It was a topic that seemed to come up regularly, even at odd times. One of the most recent was at a date-night cooking class with Anthony.

It was Valentine's Day, and he'd planned dinner at a new cooking school in a hip part of town, in a building with colorful mosaic tile décor and exposed brick walls. One thing I loved about him was how multifaceted he was. He'd majored in accounting and loved spreadsheets, was a sports aficionado who played basketball and did CrossFit weekly, but he also enjoyed creative endeavors like building a doghouse for Stella, drawing, learning to cook, and planning parties and fund-raising events. He even had a sleeve tattoo on his left arm, a bright, whimsical circus complete with an elephant balancing on a ball, a leaping tiger, and a ringmaster choreographing the merry chaos. The scene symbolized his large, extended immigrant family, and the ringmaster represented him. He'd gotten the tattoo shortly after his younger brother, a teenager, got arrested for trying to outrun the cops, and he described the image, and the process of getting it, as a cathartic way of processing what was happening in his family and his own attempts to be the one to make things right and keep things under control. (Eventually, agreeing that he needed structure and discipline, his brother joined the Marines.) The first time Anthony met my mother when she was visiting Denver, he wore a long-sleeved button-up shirt and a sweater to cover the tattoo. Over dinner, though, my mother spotted some bright green and yellow near his wrist as he reached for the salt. "Let's see your tattoo," she said, her green eyes glittering with curiosity. Anthony glanced at me, obviously nervous. I nodded. He pulled up his sleeve and showed my mother the artwork, explaining what it all meant. To his great surprise, my mother loved it. (His grandparents were horrified by the tattoo, saying it made him resemble a convict.) "What a whimsical and creative way to deal with your family history!" she said in approval. "It's wonderful!" In spite of the fact that I'd never dated anyone with tattoos and never imagined I would until I met Anthony, I agreed.

At the Valentine's cooking class, the cheerful chef-instructor hung aprons around our necks, handed us cocktails, and led us through the step-by-step process of cooking oysters Rockefeller, baked salmon, and a magnificent chocolate soufflé. As we were eating the delicious results of our labor with another couple whom we'd just met, one of the women said the word "bullying" in passing. It was part of a brief anecdote about another topic, but the word caught my attention. Without thinking, I oddly blurted out, "I was a bully." The table immediately fell silent. I swallowed and did my best to explain what I'd done as a kid and that I regretted it, but I felt like an awkward employee with the habit of making uncomfortably personal admissions at business meetings. The woman who'd mentioned bullying barely spoke to me for the rest of the night. I guessed maybe she'd been at the opposite end of the bullying spectrum as a kid and wrote me off as a result.

Later, once we were in the car, Anthony said, "You know, you might not want to bring up the whole bullying thing with strangers. It's a little . . ." At first I got defensive. I said I was just trying to make conversation, and point out that people who were mean at one point in their lives weren't necessarily bad people. I'd told him about Liz before, and he'd listened and said he understood, even though my private school experience couldn't have been more different from his urban, inner-city schooling in Massachusetts, where starting at the age of eight, he routinely got jumped by boys who wanted his Nikes or Red Sox baseball hats. "I get it, babe, but it was just weird to mention it in that setting," he told me in the car now. He was right. It was odd, and as my psychologist mother would say, a sign of something "unresolved." This ability to observe each other's quirky flaws, and even call each other's attention to them in (mostly) gentle ways, was one of many things I liked about my relationship with Anthony. It's rarely pleasant to have someone point out the ketchup all over your face—or some graver self-sabotaging foible—but when he did it, it wasn't insulting, but merely truth telling out of love and generosity. After I embarrassed myself at the table that night, I began thinking about what I should do about the fact that my middle school mistakes were still haunting me.

I wondered if I should apologize to Liz again, though I'd once read something about how apologizing to someone you've bullied can be counterproductive because it can take the form of pressuring them to forgive in order to assuage your guilt. Once in high school, while a group of us were gathered around chips and guacamole in someone's kitchen, I turned to Liz and said something like, "I'm really sorry I was so terrible to you in the sixth grade." She shrugged it off, waving the apology away as if it were a gnat circling her face. "It doesn't matter," she said. That exchange certainly did little to bridge the chasm between us. She remained guarded and distant, and I couldn't blame her. The days of sitting together at field trips, carpooling to school, and taking combined family trips were long over.

A few months after visiting Karen, I decided to reach out to Liz again. I figured that maybe now, as adults, we could talk about what happened from a more mature perspective, that maybe I could make another attempt at apologizing for being such a jerk, without pressuring her to rehash something she didn't want to or to forgive me. I found her on Facebook, which showed that she was now a married mother of four. I wrote her a note asking if she would be willing to talk. A week or so passed, and I didn't hear anything. Just in case she didn't see it or forgot, I sent a follow-up message. To this, I got an instant reply. *I'm sorry I forgot to respond, Megan,* she wrote. *I got your e-mail and then totally spaced it. I don't want to talk to you about it. It was so very long ago and we are both different people more than two decades later. I am happy to be digital pals, but I have no interest in rehashing 6th grade.* I replied that I respected that, and thanked her for responding.

I mentioned the Liz episode to a therapist once. When she asked what was going on in my life in sixth grade, I told her that my sister had left for college, and that at around the same time, my best friend's father killed himself by hanging in the family basement. The therapist suggested that I bullied Liz as a way of trying to make myself feel powerful and connected at a time when I felt alone and powerless. That made sense. And yet, when I thought about it, ditching Liz wasn't the first time I put others down in order to feel better about myself. In the fourth grade, I got in trouble for pouring a cup of fluorescent orange Tang onto the flaxen, white-blond hair of a boy in my class. In third grade, I put tacks on two students' chairs, but was thankfully discovered before anyone sat on them.

By college, I'd moved on from such juvenile pranks and thought I'd become a pretty nice person—that is, until a friend called my attention to my nasty habit of exclaiming with shock and horror when someone didn't know something that I thought was common knowledge. "You don't *know* who that *is*?!" I'd say, mouth agape, when a friend admitted she'd never heard of someone like Margaret Sanger or Billie Holiday. Ignorance of certain films or books met with similar reactions. "You've never *read* that?!" I'd say. "That's *ridiculous!*" Once called out, I began to notice myself doing it. I was surprised and embarrassed. I apologized to a lot of people, some of whom admitted that I'd made them feel tiny and stupid.

In addition to acting mean as a way to feel powerful, I realized through talking with my mother that I also did it to feel smart and competent when I felt daft and inept. Growing up as a sensitive kid with brilliant parents, and surrounded by highly gifted peers, I often felt slow. I struggled with math, sometimes crying, panicked and frozen, during tests, and while I excelled at individual sports such as track and skiing, I lacked the spatial awareness and coordination necessary for ball handling in sports like soccer and basketball. To puff myself up, my automatic response was to put others down, especially people who reminded me of the shyness, ignorance, or incompetence within myself that I was so desperately trying to banish.

My knee-jerk "mean girl" reaction was as natural as the age-old human instinct for aggression and revenge. But just as revenge has become less productive in a civilized, complex world that depends on cooperation and interdependence, my meanness failed to get me what I wanted or needed. Sure, maybe I felt justified and empowered for a brief moment, but the long-term effect of bullying and belittling was guilt and shame.

My first, incomplete apology to Liz was the first step I took to redeem myself. But redemption is defined as "to make better," not just to admit you screwed up. "An apology is a statement of intention to redeem oneself, and the beginning of a conversation about how this can be done," write Flores and Solomon. Jay Heinrichs, a classical rhetoric expert, says the most important part of fixing screwups is setting forth a new, inspiring future. You do that by admitting that you fell short of your high ideals and laying out your plan for how you'll honor them moving forward, he writes in his book, *Thank You for Arguing.* If people remain guiltily focused on what they did wrong for too long, Heinrichs points out, they seem to shrink. The association of apology with either an obligatory yet uncaring "sorry" or with a groveling shame-fest that makes the apologizer feel—and look— like a tiny mouse, leads many of us to shy away from the act altogether.

The key is striking the right balance between remorse and rededicating yourself to your high standards. For instance, Heinrichs recommends this type of response after a professional screwup: "Boss, you know what a detail-oriented person I usually am. In this case, though, I didn't live up to that reputation. My mistake drives me crazy, and I'll be even more fanatical about details in the future." One dramatic example of this in the corporate world is the spectacular near-death plunge that nearly killed Netflix in 2011, and the apology-revved recovery spearheaded by its chief executive, Reed Hastings. When the company announced it was dividing its DVD and streaming operations and raising prices, its stock price began to plummet, eventually falling from nearly $299 per share in July 2011 to just $53 a year later. Thousands of angry letters from customers poured into Netflix HQ, and stock traders wrote the company off as a goner.

Hastings posted on the Netflix blog on September 18, 2011. Starting out by saying he messed up, he wrote, "It is clear from the feedback over the past two months that many members felt we lacked respect and humility in the way we announced the separation of DVD and streaming, and the price changes. That was certainly not our intent, and I offer my sincere apology." He explained that the move was a push to remain current in its shift to digital, avoiding the spinouts of companies like Borders that failed to evolve. However, he acknowledged that he did a clumsy job of executing the move and communicated it poorly to his customers, pledging to do a better job of serving customers and communicating with them.

The apology impressed certain power players such as Wall Street analysts. Hastings knew that was just the beginning of his work, however. "We had to earn their trust by being very steady and disciplined," he told the *New York Times* in 2013. "I couldn't say for sure we'd recover. But I was confident that our best odds were to be very steady and focus on improving the service."

It worked. By April 2013, Netflix announced that it gained three million global subscribers in the first quarter and revenue for the quarter exceeded $1 billion, a company record. The stock price, meanwhile, was up 135 percent, making Netflix the best-performing company in the Standard & Poor's five-hundred-stock index. By April 2014, Netflix had surpassed YouTube as the top online video site, 69 percent of subscribers said they were unlikely to leave the service, and its original content, such as *House of Cards*, was drawing additional customers.

Compare Hastings's response to the disastrous stonewalling that characterized General Motors' reaction to its faulty ignition switches that caused crashes leading to more than a dozen deaths. Even though the company had evidence starting in 2001 that the switches malfunctioned, GM continued to install them in vehicles for another decade, until forced by lawsuits and investigations to issue a recall of 2.6 million cars in early 2014. In April, CEO Mary Barra finally issued an apology to a congressional committee investigating the fiasco, and to the families whose loved ones were killed. Yet she never explained why GM failed to fix the lethal switches, and bereaved family members dismissed the apology as too little, too late. Who would trust a company that refused to fix a mistake that was killing its customers for more than a decade, and when it finally admitted wrongdoing, continued to hide the truth?

Hastings's approach, like Karen's, inspired trust and restored dignity.

Which is precisely what the apology experts recommend: Show concern, talk about high standards, and fix the problem. I wasn't sure how to do that with Liz and my past as a bully. How could I fix something that I did so long ago, and to someone who didn't want to talk to me about it? I knew one option was to donate time or money to some sort of anti-bullying cause, but that didn't feel personal enough. One day, part of the puzzle fell into place while I was driving through Denver in my Subaru, listening to National Public Radio. The show was about how and when children develop empathy, and one of the producers spoke to a man who told a childhood story: When he was six, he and a friend were riding their bikes when they crossed an intersection. Once he was on the other side, he heard a *thwack*, and turned to see that his friend had been struck by a car. The boy tried to stand, but one of his legs buckled beneath him, broken, and he mouthed "help." Instead of turning around and going to his friend, the six-year-old continued home. When he got there, he didn't mention what happened to anyone, and his mother found out from the other boy's family that they'd been together at the time of the accident.

"It always haunted me," this man told the producer. But it did something else, too. It served as a reminder of how he'd fallen short in a fundamental way, a way in which he never wanted to fall short again. The memory of abandoning his friend in the intersection became his motivation to be a loyal and caring friend. Today, this man is known as the guy you'd call to pick you up in the middle of the Mohave Desert at three a.m. during a dust storm.

As I listened to the story, I felt hot tears of recognition rolling down my cheeks. It all came back—the dry, brown lawn, Liz's face as I ran from her with my friends, my cutting remarks. I realized that after I ruined our relationship, I worked hard to be a loving, trustworthy friend, and when I fell short of that standard, I apologized and corrected my missteps. Upon learning in college that through patronizing remarks I was yet again assuaging my own insecurity by making others feel belittled, my friends generously forgave me, and I pledged to be the kind of person who makes those around her feel bigger, not smaller.

Sitting in the car, I saw clearly for the first time just what that pledge made possible: I had a network of close friendships with people scattered across the country and the world, and they were more precious and sacred to me than anything in my life. I had one group of girlfriends that met monthly to empower each other in various career and personal goals. I had another comprised of zany, brave female writers, and yet another of hard-core Colorado adventurers, always up for a powder day on the slopes or a long hike in the backcountry followed by beers. I'd been in the weddings of half-dozen friends and attended half-dozen more, some in places as far away as Guatemala. I had one writer friend I hadn't even seen in six years—she now lived in Peru—but we spoke via phone every few weeks. Like my mother, I had become the kind of person people call when they're uncertain or afraid or devastated, the one they tap for advice and support. I felt exquisite gratitude for that, for how far I'd come from the girl who mercilessly turned on a friend.

I suddenly realized that even if Liz never forgave me, even if that situation was never fully "resolved," I could forgive myself. I had done everything I possibly could to make that mistake, that series of human flaws, into the raw material for the kinder person I was busy becoming. I doubt I would be the friend I am today if it weren't for those failings and the hard work and dedication they spurred in me. Even so, no matter what happened, I decided Liz deserved a better apology than the one I attempted in high school, and that it should be given freely, with no request of her.

There's no need for you to respond or for us to talk, I wrote this time.

It is about sixth grade, but it's not rehashing, at least that's not my intention. I wanted to apologize—truly—for excluding you from our group of friends. And if there were other things I did that were hurtful, things I may not even recall at this point, I apologize for those, too. I realize, of course, that we both have moved on, and that you have created a beautiful life for yourself and your family. I realize sixth grade probably seems like another life—it certainly does to me. And yet, I have always thought back to middle school and regretted suddenly excluding you and being un-kind. I felt awful and sad about it and wondered why I did it. After all, I've always prized my memories of our times together as kids—carpooling, admiring your musical prowess at camp, that family vacation to Colorado Springs.

After a lot of reflection, my answer is the one that most peo-ple would guess: I was feeling powerless and lonely for a variety of reasons, and being mean was a childish attempt to feel power-ful and connected. I felt insecure, and I acted that way in an at-tempt to master that feeling. That's not an excuse, of course, it's only an explanation. If I could, I would go back to those days and alter my behavior. While unfortunately I can't do that, I will always feel sad about it and work to increase compassion, my own and others'. I also realize that since middle school, I have worked really hard to be a loyal friend. That doesn't mean I don't still screw up and need to apologize for things, it just means that in some way, that middle school behavior contributed to the development of my conscience. Anyway, that is all. I hope this hasn't upset you or seemed unnecessary—it's just something I wish I had said years ago. Thank you for reading, and all my best, Megan.

As I pressed send, I felt a sense of relief. I didn't expect a reply or feel that I needed one, but a few days later, I received this message:

This apology means a lot to me. It is never too late to say sorry for a wrong committed. While I let it go (because what's the point of hanging on to it), there is some part of forgiveness that isn't com-plete until someone acknowledges the hurt they caused. It's a relational part, the part that allows hurts to shrink and relation-ships to repair. Thank you, Megan. All my best, right back at you.

4

A Reckoning of Origins:
Forgiving Our Parents

Rebecca Baines stands out in a room. Tall, lean, and muscular, with long brown hair and a bright, wide smile worthy of a Crest commercial, she is beautiful; but more striking even than her beauty is the light she seems to exude. She's quick to laugh. She likes to tell stories and hear them. Take her to a party where she doesn't know anyone, and soon she'll be surrounded by a group, absorbed in conversation.

The shining social ease that's so apparent now, in her early fifties, wasn't always part of Rebecca's personality. Growing up the third of four children, two boys and two girls, she was shy and quiet, the obedient daughter of a United Methodist minister. Her parents met at a Bible college in Texas, and they moved the family around the country as her father hopped from one church post to another. Her dad, a member of the Native American Tlingit and Tsimshian tribes in Alaska, worked for years to perfect his elocution and eliminate his native accent. By the time he became a minister, he didn't need a mic to fill a church with his warm, golden baritone. He also loved to sing, especially performing his favorite hymn, "How Great Thou Art."

As a girl, Rebecca loved to sing, too. When they lived on the edge of the woods outside Anchorage, she would hike up a nearby hillside and sing while gazing out over the trees and the ocean beyond. She loved the sound of her voice carrying on the open air. When the family lived in Glendale, Arizona, her parents managed to buy a retired racehorse, and after school Rebecca would ride bareback on the half acre of arid land surrounding their house. Her thoroughbred was a mare named Watoosie. Watoosie had a rare quality for a horse: She didn't abide men. During her racing career, Watoosie was known to buck off the male jockeys and finish the race alone. Yet when a woman climbed on her back, she seemed pleased by the companionship. Everyone guessed that Watoosie must have had a bad run-in with a man. Much later, Rebecca would joke that maybe she and the horse got along so well because they had that in common.

As Rebecca grew from a kindergartener who loved her black-and-brown plaid dress with lace trim into a serious young woman with dark hair that grew past her waist, she attended church and earned As. And then, once she'd been away from home for a few years for college, everything changed. She started having flashbacks during her first year at the University of New Mexico School of Medicine. At first, the scenes were clipped and disjointed, like the fragments of memory that arise in the haze of a hangover. But then, the flashbacks became horrifyingly complete. They featured her father, the United Methodist minister who organized church charity auctions and sang "How Great Thou Art," entering her room at night and raping her. In the most recent memories, she was sixteen. In the most distant, she was a toddler.

Rebecca is a friend. I asked her about her story because I wanted to know how people who have endured difficult childhoods forgive their parents (if they do), and whether doing so was helpful. For me, this was never an issue I had to face. There was nothing for which I had to forgive my parents, because they were incredibly generous and supportive. The only time I remember ever being truly angry at my parents was once when I was about six, and I hid in the bathtub for about an hour in hopes that they'd think I ran away and immediately feel terrible about whatever it was they'd done (I have no idea what it was). Life is challenging enough when you've had a charmed childhood, I figured, so how do people cope after growing up with parents who have hurt, disappointed, or neglected them?

Even for people who haven't had traumatic childhoods, harboring resentment against parents for more seemingly trivial things, like making light of our feelings or missing a dance recital or a little league game, can become destructive over time. Going back to what Luskin, the cofounder of the Stanford Forgiveness Project, said about the damaging physiological effects of holding a grudge, it's worth remembering that a grudge is a grudge, whether its origin is extreme (sexual abuse) or benign (forgetting our science fair presentation and then making light of it). The question of forgiving parents struck me as especially momentous, given the power that parents wield in our lives. Who could possibly be more influential to children—for good or for ill—than their original caretakers? And when that influence is harmful to any degree, how do you forgive?

To explore that question, I interviewed twenty people who say they've forgiven their parents, and several who say they've struggled to forgive. There's Loretta, whose mother tried to kill her more than once, and Genea, whose mother called her a "cow" and a "deviant" for coming out as a lesbian. There's Diego, whose absentee father appeared occasionally to make and break promises, and Kyra, whose father left her family and started a new one. Those I interviewed who did forgive didn't say it was easy. They did say that doing so provided myriad benefits, from peace of mind to self-confidence and better relationships with everyone from friends and relatives to spouses and lovers. I noticed that their stories showed striking commonalities with the research of the past two decades on happiness and psychological resilience. (While happiness refers to the maintenance of a positive emotional state, resilience describes why and how some people in "high-risk" conditions such as poverty or abuse become productive and fulfilled in spite of harrowing childhoods.)

It's important to emphasize here that forgiveness and reconciliation are two different things, and that it's possible to forgive without reconciling or having a relationship with an offender. Rebecca would ultimately choose to reconcile with her abusive father, but he was at that point nonthreatening. As a family friend and psychology professor once told me, "If I step on your toe and say 'sorry,' but continue standing on your toe, you're not going to say, 'It's okay, I forgive you,' you're going to tell me to get off your toe!" If someone continues hurtful behavior and it's unhealthy to be around them, setting firm boundaries—from not talking to them on the phone to not seeing them at all, ever—is vital. Forgiveness that seeks to rule out safety or justice is not forgiveness at all. And you don't necessarily have to have a physical or verbal resolution with the person, either. Though it may be more difficult, it's possible to forgive someone who is absent, whether because they're unsafe, imprisoned, or deceased, just as it's possible to forgive someone who is unrepentant.

As I reviewed my conversations with these roughly twenty people, aged twenty-two to sixty-five, I saw similarities not only in the benefits they received for forgiving, but also in *how* they forgave. We'll explore that process in the following pages. For Rebecca, like Azim and most of the people in this book, forgiving was a process, not a one-time act. Sometimes it didn't even feel or seem linear at all, but up and down, erratic and fluid. By and large, though, that process began with acknowledging the truth, and then setting about healing from it.

Many people who suffer severe sexual abuse as children repress it in order to cope, recalling the trauma in young adulthood or even later. Rebecca's flashbacks usually came at night, as she was drifting off to sleep. There were images of her father forcing himself on her in her twin-sized bed and memories of crying alone into a pillow afterward. Sometimes she even felt the searing pain and the breath on her face. She began forcing herself to study through the night to stave off the sickening flashbacks. Other times, she would drink wine to numb the horror that lay in wait. She couldn't eat and grew rail-thin. She cried uncontrollably, often for hours each day. She would sit reading her copy of *Harrison's Principles of Internal Medicine*, fat tears splashing onto the pages and smudging the words.

Had the situation been different, she might have convinced herself that she was merely having nightmares. But something had happened recently, before the first flashbacks exploded into her consciousness. Her father pled guilty to criminal sexual penetration of a minor. That minor was his stepdaughter, whose mother he'd married after he and Rebecca's mother divorced. For weeks, Rebecca resisted believing that he had done such a thing, much less admitted to it. She wrote him letters to pledge her support, signed them "Love, Rebecca," and mailed them to Cochise County Jail in Bisbee, Arizona.

Yet the flashbacks grew longer and more frequent, ambushing her day and night, like a relentless stalker whose mission was to systematically shatter her sanity. When she caught a glance of herself in the mirror, she saw a gaunt, haunted girl, desperate for escape. Then her father, having served a jail stint for the original conviction, was apprehended for molesting his stepdaughter again while on probation. The news annihilated any doubts about her father's culpability, and she could no longer hold her memories back. One night, she drunkenly called her sister in Alaska and said she didn't want to live anymore. Her sister told their brother, who persuaded their mother to fly to Albuquerque to help check Rebecca into a psychiatric hospital.

For days, Rebecca awoke to fluorescent light beaming in from the hallways, where lost-looking patients wandered the halls. *Just days ago I was in med school. How did I get here?* she would think. Her days were filled with intensive group sessions, one-on-one therapy, art therapy, and lots of bland, colorless food. She met an old veteran who wore the same brown mechanic jumpsuit each day, an anorexic woman who drank Ensure in the cafeteria instead of eating, and a woman who repeatedly mentioned her "five-year-old." It took a while for Rebecca to realize that the woman had multiple personality, or dissociative, disorder, and was referring to her five-year-old personality, not an actual child.

Soon she switched to an outpatient program that required daily therapy but allowed her to go home at night. As she progressed, she noticed herself starting to laugh and smile again. She faced a new problem, though: a growing number of mysterious physical ailments, including rashes, immune deficiency, and inexplicable pain that would eventually be diagnosed as fibromyalgia (this isn't uncommon—victims of childhood sexual abuse are at elevated risk for a host of illnesses, from heart problems to mood disorders). She dropped out of medical school and worked half-time as a massage therapist while living with relatives to cut expenses.

Over the decade that followed, Rebecca continued intensive psychotherapy. And, despite the fact that she didn't speak to her father for long periods and that he was incarcerated for sexually abusing several children, including a cousin, she wanted to be able to forgive him. While she briefly considered filing charges, she didn't know how she would prove her allegations, and the thought of undergoing such a process seemed to pose an insurmountable effort. Besides, she thought, her father would likely spend the rest of his life in prison, anyway.

"I could see what the anger was doing to me psychologically, and physically," she says now, at fifty-two. "I wanted to forgive him. I knew to survive I had to do it." In addition to depression and fibromyalgia, she suffered from hormonal imbalances, and she felt the problems were related to the bitterness she harbored. "If my dad went to his grave with me despising him, you could say that would be appropriate," she says. "But I knew I couldn't hold on to the rage and hatred and have the life I wanted." As we discussed earlier, science supports Rebecca's intuitive sense about this: Prolonged anger and rage play a role in various health problems, especially mood disorders and heart conditions. Yet reaching her goal was far from easy. The first time she wrote to her father in prison and declared that she forgave him, he accused her of fabricating the abuse, which enraged her all over again.

At a personal growth seminar months after that first frustrating attempt at forgiveness, Rebecca told her story to a room full of people. As her voice carried, she felt a heavy weariness at the sound of it. She was tired of the disgusting tale and the way it made her feel. When she finished, the seminar leader looked at her and said, "Rebecca, do you get that there's nothing wrong with you?" She nodded, knowing she should certainly feel that way, after all the years of therapy and the time and distance between her father's crimes and her current life. But the facilitator continued to look at her, compassion in his eyes. "Rebecca," he repeated slowly. "Do you get that there's nothing wrong with you?" She blinked. He said it again. And again. Suddenly, she really did get it. She felt a loosening in her throat, as if a noose had been cast off, and calm spread throughout her body.

For the first time, she actually had the visceral experience of what she had known intellectually for so many years—that even though her dad abused her, it wasn't her fault and it didn't mean she was worthless. She felt an exhilarating sense of lightness. When she got home and did the things she normally did—feeding her cats, cooking dinner—she still felt totally different. "I noticed that the anger and bitterness was gone—completely gone," she says. "All I can say is that I continuously set the intention to forgive . . . and God gave it to me, it just washed down over me."

Rebecca wrote her father again and said that even though they disagreed about what happened in the past, she loved and forgave him. This time, he replied that those were the best words he'd ever heard. Soon after, he was diagnosed with terminal brain cancer. Rebecca and her sister wrote numerous letters to the department of correction and the courts and eventually managed to convince the judicial system to release him from prison. When they arrived to retrieve him, they were shocked to see his emaciated frame. His bones seemed on the verge of jutting through the skin, and his head looked tiny and shrunken. They brought him home, to Rebecca's sister's house in Alaska, and nursed him.

One evening before he died in the guest trailer they shared, he looked Rebecca in the eye and said, "Honey, for all the pain and trauma I caused you, can you ever forgive me? I'm begging you. Please forgive me. I'm so sorry." As he sobbed, she told him she had already forgiven him. This time, it felt different, even from the epiphany at the seminar. In the past, forgiving her father had often meant repeatedly setting an intention that often felt distant and intangible, the snow-capped peak of a mountain she hoped to scale but couldn't quite make out through the storm. Other times it was a fleeting feeling, generous and peaceful, that evaporated like mist. While she had forgiven him—she wouldn't have nursed him in his final days otherwise—this time, as she said the words, she felt and knew them to be wholly and definitively true, in the real and simple way that had eluded her until now. It was almost the way saying your name feels, without hesitation or doubt or effort.

Afterward, she was overcome by a profound sense of peace. Within that calm was a feeling of solidity, like an old tree with a wide trunk and deep roots reaching down into the heart of all that ever existed and ever would exist. "I felt so incredible about the person I had become, because I'd done the impossible, right?" she says. "My self-confidence skyrocketed."

There's no exaggerating the importance of the parent-child relationship and the ways in which it reverberates throughout our personal development as children and young adults. In his landmark book *Childhood and Society*, famed psychologist Erik Erikson described a series of phases through which all of us pass in our lifespan, each one key to developing certain qualities. The first one, infancy, is called "trust versus mistrust." Since infants are completely dependent, those whose needs are met in a caring and consistent manner learn to trust the world and others, while those whose needs are not met learn to mistrust. As children proceed through the subsequent stages—learning to do things for themselves and how to interact with peers, for instance—their communities also mold the ways they learn to deal with the world, but parents continue to play a large role.

Parents not only affect the ways in which we develop into adults; they also influence our perception of ourselves. In the psychological landscape of toddlers and small children, everything revolves around them. So when bad things happen, they often assume that they themselves are the reasons or the causes. (When parents divorce, for example, children often think it's their fault or that they could have done something to prevent it.) We also live amid the pervasive cultural notion—supported partially but not entirely by biology—that we are products of our parents.

In his brilliant book *Far from the Tree*, Andrew Solomon explores the way certain people, upon finding that they are fundamentally and radically *unlike* their parents, form "horizontal" identities by seeking communities of others who are like them. (To make the point, he spends time with the deaf, among other groups.) He wouldn't have had to write that book if our parent-based, vertical identities—or the notion that our self-concept is a direct offshoot of our parents or our relationships with them—were not starkly present. Some people strive to be like their parents while others resolve to be nothing like them, but more often than not, the words "like them" or "not like them" become the dominating mantra of our march toward adulthood. In scholarship, career, relationships, and parenting—even in personal hygiene and style preferences—we tend to chart our course at least in part based on our parents, or on our *perception* of them and how they saw *us*. (Like Rebecca, most people who were mistreated as children assume that it was because they deserved it or were defective in some way.) We tend to measure ourselves against them as we go, whether by imitating or avoiding their behavior and traits.

Historically, the cultural importance of origins has been paramount. In any number of eras and places, the circumstances of your birth dictated who you were and who you could be. Under the laws of ancient Rome, babies born to free parents could never be enslaved, while babies born to slaves would be hard-pressed to live a free day in their lives (a reality that persisted through institutionalized slavery until the late nineteenth century). Babies born to prostitutes were long marked with shame, as were bastards. In feudal England, a boy born to a queen was undoubtedly a prince, while any child born to peasants was doomed to his parents' fate. In most Jewish families around the time of Christ, a boy born to a baker would be expected to become a baker himself, just as the sons of scholars, welders, or rabbis would likely follow in their fathers' footsteps as well. As for girls in most feudal societies, parentage determined marriage and thus life, as they were used as pawns to enhance the status of their and their husbands' families. One's "blood," and its defining power and constraints, is one of the most loudly resounding literary themes throughout the ages, from *Oedipus* to *Romeo and Juliet* to *Oliver Twist*.

Over the past two hundred years, a growing value has been placed on self-determination and the "self-made," particularly in the individualistic United States. This momentous shift toward free will is scientific as well as cultural: We've learned an enormous amount about how genes and environment contribute to our traits and interact with one another, and about the ways in which behavior can change the brain (think cognitive behavioral therapy and the more recent concept of neuroplasticity, through which new habits create new neural pathways). And yet, to some degree, we are and will remain our parents' children. We will always have their genes, and we will forever be marked by what they did or did not do. So, what does all of this have to do with making peace with one's parentage, and what does it have to do with forgiveness? As a friend of mine recently remarked, "If you can't have compassion for the source from which you came, how do you ever expect to accept yourself?"

And yet, while people assume it may be helpful to accept their parents and what they did or didn't do, actually doing that can prove difficult—especially for people whose parents have died, gone to prison, or suffer from dementia, making an in-person resolution impossible. Besides, isn't it natural to be angry if, like Loretta, your mother tried to kill you, or, like Diego, your father disappeared and reappeared only to disappoint you once again? I directed this question at my mother and several other psychologists, since they spend a lot of time helping people recover from toxic childhoods, or from the damaging parts of mostly positive ones. My mother said that while it is indeed natural to be angry and upset, getting stuck in those emotions is similar to being unable to grieve properly.

Normally, people experience various aspects of grief, which include denial, shock, depression, anger, and acceptance as they work through their feelings over a loss, but when people become stuck in depression or anger, they usually also find themselves unable to forgive, or to reach that final stage of grief—acceptance. While the psychiatrist Elisabeth Kübler-Ross defined these as chronological stages based on her work with terminally ill people, more recent research shows that people who have lost a loved one or experienced some other traumatic event usually go through these phases in nonlinear order, often experiencing several of them in the space of a few days. And yet, once people have completed their grieving, they arrive at acceptance, which shares many hallmarks of forgiveness. The forgiveness process is similar to the grief process, then, as both aim for acceptance and can vary in duration and intensity for each person, depending on personality, brain patterns, and circumstance.

Just as grief doesn't normally hew to those neatly defined, chronological stages, forgiveness can be a long, nonlinear process rather than a one-time event. In ways that we'll explore later in this book, forgiveness more often takes the form of a constant practice than a single cathartic experience. One day you feel at peace with someone, as if you've forgiven them, and probably you have, but the next week something reminds you or takes you back and you have to choose to forgive again, in that moment, on that day, in whatever way you can.

A longtime friend of mine was abused by her father, who has since died. When I asked her about the concept of forgiveness and how it has played out for her, she sent me this letter:

> I have to say the word "forgiveness" occurs to me as a demand and lack of patience for the process of healing. Perhaps I'm not defining it in a living, breathing way, but I find it to be a very abstract idea that people who haven't suffered gravely gravitate to. No one I know who has experienced abuse has ever used the word "forgiveness." It's not a topic that we share; instead we share the endurance required to feel our feelings and the rigor involved in girding up our loins for another layer of healing and the will to give ourselves the very best present and future we can. We talk about how we didn't deserve what we experienced but we are somehow responsible for correcting it, because if we don't, our lives will be consumed by the fire of someone else's misdirected power over us. . . . Because I'm still experiencing new memories [of abuse], the phenomenon of forgiveness—which to me implies completion—is irrelevant at this point in my life, and perhaps for some time to come. Each new memory takes me back to square one and I have to start all over. So my "stage" in the "forgiveness process" depends entirely on my day, what it brings up, the degree to which I'm entirely present or paralyzed in abuse-born fear, which takes time to extinguish, which takes time away from the present, but which is ultimately very worthwhile. Even when I am at peace—and praise

*God I have oceans more now than ever before—I still carry ill will
toward my father for abusing and abandoning me and wish him
an eternity of torture and suffering, despite my missing and loving
him.*

As my friend so eloquently points out, particularly for people who
have suffered severely at the hands of those they trusted the most, concep-
tualizing forgiveness as a destination at which one "arrives," or even as a
process that can be completed once and for all, can be worse than useless.
After all, if forgiveness means giving up resentment, it doesn't follow that
resentment disappears forever. Perhaps it means that when it crops up once
more, you can let it go once again.

The pervasive idea that grieving, recovering from trauma, or forgiveness are—or should be—tidy processes that adhere to certain time frames
or deadlines leads to a lot of problems. One of them is that we underesti-
mate the time and effort it can take to recover from life's hits, and therefore
assume that if we don't feel right, we must be clinically depressed, anxious,
or suffering from some sort of anger disorder. Even clinicians have trouble
distinguishing between grief and major depression, two different conditions that are often confused. While normal grief shares qualities of major
depression, including sleep and weight loss, tearfulness, and lack of con-
centration, there are important distinctions. People with major depression
tend to view the world and themselves through a pervasively negative lens,
tormented by feelings of hopelessness and despair, as well as self-loathing.
Those in the midst of grief, however, have episodes of sadness that alternate
with more positive feelings, such as cherished memories or the belief that
they'll return "to normal" at some point. Their symptoms are triggered by
reminders of the loss or trauma, as opposed to being pervasive and ever
present. That said, sometimes normal grief turns into what psychologists
call "complicated grief," marked by symptoms such as an inability to accept
the loss or trauma and return to normal functioning after six months or
longer, suicidal thoughts, and persistent bitterness, denial, or anger.

My mother says that many people who come to her seeking treatment for depression or angry outbursts actually suffer from complicated grief, not a mental health disorder requiring medication. The treatment, she says, is often grief or trauma counseling, which eventually brings acceptance, peace of mind, and forgiveness. Many of these patients discovered that they'd never adequately grieved the loss of a parent, especially when that parent happened to have been abusive or neglectful, which can make grieving more complex and difficult. (People may feel guilty thinking negatively about their deceased parent, so they cease thinking about them or processing their feelings at all, for example.) Sometimes, the loss had occurred years or even decades earlier, but my mom helped them work through their feelings about it in therapy, eventually resolving their symptoms. For people whose parents are deceased or absent, she has found one exercise to be especially helpful: She has patients write a series of angry letters listing all of the violations the parents committed against them and the impact the abuse has had on their lives. Then she has the patient write a "Letter of Liberation," which stresses that while their parents' behavior was incredibly damaging, they now choose to forgive the parents and themselves. The goal is to declare their freedom from the past and their independence, not as victims or even survivors, but as people with a right to thrive in a new, fulfilling life.

She's found that this sort of virtual resolution can be just as effective as an in-person one.

Whether a parent is dead or alive, lack of resolution can be detrimental. Since prolonged anger and resentment take a toll on the body, when the subject of that anger is a parent—a central fixture in one's life—the effect can become magnified, bleeding into one's overall view of life and any number of other relationships.

I was dining with friends in Colorado when the topic of this book came up. Kate, an elderly woman who was raised with a cold, distant, and often cruel mother, said she would never forgive her late mother because her behavior was unacceptable and her mother didn't deserve her forgiveness. I listened and accepted her point. After all, she is someone I respect, and forgiving one's parents is very personal.

Yet soon after, something struck me. When Kate talked about her mother and the frigid North Dakota steppe where she'd grown up lonely and forlorn, her smile—understandably—became a grim, set line. Her voice took on a steely edge. But here's the thing: This happened not only when she talked about her mother, but also sometimes when she talked about other things. Landscaping. Travel. Holiday plans. Soup, even. At these times, her voice became a lacerating whip. And the person most often on the receiving end of that whip was her beloved husband of fifty years. She snapped and poked while he dodged and sighed. *What was he thinking, buying that plant? Why would he suggest such a preposterous plan? Just who did he think he was, anyway?* As the barbs flew, I got the uneasy feeling that my friend's rigid refusal to forgive her mother might have something to do with the hostility she was dishing out on her husband.

Luskin, of the Stanford Forgiveness Project, tells of a woman in one of his workshops who showed a similar pattern. Marilyn was so consumed by her sadness over being raised by an emotionally detached mother that she was unknowingly repeating the same pattern of neglect with her own children. It was impossible for Marilyn to be fully engaged with her kids while she remained wrapped in a blanket of sadness about her upbringing. Marilyn also blamed her mother for every problem in her life. She had trouble establishing close relationships with men and blamed her mother. She suffered from depression and blamed her mother. She didn't finish college and struggled to find work, and she blamed her mother for that, too. Remember, thinking about a grudge floods the brain with stress chemicals, and over time hobbles the part of the brain responsible for problem-solving. So the more time Marilyn spent reacting to how her mother wronged her, the less time and energy she had to solve her own problems.

People who harbor resentment about the past have much in common with those at risk for depression and general unhappiness. Dr. Martin Seligman, the University of Pennsylvania professor known as the father of the "positive psychology" movement, has identified the qualities—inherent and learned—of both happy and unhappy people. The latter, he says, fall easily into what he calls the three *p*'s of poisonous thinking: They take things personally, they view setbacks as pervasive (as in, this *always* happens to me! or, it's *never* going to get better), and they're pessimistic, tending to focus on the negative and expect the worst.

Unhappy people also tend to ruminate, or compulsively focus on what's causing their distress, thinking repetitive thoughts about negative past experiences. Susan Nolen-Hoeksema, a researcher at Yale University, showed that people who reported ruminating more frequently, thinking thoughts such as "Why do I have problems other people don't have?" when feeling sad, were more likely to have elevated symptoms of depression a year later than people who reported thinking such thoughts less often. She also found that ruminators develop major depression four times as often as nonruminators. Similarly, Benjamin Hankin of the University of Denver found in a 2011 study that adolescent girls who reported high rates of rumination were more likely than their less ruminative peers to have depressive episodes, and that those episodes lasted longer.

While some people repress pain and fail to heal because of it, others dwell on the source of their pain so thoroughly that they become prisoners to it. No wonder the other linguistic meaning of "rumination" happens to be the process whereby cows and other members of the ruminant family regurgitate the same food over and over again in order to digest it. One byproduct of cows' "chewing the cud"? It exudes methane gas, which erodes the ozone layer and pollutes the atmosphere.

If you consider how large parents loom on our emotional, psychological, and social lives, and combine that with the dangers of rumination and pessimism, it's not difficult to see how blaming one's progenitors can be a direct road to misery. So, what to do?

The some twenty people I interviewed all took similar steps, which we'll explore below.

Finding Empathy

The first time Loretta's mother tried to kill her, Loretta was eight. She was playing with her three younger sisters in their nursery when their mother, a statuesque beauty who loved to paint, exploded into the room in a rage. Loretta recognized the wild-eyed look and bolted down the hallway. Her mother grabbed a hammer and clutched it over her head as she pursued Loretta, who was running out the door and toward the safety of the neighbors' yard. The second time, Loretta was riding shotgun in the family sedan while her sisters sat in the backseat. The children were arguing about something, and suddenly her mother shouted, "I can't stand it!" and veered off the road and onto the edge of a ravine. As the car teetered precariously, her mother hollered, "I'll kill us all!"

As Loretta grew older, she began to notice that people would recoil from her mother at the store or on the street, edging away from the irrationally exuberant torrent of words that poured out of her mouth in a nonstop staccato. As a teen, Loretta did everything to distance herself from her mother. When her parents divorced, she moved in with her father and didn't speak to her mom for a few years. But then she would reach out again and visit. She'd arrive hoping her mother would be that "normal mom" she'd always wished for, but her mother was still prone to manic nonstop talking, or wrapped in a cocoon of desperate sadness she couldn't explain.

Eventually, Loretta realized that her mother was incapable of changing. She would never be the "normal mom," but only the mother she was, the one who during Loretta's childhood sometimes had to "go away" to a hospital where they treated her "nervousness" with electroshock treatments. As Loretta's children grew from infants to toddlers to adolescents, she would often think about her mother at certain moments when she was doing something differently than her mother would have, like responding in a calm yet firm voice when her son disobeyed her, instead of breaking into hysterical tears like her own mother sometimes did when Loretta was a child. Something about these memories, about stepping outside of herself for a moment and observing just how differently she behaved from her own mother, slowly helped her conclude that her mom had done the best she could to raise the four of them when she was barely capable of taking care of herself. As Loretta grew older, she did her best to love her mother as she was.

Years later, long after her mother died, Loretta's eldest son was diagnosed with bipolar disorder. She sat in the doctor's office reading the pamphlets the psychiatrist gave her, and phrase after phrase leapt from the page: *mood changes; talking very fast, jumping from one idea to another; behaving impulsively and engaging in pleasurable, high-risk behaviors; thinking of death or suicide. . . .* All of it described her mother, and the pamphlets mentioned that the condition often ran in families. Loretta was overcome with a wave of compassion, struck by how her mother had suffered for so long with a disease whose causes and treatments hadn't yet been discovered. She felt grateful that she had found a way to forgive her mother while she was still alive.

Empathy, the ability to understand and share someone's feelings and perspective, is as key to forgiving parents as it is to forgiving anyone else. In 1997, McCullough and a team of researchers had 239 undergraduate students fill out surveys about a situation in which a friend, relative, or romantic partner had hurt or offended them. The questions designed to measure their empathy levels were based on a scale used repeatedly by scientists who studied the "empathy-altruism link," which confirmed that people are more likely to help those with whom they empathize. To determine whether that holds true for forgiveness, too, the researchers had the students rate items such as "I wish him/her well" and "I have forgiven the person" and others to measure behavior, such as "I took steps toward reconciliation," or "I avoid them."

The researchers found a correlation between empathy, forgiving, and conciliatory behavior toward the offender, and decided to explore it further. They selected 136 of the original study participants who had expressed a desire to forgive someone who had hurt them. Half attended a seminar on empathy, where they did writing exercises surmising their offenders' motivations or psychological states, and reviewed times when they sought forgiveness from others. The other half—the control group—attended a seminar about the merits of forgiveness, but not empathy. The first group proved more likely to forgive in a postseminar assessment than did the control group. In addition to establishing links between empathy and forgiveness, the experiment confirmed the finding in multiple experiments that forgiveness can be increased through clinical intervention.

While there's scant research on forgiving parents specifically, Robert Enright of the University of Wisconsin measured the effects of a six-day seminar on forty-eight college students who reported growing up "love-deprived." While one group received a six-day workshop focused on forgiveness—including exercises that focused on empathizing with parents—the control group received a leadership development training. One week after the workshop ended, the forgiveness group reported a higher willingness to forgive, as well as increased hope and self-esteem and decreased anxiety compared to the control group.

Okay, it makes sense that if you can empathize with an abusive or neglectful parent, forgiveness is likely. Yet isn't it easier to empathize with someone who, like Loretta's mother, was or is ill? The answer is yes. McCullough's list of factors that make people more forgivable includes situations in which the offender is sick or has fallen on hard times. And yet, psychological researchers like Enright insist that it's possible to extend empathy to others, as well.

When I spoke with Dr. Kyra Gaunt, a sociology and anthropology professor at Baruch College at the City University of New York, this seemed to hold true for her. After her mother got pregnant at nineteen, Kyra's father left. Kyra spent much of her life feeling abandoned, and at forty, with her mother's help, she tracked her father down. In conversations with both him and her mother, she learned that soon after her parents discovered the unwanted pregnancy, her mother told him, "You don't have to stay." While Kyra still had her opinions about his decision to be uninvolved in her life, this information indicated to her that a feeling of being unneeded or unwanted may have played a role in driving him away. Knowing that, she took his absence less personally.

Seligman, the happiness research pioneer, found that the people most likely to be happy and to flourish in spite of circumstances don't take negative words or deeds personally. And for nearly everyone I interviewed for this chapter, refraining from taking their parents' shortcomings personally was a key component of their resilience and ability to forgive.

Diego, thirty-four, was born to teen parents in an inner city, and though his father lived minutes away, he rarely saw him. He longed for attention from his father, who was known around town as a popular ladies' man who had "the gift of gab" and "could sell ice to an Eskimo." Yet by the time Diego hit adulthood, what he'd gotten from his dad was a litany of broken promises: missed baseball and football games, and a pile of student-loan debt. When Diego became the first person in his family to be accepted to college, his father, a high school dropout, promised to help him with his loan payments. ("Go ahead and go, we'll take care of it later," his father said of the private college tuition.) After Diego graduated, his father invited him to the car shop where he worked. Ceremoniously, he handed his son a grease-smeared binder crammed with papers. In it were five years' worth of grant applications for low-income students, loan statements, and notices of default. Most of it was unopened. "That's all I got," his father said, beer in hand, as if it were a gift. The debt totaled more than $100,000.

Diego is a friend, a hardworking, dedicated, and kind man. When he told me this story, his eyes filling as he recalled the sickening realization of the debt he'd unknowingly incurred, I was disgusted and outraged. I wanted to grab his father by the neck and shake him. After all, he didn't have any sort of mental illness or other disorder. "How could you forgive him?" I asked, incredulous.

"Well, he was nineteen when he had me," Diego replied. "I wasn't ready to be a father when I was nineteen. Plus, I've kind of outlived him now. I mean, he never finished high school or moved away from home, and I have two master's degrees and have traveled and lived in lots of different places." When he turned thirty, Diego went out for drinks with his dad and asked him why he wasn't around when he was growing up. His father, the guy with the big shiny truck, the one who everyone liked to see at the bar, took a swig of beer and looked down. "I didn't want you to be like me," he said. Despite his father's tendency to exaggerate or even lie if it made for a great story or a good excuse, Diego was moved. It was something about his father's expression, maybe the way he looked down in seemingly genuine embarrassment. Diego figured that for all the years he'd been yearning for his father's attention, assuming that his father didn't provide it because he

didn't care about him, the truth was that his father felt unworthy and incapable of being a parent in the first place. This awareness made him feel
compassion for his father. He wasn't condoning or excusing his father for
disappointing him, but he could accept it and forgive him for it.

Untying the Knot: Forging Your Own Identity

I noticed as I interviewed more people that somehow, forgiving their parents enabled them to forge their own identities. Whereas before they forgave, their perceptions of themselves were directly tied to their parent or
how they'd been hurt, afterward they felt a newfound freedom to define
themselves and their potential on their own terms.

Ginger, whose father left her family and was later convicted of molesting at least three minors, struggled to imagine how she could ever amount
to anything as the daughter of such a man. Though her father told her he
left her, in part, because he didn't want to "do that" to her, she was still the
daughter of a pedophile. "I felt like I was nothing. How could I be anything
when I come from all this disgusting stuff?" she told me. It was only when
she learned that he had been sexually abused as a child that she began to
develop some empathy for him. She accepted that she couldn't change him
and stopped blaming him, which allowed her to realize that she'd been
feeling "disgusting" by association—and that she didn't have to. Yes, her
father had hurt children, but she wouldn't. Her father left her, but that
didn't mean she wasn't worthy of love. She has since worked as a mentor for
abused children, determined to share what she discovered on her own:
Regardless of your background, you can lead a life of your own choosing.

Genea's mother started hitting her when she was eight. She would drag
her daughter into the kitchen by her hair or slap her in the face. Later, when
Genea came out as a lesbian at nineteen and began living with her current
wife, her mother screamed and called her names like "deviant" and "cow."
Nonetheless, Genea tried to keep in mind the stories she'd been told about
her grandmother, who ridiculed her mom when she was a girl, beating and

berating her. Her mother was a product of her childhood, Genea repeatedly told herself. For a long time, Genea didn't want children because she was afraid that she would be like her mother. "Once I could start to forgive my mom," she told me, "it made it possible for me to say, yes, actually, I want kids. I can be a good mother." Genea and her wife are now foster parents.

I was fascinated. Why, and how, was forgiving a parent linked to forming your own identity apart from them? Vivian's story provided more insight.

When Vivian was twelve, her father confessed that he had fallen in love with her mother's half sister. With a tortured expression, her father admitted to having an affair with the woman while she was staying in their home. Soon after, Vivian's mother found her father sitting in his Chevrolet Impala in the garage, dead of carbon monoxide poisoning. That moment, running into the garage behind her mother and hearing a scream without knowing if it was hers or her mother's or both, echoed throughout Vivian's life for decades. From her teens through her thirties, she felt alternately numb and enraged at her father for his affair and suicide, but she also felt guilty about her anger, hating herself for feeling that way.

She eventually sank into depression and alcoholism, both of which ran in her family. She moved constantly, leaving jobs and men behind. "I was always scared that I'd do what my father did to someone else, that I was poisonous," she told me. Then, through Alcoholics Anonymous, Buddhism, and therapy, she began to understand that her father had been severely depressed and an alcoholic, and she saw that he didn't intend to hurt her or her mother. In turn, this helped her see that she wasn't to blame, either. "I realized that I didn't cause his death, that I didn't have to blame myself anymore, and that I didn't have to follow in his footsteps," she said. One day she rode her bicycle down a steep hill with her arms in the air, euphoric. "It was such a release," she said. "I finally knew that I was okay, that I could create a vision and goals that were really mine." She bought her first home, got a job she actually liked, and fell in love with the man who is now her husband of fourteen years.

As I listened to these stories, I kept imagining this image: A thick, ropy umbilical cord had somehow been cut through forgiveness, setting the person free. It reminded me of something I'd heard about certain indigenous cultures believing that blame *ties* you to the object of your rage. I researched the anthropological literature and learned that the ancient Hawaiians believed that an offense created a state of sin, or *hala*, which was represented metaphorically as a cord binding the offender to the offended. To untangle or untie this cord, they would do a series of purification prayers, or *huikala*.

Perhaps the most famous example of this concept can be found in the Lord's Prayer, from Jesus' Sermon on the Mount in the Gospel of Matthew. There may be more to the King James Bible version of the line "Forgive us our debts, as we forgive our debtors." That wording is the result of Aramaic, the language spoken in first-century Israel, being translated to Greek and then to English. The original Aramaic sentence, according to Aramaic biblical scholars such as Rocco Errico and Neil Douglas-Klotz, was *"Washboklan khoben: aicanna dop khnan shbakn lkhayaven."* A literal translation of this is "Free us from our offenses, as we have forgiven our offenders." But the Aramaic word *shbakn*, translated here as "forgive," also means "to free," "to untie," and "to release." Which is why Douglas-Klotz argues that the most complete translation would read, "Loose the cords of mistakes binding us, as we release the strands we hold of others' guilt," or, alternatively, "Detach the fetters of faults that bind us."

If forgiving releases the fetters thát bind us to our faults and those of others, then by forgiving our parents, we cut the ties to our anger and bitterness and disappointment, but we also cut the ties to whatever limiting perceptions of ourselves are derived from our parents and our past. While I didn't have ties of resentment to cut with my parents, I did have ties of guilt to cut when it came to Liz. And it was true that when I received that message from her, the one acknowledging my apology and in a way, forgiving me, I did feel a new sense of freedom. There was a physical sensation of relief, like letting out a long breath that you've been holding for years. I thought about it less often, and when I did, the tightness in my chest that had always accompanied the memory was gone. As I reflected on the stories of the people in this chapter, I realized that, like most of them, I'd acquired a new freedom in the way I viewed myself and my life. While I was still driven to "comfort the afflicted," magnify marginalized voices, and sow compassion through my work, that drive was no longer couched in a crusade of atonement, in which some small part of me was still trying to prove that I was worthy or good in spite of my deplorable behavior back in the sixth grade. Now, I was simply passionate about what I was passionate about, and there was something pure and whole about it.

Shifting Focus

Well-being researchers like Martin Seligman link optimism to forgiveness, because forgiveness means replacing negative, resentful feelings with more positive or at least neutral ones, and it can lead to a more positive view of the person who hurt you, the situation, or yourself. As I reviewed the conversations I had about forgiving parents with nearly twenty people of diverse age, gender, ethnicity, and sexuality, I noticed that all of them had shifted their focus in four major ways.

Seeing the Good with the Bad

A friend named Rosa has a father with a drinking problem. While her mother battled breast cancer, he was at times so drunk that even when he lay in bed beside her, her mother had to call Rosa for help. Once, Rosa's car broke down on a weekend night, and she called her father for a ride. He arrived slurring and stumbling, but Rosa, reverting to I'm-a-little-girl-and-he's-Dad mode, got in the car anyway. As they swerved across lanes of traffic, she berated herself for letting him drive her. They managed to arrive at her parents' house safely, and he loaned her their Buick. The next morning, he called her to ask if she had taken the car, oblivious to the night's events. She was livid.

Knowing that he refused to get the help he needed to stop drinking, I had trouble understanding how she could forgive him and continue to include him in her life. She explained that she no longer rides in the car with him if he's been drinking and doesn't speak to him on the phone after a certain time of night. Yet she sees him often and makes a habit of continuously forgiving him. Why? I asked. His drinking, she replied, "is just a piece of him. It's not all of who he is. He's also business-minded and successful, he came from an impoverished first-generation Mexican immigrant family and suffered severe abuse at the hands of his father, and still he became the first of his family to go to college. He's a corporate executive, and he's been a mentor for me in human resources and law."

That phrase kept popping into my mind: "It's just a piece of him." This reminded me of Loretta, whose mother was bipolar before it was discovered as a treatable condition. When Loretta forgave her, something happened. She was flooded by snippets of memories that she had completely forgotten: Her mother putting down her paintbrush to painstakingly fix Loretta's broken doll, for instance, and the time her mother made Loretta and her doll matching green-and-white taffeta dresses for a fourth-grade party. She also noticed something else: While many of her peers in the sixties confronted limiting parental expectations about what women could achieve, she realized that her mother never told her that she couldn't do something because she was a girl. She'd once mentioned running for president, and her mother nodded her enthusiastic approval, as if Loretta were announcing her intention to set up a lemonade stand outside. "The grandiose thinking that was part of her disease was in some ways a gift," Loretta told me.

These perspectives shocked me. I'm a lover of rules and standards, someone who tends to see in black and white. I was reminded of something Luskin, of the Stanford Forgiveness Project, talks about: "unenforceable rules." An unenforceable rule is an expectation that you have no power to enforce, a standard often articulated as a "should." Common ones include "Parents should be loving and supportive" and "People shouldn't lie to me." While most of us might agree with these statements, we can't force them to be true. Rosa clearly decided that, rather than spending her time attempting to enforce an unenforceable rule, she'd enjoy her father's good qualities while mitigating the bad ones as best she can.

Reinterpreting Wrongs

When Genea's mother called her names for being gay and asked why she would choose to be "that way," Genea didn't speak to her for eight months. For several years afterward, Genea's mother tried to set her up with men and referred to Genea's wife as "that white girl who made you how you are." Though Genea was hurt and angry, she made continued efforts to stand up for who she was and whom she loved, while forgiving her mother for reacting the way she did. "I tried to keep in mind that everyone has hopes and aspirations for their children, and I was clearly shattering one of hers," she told me.

One thing that enabled Genea to forgive her mother and continue to have a relationship with her was that she reinterpreted what might have been driving her mother's reaction to her sexuality. "It was the midnineties when I came out," she says, "and homosexuality really wasn't very accepted, especially in the black community. I thought, well, maybe she's expressing concern for me. Maybe she's afraid for me."

Over the years, her mother changed. Because Genea was able to develop some understanding of her mother's cruel and ignorant comments, while still calling them out as unacceptable, her mother was able to gradually work through her knee-jerk reactions to Genea's homosexuality. She's now close to Genea's wife, calling to talk to her on the phone and ensuring that she's included in family photos. Recently, Genea's mother discovered that her favorite teenaged barista had been kicked out of her parents' home for being bisexual, and she helped the girl move and bought her a care package for her new apartment.

Recognizing What You Got from the Hard Parts

When Diego talked to me about his absentee father, from whom he longed for guidance on everything from sports to cars to girls, he would get a wistful look on his face. "Whenever I would see a strong, successful man, a guy I respected," he said, "I'd always think, 'He must have had a great father.'"

That unfulfilled desire for guidance became a powerful motivator. It drove Diego to seek knowledge and support from men who were capable of giving it when his father was not. He learned about leadership and strategy from his baseball coach and about discipline from his football coach. He played catch with his uncle. As an executive assistant to a local political leader after college, he learned from his boss about how to buy a suit and tie, how to talk to people at dinner parties, and to always put his car keys in the same pocket so he wouldn't lose them.

Diego regretted that though his father worked construction for years, he didn't teach him anything about it, so he worked summers framing houses. After the college loan disaster, when he felt deflated by yet another of his father's false promises, he got a job working as a financial aid adviser at a university, where he learned and taught others about the financial aspects of higher education. He also managed to pay off $50,000 of debt in four years. In many important ways, the painful experience of not getting what he needed or wanted from his father taught him how to go out and get those things for himself. "I'm grateful for having found the answers to a lot of my own questions," he told me. "There's a sense of pride in the fact that I've done a lot with the cards I've been dealt."

One evening when Anthony came over for dinner after work, I told him about the conversations I'd been having, particularly the one with Diego. He nodded knowingly. Born to teen parents himself, he knew what it was like to have parents who weren't capable of providing what others could. His grandmother and grandfather, who immigrated to Boston from Portugal in the sixties and worked as a teacher and a factory worker, respectively, stepped in to help raise him. Like Diego, Anthony said that while some of his childhood experiences were extremely challenging, many of them benefited him in the long run. (Instead of having a bike delivered at Christmas, for instance, he spent months saving for a bike by working extra hours for a tent-rental company and felt a deep sense of pride when he finally bought it.)

I was impressed by his ability to view those things he lacked as assets. To me, someone who'd struggled to be optimistic my entire life despite having myriad opportunities that most people don't, this took grit and spirit and creativity. It embodied the kind of resilience that psychologists refer to when talking about people with tough childhoods who "beat the odds." As I looked at Anthony sitting there in his suit at the end of the day at his corporate job, I felt a deep sense of admiration. Here was a guy who grew up in Lowell, Massachusetts, the hardscrabble neighborhood where the movie *The Fighter* was filmed with Christian Bale and Mark Wahlberg, and became the first person in his family to go to college, then graduate school. He paused to think, his fork poised above the salmon dinner we'd made on the grill, and said, "I don't know. I think maybe life gives you what you need."

Being the Hero in Your Own Story

By using his father's absence as an opportunity, and appreciating the discipline and drive that he developed as a result, Diego is sailing his own ship, charting his own destination and adjusting the sails as he goes. Instead of being the victim of his fatherless childhood, he's using it as motivation to become the man that he wants to be. This is the stuff of the American Dream, the very spirit of what we call "free will."

Forgiveness, it turns out, is more about the future than the past, perhaps especially when it comes to forgiving parents. While parents play powerful roles in shaping who we are, who we become is up to us. Seligman identified what he calls the 40 percent rule: Fifty percent of what determines our mind-set and mood is genetics, 10 percent is determined by experiences and circumstances, and 40 percent of our mind-set and general mood settings are determined by us—by our habits and deliberate choices, by our thoughts, emotions, and actions over time. Forty percent isn't bad. Forty percent is almost half. Recently, when a relative of Anthony's was complaining about her life and asked how he's "done so much," referring to his living in various parts of the country, traveling, and earning two advanced degrees, he told her, "You want happiness? You gotta go out and fucking get it."

One way to forgive the past and chart the future is to recast yourself as the hero, not the victim, in the narrative of your own life. Rebecca cast herself as a woman who overcame childhood incest to become a massage therapist and energy healer who speaks openly about her experience because she wants to be an example for other survivors. On that grim night when she called her sister and admitted that she didn't want to live, she figured she would have to spend her whole life trying to recover, and that by the time she did she would probably not have time left to have a decent life. Yet later, she began to think differently. "If I can get through this and even help one other person," she told herself, "then it would be worth the pain and the journey." And part of being a hero, not a victim, is learning how to forgive even in the absence of apology or remorse. Rebecca's father apologized only after she had forgiven him, after she'd been actively working to forgive him for years. And she certainly didn't make her forgiveness contingent upon his apology. When it came, it was an unexpected blessing, but she was committed to forgiving him first and foremost for herself. As Azim likes to say, refusing to forgive until someone apologizes merely keeps you stuck in "the victim mentality," squirming at the mercy of someone else's choices or feelings.

As a psychologist, my mother has long been a fan of a concept developed by the mythologist Joseph Campbell. Campbell studied Carl Jung's idea of archetypes—universal human patterns of behavior—and the mythology of world cultures to conclude that all stories essentially boil down to one core tale that humans have told and retold since the dawn of civilization. He called it the Hero's Journey. In it, the Hero, whether Odysseus or

Luke Skywalker or Hester Prynne or Dorothy from *The Wizard of Oz*, embarks (for reasons outside his control) on a journey of adventure and transformation. The hero encounters battles and monsters, fighting and struggling and, in the process, becoming stronger. Propelling the hero along is the necessity or promise of a magic elixir, which can symbolize everything from a literal cure for a disease to personal fulfillment. As Campbell described in his classic book *The Hero with a Thousand Faces*, we relate to those stories and watch and read them repeatedly because all of us are on a Hero's Journey of our own.

Those I interviewed about forgiving their parents had unknowingly cast themselves as the heroes of their stories, using the disappointments of their childhoods in the same way that Odysseus used his encounters with the Cyclops to become stronger and more determined to return home from the Trojan War.

Diego says the self-reliance he got from basically having to father himself led to self-confidence and pride, a sense that whatever comes, he'll be able to face it. For people like Rebecca, the act of forgiving itself is a triumph, evidence that she is capable of anything. Vivian says the experience of her father's suicide helped her find compassion for herself and others, and as a result, she nourished a love of acting. Today, she runs an acting school and performs in theater, television, and film. Without the empathy she gained through suffering, she says, she wouldn't be able to step into the skin of an imagined person, or perform her own story on stage.

Kyra, the Baruch College professor, also performs, and was selected as one of the original TED fellows. She sees her ability to forgive her father for being absent, like so many black fathers are, as a gift to offer to the black community, helping other black women to release the resentment that she believes often poisons their relationships with fathers and partners and contributes to the cycle of fatherlessness. As a TED fellow, she is developing a "vocal memoir" performance that describes this release as ceasing to "carry bitterness we set at the feet of future paternities."

Most of the people I interviewed also said that forgiving their parents enabled them to enjoy the best parts of their parents, whether they were still in their lives, or not. Ginger, who forgave her father for molesting children, ended their relationship when he persisted in getting drunk and yelling at her over the phone. But she says she still enjoys her favorite memories of him: cooking her banana pancakes, taking her out on his motorcycle and letting her stand barefoot against his back, her plump toddler feet touching the leather seat and her arms outstretched in the wind. Loretta says she found peace in being able to enjoy the time she had left with her mother without expecting her to be different. "The more I forgave, the more I remembered and was able to treasure the good moments when she got to be the mother she wanted to be," she told me.

Not only did forgiving improve their relationships with the parents in question—it also seemed to improve other relationships. As Diego forgave his father, he stopped erupting in angry tirades at his stepfather. When Vivian forgave her father and later, the relative with whom he'd cheated before his suicide, she was able to calmly share with her husband the anxious feelings that arose when a colleague flirted with him—a major difference from her longtime habit of flying into a rage any time she felt jealous.

After listening to these people's stories and observing their lives now, my judgments about whether their parents deserved their children's forgiveness became irrelevant. Because when these wise people talk about their parents, they sound like a lot of the icons my generation grew up revering, people like Martin Luther King Jr., Maya Angelou, and Oprah Winfrey. They sound like the hero with a thousand faces at the transformative end of a very long journey.

5

The Ecology of Trust:
Forgiveness in Intimate Relationships

Love is perhaps the area of life most ripe for betrayal, not to mention the more mundane challenges of living with someone intimately over time. Given the prominence of love relationships in most people's lives, and the resentments that can pile up, I wanted to explore the role forgiveness plays in marital and relationship health. My reasons were partly selfish, of course. As a child of the "Divorce Generation," my parents and most of my friends' parents had split up, and I'd gone through at least a half-dozen long-term relationships and breakups myself. At this point in my research, Anthony and I had been together for about nine months, and we'd started to discuss next steps. We planned for him to move in with me when my roommate moved out. During these discussions, it wasn't uncommon for one or both of us to grow skittish and worried. One issue was Stella, his hundred-pound brindle mastiff, whom I loved but to whom I was unfortunately allergic. I'd gotten used to taking allergy medicine when I was at his place, and developed the habit of washing my hands before touching my face so that my eyes wouldn't immediately swell shut. We would eventually compromise by keeping the bedroom dog-free, vacuuming a lot, and letting her stay outside as much as possible, but it took more than a few tense conversations to figure that out.

Beyond the dog problem, which would turn out to be a simple material compromise, we were concerned about how we'd sustain the relationship long-term, since we'd both gone through a lot of breakups and were both children of divorce. Anthony was especially puzzled by my parents' split. While his parents accidentally got pregnant with him in high school and never attended college, mine had waited until their midtwenties to marry, shared common interests, earned advanced degrees, and enjoyed thriving careers. If they couldn't make it work, he initially wondered, how could anyone? Having lived with my parents for the first eighteen years of my life and then watched them divorce when I was twenty, I was at least mildly aware of the problems that finally choked off the lifeblood of their relationship. I puzzled over it for a few years and underwent a year of therapy, but ultimately, I concluded that it's fruitless to attempt to fully understand the invisible nexus of factors that comprise the bond between one's parents and then cause its dissolution. As the people in the last chapter made clear, at some point you have to stop glancing over your shoulder and chart your own course. As Anthony and I looked toward the future, I still harbored some cynicism, but I was also a romantic, seeking love and answers about what makes it "work." How central is forgiveness to that equation? I wondered.

To explore that question, I interviewed fifteen couples who have been reportedly happily married for between ten and thirty-five years, and have forgiven each other for things large and small. I also reviewed the social science research on what makes love last. When it comes to forgiveness in love, I would discover, the key is to use it in the right ways, at the right times. Forgiveness is key to sustaining a healthy union, but only if used by both partners as one tool among many, including the ability to take responsibility for hurtful actions, empathize, and apologize. The happy, long-term couples I interviewed reported that seeking and granting forgiveness are reciprocal in their relationships.

The revered marriage researcher John Gottman, who has studied thousands of couples in his famous Seattle "Love Lab," says there are four main habits that spell trouble for any relationship, all of which imply some level of resentment or blame: contempt, defensiveness, criticism, and stonewalling (refusing to communicate). Conversely, his research also illuminates one component shared by all happy marriages or partnerships: mutual trust. In this chapter we'll explore not only how to rebuild trust after it has been violated, but how to cultivate and maintain it to begin with.

From day-to-day annoyances to large disappointments, the couples I interviewed told me that seeking and granting forgiveness was an integral part of maintaining and rebuilding trust. That dovetails with what researcher David Fenell discovered when he interviewed 147 reportedly happy couples married for more than twenty years. They said the willingness to forgive and be forgiven was one of the chief factors that helped them sustain their relationships, along with loyalty and respect. Since then, other social scientists have weighed in on the role of forgiveness in marriage, finding strong correlations between the ability to seek and grant forgiveness with reduced conflict, as well as with strong commitment and relationship closeness.

And yet, there is such a thing as being *too* forgiving. Florida State University's Jim McNulty identified a pitfall when it comes to forgiveness in marriage: If it's unequal, it can be dangerous. McNulty examined spouses' tendencies to forgive transgressions over the first two years of seventy-two marriages. He found that in couples with less frequent conflict and "hostile behavior" to begin with, forgiveness worked to resolve and prevent conflict. But in couples with more frequent hostile interactions such as sarcasm or insults, forgiving led to more—not fewer—hurtful comments or actions, with one spouse more likely to lash out and the other more likely to roll over and take it. He dubbed this "the doormat effect." McNulty's findings reminded me of the colleague of a friend. About every other year, this woman's husband is found to be cheating (often while she's pregnant with their next child), and after a period of weeping and yelling and brief separation, she takes him back and accepts his supposedly contrite apologies.

It turns out that arguing and temporary anger, as well as the withholding of forgiveness and the willingness to leave if necessary, are important ways to regulate harmful habits and broker creative solutions. When I told a friend about McNulty's findings, she observed that the rose, that long-standing traditional symbol of romantic love, happens to be one of the few flower bushes with thorns. Countless clichéd lyrics use thorns to represent the risk of heartbreak in love, but my friend saw a different metaphor. Just as kindness is key to sustaining love—of others and self—so is the ability to say no (or "Hell no, not until the Pope rides a purple Pegasus over New York City"), to tell your partner when you're too angry to speak, and to be willing to walk if you consistently find yourself hurt or disrespected.

So, how to achieve the balance of being forgiving enough, but not too forgiving? I've certainly been known to veer to either extreme in my own romantic history, at times tolerating damaging behavior and other times dismissing someone altogether when he didn't call precisely when he said he would. As I researched this chapter, I confronted my own love history and my most recent breakup, as well as the relationship I was in the process of building with Anthony. Little by little, I began to get a sense of what it means to cultivate an environment that nourishes mutual trust, forgiveness, and genuine apology.

Forgiveness and Infidelity

When it comes to betrayal and forgiveness in relationships, the most extreme and the most immediate scenario that usually comes to mind is infidelity. That topic came up in several of my interviews, particularly in the case of one couple, Danielle and Jerry. A mutual friend mentioned to me that he knew a couple who were rebuilding their relationship after an affair. He put us in touch, and they were willing to talk to me about what they'd gone through.

The day Jerry told his wife was a warm September Sunday, the sun shimmering over the Southern California foothills surrounding their spacious home. Danielle returned from yoga to find her husband sitting on their flagstone patio by the pool.

"I need to tell you something," he said. His wiry cyclist's frame appeared folded in on itself, as if he'd shrunk. The tense expression on his boyishly handsome face stopped her short.

"Okay . . . ?"

"I'm in love with Holly."

Nothing. She felt nothing, but the sage and juniper-dotted hills around them seemed to undulate like waves. Then came relief. It struck her as odd at first, but she realized that she felt relieved because she had long known on some level that something was wrong, and now she knew she'd been right. Then came the rage. "Holly?!" she yelled. "In *love* with her?!" Danielle, a soft-spoken woman with short, stylish bleach-blond hair and blue eyes who resembles a petite Charlize Theron, yelled and paced, unable to stand still. Jerry, her husband of thirty-five years, had just confessed that he'd engaged in a two-year affair with one of their friends.

It began on a couples' camping trip. Holly kissed him while they were washing dishes together, Jerry said, and he was flattered. Afterward he considered telling Danielle, but something stopped him—the thrill of feeling so wanted, the adrenaline of keeping a secret. The relationship escalated in small increments until they were spending weekends together when their spouses were out of town. When something bothered them about their partners, they confided in each other and grew ever closer. He hated himself for it, he told Danielle now. He ended it several times, but never for long. He repeatedly told Holly he wasn't leaving his wife, he said, but eventually, he became confused. The more he hid from Danielle, the more distant they became. Maybe he really was in love with Holly, he wondered. He didn't know what to do.

Danielle stood in the patio doorway, frozen. Memories of the past two years flew through her mind: that night when they had a party and she thought Jerry and Holly looked a little too cozy, the times she and Les sat talking at the campfire while Jerry and Holly gathered wood, the conversations she and Jerry had had about how they weren't as close anymore and hardly had sex. The knowledge that he had done this and lied about it for so long, that Holly had been her friend, and that for the past year her husband had allowed her to rack her brain trying to figure out what was wrong with their marriage while all the while he was actively destroying it—it made her want to set him ablaze. She leaned in to her husband's face and hissed, "Why don't you take your fancy car and get the hell out of here."

This was what Jerry had expected. He felt horribly guilty, but part of him also felt relieved to have finally told the truth.

Danielle returned to pacing and slamming doors. But then she stopped. Just as thoughts of his betrayal flashed in her mind moments earlier, now came the memories of their life together: Meeting and falling in love in college when they were both competitive gymnasts, moving to California and spending decades building a successful sales business, all of the conversations and mountain adventures and throwing parties and supporting each other through the losses of parents and friends. The fact remained: For better or worse, she loved him. She didn't want him to leave. At least not before they explored what happened and whether their marriage could possibly be salvaged.

A calm came over her as she sat next to him at the patio table. "I just want you to know that I can forgive you," she said.

Jerry looked shocked. Danielle was surprised, too—she hadn't contemplated this sudden turnabout, but here it was.

"If you leave our marriage now, you're making the biggest mistake of your life. Everything you want is right here," she said, looking out at their backyard and the rolling hills and endless sky beyond. "Whatever happens, let's take this opportunity to explore how this happened so it doesn't happen again."

On the day he told Danielle about his affair, Jerry was thinking he would move out, either into a place alone, or perhaps with Holly. But then Danielle said she could forgive him and collapsed on the couch. "I anticipated the yelling but never the forgiveness," he told me, a year later. "And then the crying—it was heart-wrenching. To know I was responsible for that." He held her as she wept, and later they took their dogs for a walk. She thought that leaving was the cowardly option. She wanted him to stay while they started therapy and sorted out what happened. He agreed. He felt like a cliché, allowing himself to be drawn into an affair with a younger woman at a time when he and his wife had grown somewhat distant, taking each other for granted and failing to address it. As the news of the affair trickled out to their circle of friends, several of Jerry's male buddies called him. Most said some version of this: "Are you totally out of your mind? You're leaving Danielle for Holly? Get it together, man."

Over the days that followed, as they sought out a relationship therapist and Danielle endured sleepless nights, sometimes dozing off only to wake at three a.m. in shock all over again, Jerry took Holly's calls and explained what was happening. She was livid. Since he'd led her to believe that he was finally leaving Danielle, the fact that he was staying, at least until they decided on a course of action, enraged her. As the days went by, she grew angrier. She sent scathing text messages. She repeatedly demanded to know if he was wearing his wedding band and ordered him to remove it. Jerry noticed that she seemed to have no concern for Danielle whatsoever, despite the fact that they were supposedly friends. He didn't like that. "I looked at Danielle and how she was handling this with such grace, and I was reminded of why I fell in love with her all those years ago," he told me. "It became clear what my choice would be." Within weeks he told Holly he was choosing his wife.

In therapy sessions and long conversations on the couch at home, Danielle and Jerry discussed what had been missing in their marriage that led to increased distance (failing to set aside quality time as a couple alone, for instance), and Jerry explored what led him to cheat and lie about it (his father took his own life when Jerry was a teen, and he realized that that event drove a lot of his insecurities, including fears about aging and death). When he found himself pursued by a younger woman, it gave him a sort of addictive escape from those fears. "I'm embarrassed to say it," he told me, "but the flattery played to my ego."

While this may sound neat and tidy, as if Danielle and Jerry just sailed into the therapist's office and sorted it all out, it was not. There were months of sleepless nights. Crying jags. Days of silence followed by shouting matches and then long, tedious conversations in the living room. Some of those conversations seemed to resolve some things, others didn't. Sometimes Danielle felt as if she was past the affair, moving on, ready to confront the future with or without her husband. Sometimes she felt she'd truly forgiven, and she'd awake with a sense of renewal and peace. And yet other times, that calm feeling was replaced by a weariness, a heavy sense of exhaustion, and she thought maybe she was just too drained to feel angry anymore. But then she'd sit up suddenly in the middle of the night having dreamed of her husband with Holly. She'd lay there sweating, anxious and furious all over again. As with most people I spoke with about forgiving extreme trespasses, Danielle's process of forgiveness was anything but linear and steadily progressive. If you plotted it on a simple graph with various levels of forgiveness on the vertical axis and time on the horizontal axis, the line would be volatile, plodding slightly upward, plunging down, bouncing up, and everything in between. Yet over time, overall, the line would inch up and up, rising toward the highest level of forgiveness little by little.

Every time they reached some new ground of common understanding about what led to the affair, it got easier. As they got better at listening to each other and doing their best to understand and validate each other's experiences, it got easier. Every time Danielle got upset all over again, but forced herself to remember why she chose to stay with Jerry, mentally reviewing all of the things she cherished about him and about their relationship, it got easier. While the moment when Danielle decided to forgive her husband was forever clear in her mind, the process was less defined. It was more like stumbling up a steep mountain, with lots of backsliding, than crossing some magical bridge to the Land of Having Forgiven. And yet, within about nine months, she—and they as a couple—found themselves in more forgiving territory. Their days were less painful and more loving, their nights less marked by agony than by a tenuous yet growing tenderness.

When I visited them a year after Jerry admitted to the affair, interviewing them separately and together, they told me they now communicate more than ever before. "We spent all day yesterday talking," Jerry said. "We never would have done that before, because we were always doing something— riding our bikes, working, hanging out with other people." I doubted things were completely resolved, even after a year, and before I even asked, they acknowledged that was true. Jerry told me he still feels terrible. "I'm having trouble forgiving myself for letting it happen," he said, hanging his head.

Danielle still sometimes wakes at three a.m., heart racing, thinking about her husband with another woman. Yet she's glad she responded the way she did. "Forgiveness was the thing that allowed me to see how much I loved him, to have compassion for everyone in the situation, including me," she said. "The easiest thing would have been to leave. It's been much harder than I expected. But it's led to incredible growth, and I don't take anything for granted anymore."

So, how do you know if not only forgiving, but forgiving and being willing to stay, is a viable option? Most people assume that an affair is an automatic relationship killer, but research shows that couples committed to overcoming infidelity have just as good a chance as other struggling couples to overcome the past. While they usually start therapy with lower happiness levels than other struggling couples, most finish with just as high a level of relationship satisfaction. Several of the couples I interviewed reported confronting infidelity at some point during their marriage, and their stories share similarities with Gottman's recommendations on rebuilding a relationship after an affair. While in the couples I interviewed the cheating spouse happened to be male, that's obviously not always the case. Estimates on infidelity in the United States place males at a higher likelihood of cheating, but women have been catching up in recent decades, reporting having affairs at an increasing rate, most likely because the sexual revolution brought equal opportunity to meet other partners outside of the home.

When Lulu, a forty-six-year-old author and public speaker, found out that Dirk, her husband of nearly twenty years, had a one-night stand while on an extended work assignment abroad (guilt-ridden and afraid that hiding something so major would most certainly ruin their marriage, he told her), she demanded to know the chronology of events that led to the liaison. Not only that, she wanted to know about every instance of flirting or attraction to another person in past years, even if it didn't lead to an indiscretion. "I took a long road trip alone after he told me, and I just knew that for me to have trust rebuilt, I first needed to know if there was anything else 'untidy,'" she told me.

While some counselors, most often religious ones, recommend avoiding the subject altogether and merely "moving on," Gottman and other therapists say that only exacerbates emotional distance and fosters distrust. Experiencing betrayal at the hands of your spouse often leads to PTSD symptoms, from sleepless nights and flashbacks to depression, anxiety, and obsessive thoughts. As with any other trauma, recovery means knowing and understanding exactly what happened and being able to grieve.

The betrayed spouse also needs apology, remorse, and accountability in order to move forward. Dirk was 100 percent clear that his one-night stand was a mistake and that he wanted to earn back his wife's trust. "It was a betrayal of her and of all of our friends," he told me. "It came down to 'I fucked up bad. Here's what I'm willing to do to make it right. If I do, will you forgive me?'" Lulu was willing. But she needed some more evidence of his commitment. They resolved that he would share what happened with key close friends and apologize to them, too. Danielle, meanwhile, needed the right to review Jerry's phone records for proof that he cut ties with Holly. Eventually, Gottman writes, the hurt spouse will need to trust without proof or suspicion, but that should never be expected immediately.

Lulu also needed to understand *why* her husband strayed. Dirk's explanation was that he was doubting himself in his career, feeling lonely in a faraway country, and starting to feel old. Cheating is usually the end result of a chain reaction of behavior that erodes trust and closeness. This includes withholding negative emotions and failing to connect through arguing, sharing, listening, and empathy. If both partners can identify that progression and restore intimacy, they have a shot. For Abi and Genea, that meant each of them exploring personal issues that were damaging their marriage, including Abi's untreated depression. For Hsiao-Ling and her husband, Jim, who admitted to an online relationship with a coworker, it meant reexamining their communication and sex life. In the end, they developed a heightened ability to listen to each other without offering advice, and became more open about attractions to other people (which, for them, made it less taboo and therefore less compelling).

As trust is rebuilt, Gottman recommends setting a clear understanding that if the cheating spouse strays again, the relationship is over. Why? People tend to adhere to commitments when they face a threat for breaking them. You know all those sales campaigns that chime, "Today only!"? That's based on research. In the classic book *Influence*, social science researcher Robert Cialdini explains that people are more likely to comply (or buy) when faced with losing something than with the promise of gaining something of equal value. When it comes to most aspects of human behavior, people rarely change their behavior unless they face consequences.

The "Ecosystem" That Allows Mutual Trust and Forgiveness to Flourish

Given the fact that cheating happens in around 25 percent of marriages, most couples won't ever confront infidelity, much less extreme violence. The smaller resentments that most of us deal with may seem trivial in comparison, but considering the amount of time couples spend together, even one persistent resentment or unresolved conflict can lead to trouble. Most of the happy couples I interviewed talked about the importance of developing habits that create a sort of ecosystem that helps mutual forgiveness flourish. From compassion to a certain type of arguing, we'll explore those habits below.

Compassion: "If I Expect Myself to Be Perfect, Guess What I Expect from Everyone Else?"

Chuck, a forty-five-year-old father of two, has been driven since he was a child. Part of his drive comes from perfectionism. As a leader in a federal government agency, he would do anything and everything to meet a deadline or check a task off his to-do list, even if it meant not sleeping for days or sacrificing family time. When he fell short of his expectations, he would spend days immersed in a cloud of self-loathing, and when faced with imperfection in the people he managed, he responded similarly. He even had the same tendency when it came to his wife, Dianne.

"My context for myself and others was, 'You must do everything it takes to achieve this goal by deadline or you're a failure,'" he said. He became aware of this when he hired a life coach to help him assess and refine his professional and personal goals, which entailed examining what was in the way of achieving these goals. When perfectionism came up in a phone conversation with his coach, she suggested he read *Loving What Is*, by Byron Katie.

In the book, Katie describes how she discovered a way to alter her perspective by applying a series of questions to any complaint. The first question about the complaint was, Is it true? The subsequent ones raised the possibility that alternative interpretations of the complaint could be true—that perhaps he wasn't communicating his ideas effectively to his boss, for instance, as opposed to his boss being just an incompetent fool trying to stymie his career. The next steps were brainstorming ways that he may have contributed to the problem and new ideas for how he could solve it. Chuck did the exercises in relation to his high, unyielding expectations for himself and others at work and at home.

As he noticed how pervasive his perfectionism was, and how it was damaging his marriage as well as his daily quality of life, he began to work on embracing imperfection. Things started to change. One thing that frustrated him in his marriage was Dianne's resistance to managing money, consistently running up a credit card balance or overdrawing her checking account. She would apologize and say she would balance an account by a certain time, but fail to do so. This made Chuck angry and resentful, which made her even less likely to follow through.

"I've had to forgive myself for not being perfect," he told me, "because if I expect myself to be perfect, guess what I expect from everyone else?" As he became more forgiving of his wife, she felt less judged. They were able to discuss it rationally and arrive at a solution: Instead of him managing their finances and paying the bills on Quicken, she would learn to do it and take the reins. It worked. "Now, she's asking me to explain certain charges," he said, laughing.

Chuck was describing an increase in his capacity for compassion, defined as "concern or sympathy for the suffering of others," with Latin origins deriving from "to suffer together." Chuck started with compassion for himself. Kristin Neff, a University of Texas researcher who has studied self-compassion for more than ten years, makes a strong link between self-compassion and relationship satisfaction. Neff defines self-compassion as self-kindness, awareness of our common humanity, and mindfulness. This means treating yourself with the patience, understanding, and care that you would give a close friend, keeping in mind that when you're enduring challenges, you're not alone (since everyone faces challenges), and being mindful, recognizing and experiencing thoughts and emotions without exaggerating or dwelling on them.

Self-compassionate people, Neff discovered, have happier and healthier romantic relationships than those who are less self-compassionate. In a study of one hundred couples, Neff and her team measured each partner's self-compassion level and relationship satisfaction, and asked each to describe their partner's relationship behavior. The results showed that self-compassionate people were described as more accepting and less judgmental, respecting their partners' feelings, opinions, and points of view instead of trying to change them. They were also described as more caring, connected, affectionate, and intimate, as well as more willing to discuss relationship problems.

Conflict Intimacy

Melissa Siig, a forty-year-old freelance writer and mother of three, recalls that her worst fights with her husband, Steve, took place in the early phase of their ten-year marriage. When they argued, it often escalated to yelling, with him leaving the house and her considering packing a bag to go stay with friends. Over time, they learned to listen to each other's views more patiently. They began to understand their own—and then each other's—needs, reactions, and "triggers" from childhood, and adjusted their behavior accordingly. Steve, for instance, an adventure filmmaker, frequently traveled for work, and he would return to find Melissa angry and withdrawn. Her father abandoned her family when she was a child, and she discovered in therapy and by writing in her journal that her husband's trips triggered the old feelings of hurt and anger. Once they discussed it, Steve took it less personally, Melissa suffered less over his absences because he assured her that he had no intention of leaving her like her father did, and they agreed that he wouldn't travel for more than three weeks at a time.

Maintaining a close bond in the face of inevitable disagreements requires a certain type of communication. While communication is a vague term thrown around so much it can seem meaningless, Gottman and his team of researchers used their observations and multiple longitudinal, double-blind studies to demystify "good communication," categorizing it into simple components: putting your feelings into words and sharing them with your partner, listening to your partner when he or she shares (without interrupting with your own thoughts), asking follow-up questions or making statements that ensure your partner feels heard and encouraged to continue, and expressing compassion. This is the core of good communication, and helps lead to emotional closeness and the ability to seek and grant forgiveness.

Research shows that it's the way couples navigate conflict that determines whether they stay together. The psychologist Steven Solomon calls this "conflict intimacy." Gottman, after studying more than two hundred couples in his Love Lab over a period of twenty years, determined that the ones who remained happily together used a high number of certain conciliatory phrases and actions during fights. These "repair mechanisms" include comments about the conversation, such as "we're getting off topic," "that hurt my feelings," or "please let me finish." They also include statements that signal understanding, or a commitment to understanding, each other's points ("I see," for instance, or "go on").

Maintaining intimacy throughout conflict keeps your connection and mutual empathy intact in spite of the unavoidable disagreements that come up in a life together, and it also makes hurting your spouse less likely. Says Kevin, a sheriff's deputy, "Why would you want to hurt that person? It's easy—just don't do something that you would have trouble forgiving yourself for, or that you wouldn't expect your spouse to forgive you for." Debi agrees. "If you're doing things that you have to be forgiven for all the time," she says, "you should wonder if you're in the right relationship."

Compromise

When spouses can maintain intimacy, even during a fight, they're more likely to act as a team. When Matt and Roberta Fotter lost their home in Hurricane Katrina and had to relocate, Matt says he was reminded of one of his wife's best qualities: her ability to play hard for "Team Fotter." "She got a job immediately, because I was looking at jobs that would pay me a third of what I'd been making," he says. "Even now, if tomorrow I said, 'I can't stand this job anymore, I'm applying to clerk at the Apple Store,' she'd support that. She'd remind me that we have to pay our bills and that I love shiny things, but she'd support me." Similarly, Debi doesn't drink alcohol because it makes her sick, but she's happy to have beer in the house since her husband, Chaz, enjoys having one after a day at work laying hardwood floors. Melissa, meanwhile, likes to have the house immaculately clean, while Steve prefers to leave clothes and dishes strewn about. Their compromise? He gets to be messy in the bedroom as long as the rest of the house remains organized. "I call it 'containment,'" Melissa jokes.

Of course, it's unwise to compromise on core needs. Psychologist Harriet Lerner recommends compromising roughly 84 percent of the time, while standing your ground on the things that are integral to your wellbeing. These nonnegotiables could be anything from regular exercise or living near family to the right to pursue a lifelong dream. When Bruce, a financial planner, asked his wife of fifteen years, Beverly, what she wanted to do for her fiftieth birthday, she was clear: She wanted a big, Bollywoodthemed costume party with a classy catered meal. She knew Bruce would rather do something more intimate, but she grew up with consistent neglect, never having her family plan anything for her birthday. So he agreed, and she got her party.

"Apology Is the Gunshot at the Start of the Race."

One evening before Anthony and I moved in together, we'd returned from a night out with friends when I mentioned that I forgot to pick up a prescription for my allergies (I'm allergic to trees, grasses, cats, and dogs). Anthony began to tease me, which I usually don't mind because his tone is loving, but this time, he crossed the line. "Jeez," he joked, "this is gonna be like living with a hypochondriac." My allergies and asthma are a source of frustration to me, because they make me feel defective and fragile, and I felt hurt, ashamed, and livid at his comment. In scientific terms, I was "flooded," meaning adrenaline shut off my frontal lobe's problem-solving capacities and set me up to respond in a, shall we say, more primitive fashion.

I wanted to tell him to go fuck himself. Instead, I left. Once I got home and took a few deep breaths, I texted him and told him that his comment made me feel judged and mocked. He called immediately. "I'm really sorry, babe," he said. "I won't joke about your health again." His expression of understanding and the remorse he showed was vital to my feeling heard and appreciated. After that, it was easy for me to let it go.

Of course, the main point of an apology or repair is the behavior that comes afterward. "Apology is the gunshot at the start of the race," Debi, a retired special education teacher, told me. "But the race is actually running." If Anthony apologized for joking about my health but continued to do it, his apology would be meaningless.

But what happens when the "race" happens to be a more core aspect of one's habitual behavior or personality? For instance, the Friday Anthony got his car towed. We awoke to discover that because Anthony had given our dog sitter his parking permit, the towing company that patrols our building towed his car during the night. When he came in at 6:30 A.M. to tell me his car was gone, I was getting ready to drive to the mountains, where there was two feet of fresh powder, to ski. Skiing is my favorite sport, hobby, and passion, all rolled into one. I might actually have a skiing addiction. I also, as I would be reminded that morning, have "only-child syndrome" (I'm nine years younger than my sister and sometimes felt like an only child growing up), wherein I prefer to do what I have planned and what I want, regardless of what might be happening—in this case, my boyfriend lacking a way to retrieve his car and get to work.

I sighed my annoyance. I huffed and puffed. I lamented that he'd given the dog sitter the parking permit when I had expressly told him the permits were enforced with a strong arm worthy of Mussolini. Then I grudgingly told him that I'd take him to the tow yard to get the car. On the way, I obsessively checked the clock on the dashboard, imagining all of the fresh tracks I wasn't getting. Once we found the yard and saw that it wouldn't open for another ninety minutes, I drove away, leaving Anthony standing, in his suit with his laptop, by a parking lot filled with rusting Chevy trucks and a pack of barking rottweilers. It wasn't until I was sitting in bumper-to-bumper traffic on Interstate 70, realizing that I would likely spend the rest of the morning sitting on the highway while other people skied away all of the untracked powder, that it dawned on me that I'd behaved like a selfish lunatic. Once I called Anthony to apologize, I had to reexamine my priorities. Skiing is important to me, but being there for the people I love when they need me is much more important.

Altering behavior after an apology can be tough. Becoming defensive or shutting down is all too easy when a flaw you've been blind to is unveiled, but if you're willing to grow in order to become a better partner and a better person, it's worth it. Every one of the couples I interviewed mentioned this. For some, it took a crisis to inspire real change. When Genea developed an emotional crush on another woman and considered leaving Abi, for example, she went to see a counselor and realized that for years, she had tolerated her wife's inability to get treatment for her clinical depression. As a result, Genea felt alone in her marriage. She earned most of the money, took care of the house, cooked, and managed the finances and scheduling, since Abi was often despondent. When Genea explained that she felt alone and unsupported, Abi finally became willing to give up her resistance to admitting she had an illness and seeking treatment. She began therapy, got on medication, and began to feel better. She apologized to Genea for being so absent in the past, and because she was taking action and getting better, Genea forgave her and continued the relationship.

Changing habits can also resolve more mundane, day-to-day issues. My friend Lara's husband, Will, learned that his habit of leaving clothes on the bedroom floor stressed her out, and began putting his clothes away as soon as he removed them. Beverly, upon learning that her children's misbehavior was bothersome to her new husband, Bruce, became stricter.

From personal experience, I know that even small changes aren't necessarily easy. Anthony once pointed out that I could be absentminded and fail to do simple things such as keep my eye on the navigation system when he was driving somewhere new, or ensure that toxic cleaning supplies were stored safely out of our dog's reach. As a card-carrying perfectionist who does everything possible to avoid disappointing people, I took this as very bad news. I cried. I momentarily shut down, feeling numb and unable to think or speak. I felt put on the spot. I called on all of my powers of self-compassion, reminding myself that everyone can improve, and that this didn't mean I was a bad person. The fact was that, as the baby of the family, I spent my childhood following my parents and much elder sister around, free of any responsibility to manage logistics or lead the way. Here was an opportunity for me to mature, and I took it, working on being more aware and spending less time daydreaming.

Forgiveness After Divorce: "I Was Finally Able to Let It Go, and It Freed My Heart Up."

Resentment after a divorce or breakup is so common that it's no longer an interesting plotline. (Besides, who could top Michael Douglas and Kathleen

Turner trying to kill each other while clinging to a crystal chandelier in 1989's *The War of the Roses*?) Yet post-split bitterness is as bad for your health as any other kind, only in addition to potentially damaging heart and brain function and lowering mood, it can wreck any possibility of starting a new, healthy relationship. (Bitterness and lack of trust may even be part of the reason that second and third marriages are statistically more likely to end in divorce than first marriages.) If you want proof, just make your most disgusted and hateful face and then check yourself out in the mirror: Is this your hottest look? Not so much.

Many of those I interviewed said forgiving their exes was key to moving forward and finding an even better relationship. Beverly, whose first husband left her after she had a stillborn baby at nineteen, says that forgiving him led to her ability to find happiness with her current husband, Bruce. "I was angry and resentful for years," she told me. "It tainted all of my other relationships. Around the time I met Bruce, my ex reached out to me and apologized. I was finally able to totally let it go, and it freed my heart up."

Marie, a retired registered nurse, kicked her husband out of the house after she began attending Al-Anon and realized that she was enabling him by tolerating his drunken tirades and days-long benders. He ended up marrying another woman after they separated, but he also got sober and became active in AA. Years later, he would thank Marie for "breaking his denial." It took three years and a lot of conversations with supportive friends, but Marie forgave him—before he ever apologized or thanked her for helping him see the light. They remained in touch, and when he did something that bothered her (arriving at a party uninvited, for instance), she found the strength to tell him what was and what was not okay with her, and then forgave him again. This meant their three children didn't have to act as go-betweens or brace for fights when they all spent holidays together. It also provided Marie with something that not all divorcees can claim: "I can be around him and not have my stomach in knots," she says. "I'm grateful for that." While Marie forgave her ex before he showed remorse, the fact that he did eventually acknowledge his mistakes and thank her for pointing them out made it easier for her to reconcile with him and maintain a relationship. If he hadn't ever showed remorse, she would still have forgiven him, but probably without reconciling and sharing holidays.

The psychotherapist Katherine Woodward Thomas, who leads online programs for people in the process of separation or divorce, says personal responsibility is an underrated part of forgiving a spouse and correcting relationship mistakes. "Sometimes people forgive in this very patronizing way, only seeing the other person's wrong behavior but not their own part in it," she told me over the phone from her home in California. "You can do that, but you won't be available to freely open your heart again because you haven't taken full responsibility for how you colluded with old patterns, and so they continue." When you realize how you contributed to a problem, you can fix it. "Even if it was ninety-seven percent their fault and three percent mine," she says, "I need to focus on that three percent because that's the way to become free of the old pattern so it never happens again." I didn't know how that applied to me, but I was about to find out.

"The Milk Is Bad. Throw It Out."

The e-mail arrived a few weeks before a Halloween party where I was likely to see my ex-boyfriend, Mike. The party was being hosted by mutual friends, and Anthony and I would be sure to encounter Mike and his girl-friend. Upon seeing Mike's name in my inbox, I felt a shiver of revulsion. Titled "reconciliation," it read: *I hope you're well. I wanted to reach out and start a dialogue in hopes of reaching an amicable understanding before we see each other at a social function.* After noting the message's stilted official-ness, my next thought was the memory of him at the improv play, drunk-enly hurling the pretend baby into the audience. To add to my humiliation, a friend of his reached out to me after we broke up and confided that while I was visiting my family over Christmas, Mike got drunk at a holiday party and flirted with several other women—supposedly attempting to sleep with at least one.

Now, eighteen months later and a year after Anthony and I started dating, I wasn't angry. And yet, I was irritated that I had to see my ex at parties, or anywhere, for that matter. Mostly, it was shame and embarrassment that I ever dated him. Nonetheless, I agreed to meet for lunch. I didn't want our first awkward encounter to be at the party, and given our mutual friends, we were likely to be attending baby showers and children's birthday parties together for years to come.

A week before the lunch, Anthony surprised me with a one-year anniversary trip to Aspen. We stayed at a beautiful boutique hotel, slept in and read, and walked Stella through stands of sun-colored aspen trees. One morning, I reached into the mini-fridge for the milk we'd bought at the store. I poured some into my coffee and noticed it billowed into flaky clouds. I smelled it, but couldn't tell if it was rancid. I had Anthony smell it, and he couldn't tell, either. I poured out my coffee and decided to try again with tea. Same thing. I concluded it was probably bad and made a fresh cup of tea sans milk. Later that afternoon, Anthony came in after a run and opened the mini-fridge to see the milk carton sitting in the door.

"Why didn't you dump it out?" he asked.

"I guess I was waiting until later," I replied.

He stared at me.

"Sorry, I'll do it now," I said moodily, taking the carton into the bathroom and flushing the bad milk down the toilet.

That evening, I mentioned that I was having lunch with Mike. Anthony acknowledged that we've all dated people who weren't a good fit, but then he looked at me and said, "I know you probably don't want to hear this, babe, but I think he probably wasn't such a terrible guy. I think in some ways, you allowed him to be at his worst because you tolerated bullshit that was beneath you."

I looked at him, speechless and blinking.

"I've done the same thing, so I'm not judging you, I'm just pointing out what I see," he continued. "It's like the milk this morning. It was bad. It looked bad, but you smelled it and then had me smell it. Then you tried it again, and it was still bad. And then you put it back in the fridge! Babe—the milk is bad. Throw it out. It was just like that with him. The. Milk. Is. Bad. Throw. It. Out."

In spite of my desire to angrily tell Anthony that he didn't have the slightest idea what he was talking about, I knew he was right. I did tolerate behavior that upset me, and it was easier to blame my ex than acknowledge that. The truth was that while I'd demonized the guy for more than a year, there was a lot more to him than the terrible character I'd sketched in my memories. For the most part, he was kind and considerate. We had great times together, hiking and skiing and camping and talking on long road trips. Like most people, he was just trying to live his best life, and when he wasn't getting fed an entire bottle of whiskey on stage and being led into a public display of private emotions, he was a decent guy who just wasn't right for me, or vice versa.

Anthony brought the "bad milk" analogy back around to our relationship. "I can be a jerk sometimes, babe, and when I'm a jerk I want you to call me on it," he said, likening his sometimes being a jerk to the bad milk that I should have rejected. "Like at dinner, I was playing with my phone at the table. That was rude. But you didn't say anything."

It was true. I was annoyed by his sudden fascination with his phone but said nothing. "Okay," I said. "Next time you're a jerk, I'll be sure to let you know."

"Good," he said.

And with that, my unfortunate tendency to turn into the kind of doormat revealed in McNulty's research was unmasked. So why, exactly, was my default to turn into a pathetic wimp in my relationships? Like most of us, it was probably something I learned without knowing I was learning it. When my father did something that bothered my mother, she seemed to react by freezing up or swallowing her feelings, only to explode later. It turns out that "freeze" is the third and least well-known, hardwired response to a survival threat, after fight or flight. Since throughout evolution women often weren't fast enough to outrun predators or strong enough to kill them, they learned to freeze in order to avoid being seen, or "play dead" to avoid being killed.

When it came to relationships, somewhere along the way I got the idea that "rocking the boat" makes things worse, and so it's preferable to just ignore something offensive, or worse, pretend you're too cool to care. As I got into my thirties, this was compounded by the fear that if I did rock the boat, I would wind up alone, with one hundred cats. (The fact that I'm allergic to cats and don't even like them just underscores how deeply this double standard notion of "the pathetic single cat lady" pervades our society.)

On the day in late October when I agreed to meet Mike for lunch, I walked into the suburban eatery we had agreed upon and immediately spotted him at a high-top in the bar area. He had a full, bushy beard now, and he'd put on weight. His smile struck me as half warm and half false, the sort of stiff, saccharine grin you'd expect from a salesperson who's exhausted but bent on doing whatever it takes to hit their magic number. As I approached, my chest constricted. I nodded hello and shook his outstretched hand. As I sat down, I concentrated on breathing and felt myself relax.

He kicked off an old-friends-catching-up conversation by asking me about my writing and teaching, and I reciprocated. By the time the server brought our lunch, however, I was tired of it. I didn't feel any of the old ire, but I didn't care to pretend we were pals, either. Surveying the tall beer he'd ordered at noon, and the enormous bacon burger topped with fried onion rings on his plate, I marveled that we ever dated at all, given our completely divergent approaches to health, among other things. "So," I said, "what did you want to talk about?"

"Well, it sounds like someone told you that I did certain things during our relationship."

I waited.

"Well, I guess people were under the impression that you thought I'd slept with four people when we were together."

I laughed. Four people? Though we were in our thirties, gossip was still apparently a game of telephone. "No. I was told that you got drunk and tried to sleep with at least one person while I was out of town."

He nodded quickly. "That did happen."

This acknowledgment surprised me. It sat in the space between us, as solid and simple as the salt shaker. Something about the admission was a relief to me.

"But nothing *actually* happened," he continued. "It was just drunken flirting."

"Honestly, it's irrelevant now," I said, surprised to find that I meant what I was saying. "I'm really happy, you seem happy, so it's water under the bridge."

He agreed, relieved.

I truly didn't care what he did or didn't do. I didn't like him, but I didn't hate him, either. I felt completely neutral. Not just that—I felt calm. It was as if, after treading water in a bottomless ocean, panting and exhausted, a sandy ground had gradually appeared on which I noticed myself standing.

As he finished his burger and I ate my tomato soup, we discussed which situations would be comfortable for us to attend together with our significant others. Double or triple dates were out, we agreed, but parties and concerts were fine. We settled the check and chatted about our Halloween costumes (he was going as the Dude from *The Big Lebowski*; I was going as an eighties character from *Flashdance*). I said goodbye, climbed into my Subaru, and drove home to resume work. My mom called, and when I told her where I had been, she said, "Oh, wow—how was that?" As I answered, my eye caught sight of an airplane cutting a white contrail across the blue sky above. "It was fine," I replied. "It was absolutely fine."

6

A Touch of Grace: Forgiveness as a Spiritual (and Secular) Practice

Rose Sposito awoke early to the sound of rushing water. She could always hear the river, but today it was almost deafening. She woke her husband, and together they walked outside to take a look. Their home sits on forty-five acres along the Thompson River in northern Colorado, outside the town of Lyons. What they saw was unprecedented: The river had flooded, and gray-blue water roared past, roiling rapids ripping trees and bushes out of the ground as it went by. It was closer to their garden than it ever had been, but seemed downslope enough to avoid an immediate threat. They looked at each other in alarm and rushed inside to start calling neighbors.

Northern Colorado was experiencing what officials would describe as a five-hundred-year flood. In the three decades Rose had lived in Colorado, water-related problems were almost always caused by the lack of it. Now, in early September 2013, the rain was falling in sheets, with no sign of letting up. In the following days, hundreds of homes would be destroyed, people airlifted from houses surrounded by water, and roads and even parts of Interstate 25 washed away. In nearby Boulder County, a twenty-foot wall of water rushed through a canyon, and when a car stopped in the white water, witnesses saw two people emerge and get swept away to their deaths.

In Lyons, the floodwaters rose as high as street signs in some places and rendered the entrance to the town impassable. People used the city's Facebook page to ask for first aid supplies, pet food, and safe haven, and Rose's home filled up with neighbors fleeing homes that were flooded or without power. (The town's electricity went down, but Rose's home is off the grid, running on energy from twenty-four solar panels and a generator.) First, a family of four arrived carrying perishable food, bags of clothes and bedding, and photo albums and framed pictures. Another ten people trickled in over the next few days. As Rose placed her neighbors' food in the refrigerator and set up makeshift beds in the living room, she kept glancing toward the rising waters outside. Every time the rain slowed and she thought it might stop, the torrents returned with even more force, pummeling the flower beds and flooding the yard with debris.

An acupuncturist in her fifties with short chestnut hair and gray-brown eyes, Rose had for decades practiced Tibetan Buddhist mindfulness meditation, sitting in silence and noticing her thoughts, letting them pass like bubbles in the ocean. The idea is to avoid resisting or engaging with the thoughts, slowing them over time to develop a stillness of mind that isn't yanked around by the ups and downs of life. Rose usually began her days on a cushion in her meditation room overlooking the river, and ended each day there before going to sleep. But as the floods encroached and more people sought haven in her home, there was no time for that.

Even so, the days and hours became a sort of meditation in action. When she looked outside and felt fear, she would notice the anxious thoughts and the squirming in her belly and take a deep breath. She would redirect her focus to her hands as they sliced onions for dinner or folded her neighbors' laundry, or to the smiles of the children as they played games in the living room. She did the same when she felt annoyed that her bathroom was occupied or spotted dishes piled in the sink, and when she reprimanded herself for feeling that way when people's homes were being destroyed all around her. Later, she would say that what got her through those harrowing days was her dedicated meditation practice, and the compassion and equanimity that it provided for her in the midst of the flood.

What does forgiveness have to do with spirituality? I'd been asking that question since I met Azim, and my need for an answer grew more insistent as I noticed that many of those I interviewed about forgiving extreme trespasses had strong spiritual beliefs. Considering the history of forgiveness as a moral concept, that's not surprising. Forgiveness has for centuries been a major theme in world religions. It forms the core of Christianity, from Jesus' appeals to be compassionate and tolerant, to his commands to "love thine enemies" and "turn the other cheek," and finally, his plea from the cross: "Forgive them, Father, for they know not what they do." In Genesis, there's the story of Esau forgiving his brother for usurping his inheritance, and the story of Joseph forgiving his brothers for selling him into slavery—a tale also prominent in the Koran.

The prophets, from Jesus to Buddha to Moses, preached the power to transform hatred through love in myriad ways and in different words, spreading a message that transcends time, geography, and culture. Consider the similarities of the following statements, gathered by Richard Hooper in his book *The Parallel Sayings*: "Love your enemies and pray for those who persecute you," from the Gospel According to Mark; "The only way you can become free is to love those who hate you," from the Dhammapada, a collection of the Buddha's teachings used by his disciples; "Practice gentleness, seek truth, give up anger, do not slander, and have compassion for all beings," from the *Bhagavad Gita*; and "In war, have mercy. True warriors do not carry arms. True fighters do not get angry. Those who wish to win should not be contentious," from the *Tao Te Ching*.

Even contemporary models of creating change through nonviolence have come from spiritual icons or people with strong spiritual beliefs. Gandhi, who gave his life in the effort to end British occupation of India and unite warring Hindus and Muslims, talked about transmuting anger into "a power that can move the world." Martin Luther King Jr. said, "Darkness cannot drive out darkness; only light can do that. Hate cannot drive out hate; only love can do that." More recently, Nelson Mandela shocked the world when he was released from prison after twenty-seven years of hard labor on Robben Island, only to reach out to the white apartheid government in forgiveness. Then there's the Dalai Lama, who refers to the Chinese, who occupied Tibet and sent him and his fellow monks to exile or prison, as "my friends, the enemy."

Long before science revealed that rather than a sign of weakness, the ability to forgive is one of the greatest strengths anyone can possess, these spiritual leaders taught just that. (Gandhi called forgiveness "the ornament of the brave.") Of course, retribution and revenge also proliferate in the world's religious traditions, with dogma perpetuating war throughout history. Yet it's impossible to ignore the fact that people capable of forgiving extreme offenses seem to have deeply held spiritual beliefs that infuse their attitudes and inform their actions.

Why the link between spirituality and forgiveness? One argument is that if you believe you'll be rewarded for behaving virtuously, either in the afterlife, as Christians and Muslims believe, or in subsequent lives on earth and via karma, as Buddhists believe, you may be more likely to adhere to a certain moral code. Another assertion is that when you're conscious of mortality on a daily basis, life becomes more precious, allowing petty divisions to fall away. *The Tibetan Book of Living and Dying,* by Sogyal Rinpoche, became a runaway bestseller in the West by highlighting the importance of contemplating death: When you avoid coming to terms with your mortality, he argued, you live in a state of denial and take most things for granted. In contrast, a constant awareness of death infuses each day with a sense of the sacred, of being fully awake and alive. As Buddhist monk Pema Chödrön says, "If death is certain but the time of death is uncertain, what is the most important thing?"

Yet there's a distinction between religious dogma and personal practices. While people like Azim and Karen use practices that are related to broader religious teachings, the practices themselves are very private. Azim didn't forgive because of a Sufi dictate, he did it because he sensed it would bring him peace, and because his lifelong meditation habit gave him the inner strength to follow through. And while Karen's chosen route to recovery, AA, refers to God and has origins in Christianity, it isn't affiliated with any particular religious doctrine. This distinction is meaningful, because while forgiveness is featured in many religions, the people I met were not all religious—but most were spiritual. The difference? The Latin origin of the word "religion," *religio,* refers to belief in a supernatural God and institutionalized ways of worshipping that God. The origin of "spirituality," *spiritualis*, is more identified with the human spirit itself, based on the word *spiritu*, for breathing or wind. It's more personal and doesn't require belief in an external deity or public participation in institutionalized religion. This approach is becoming increasingly common in the West, where polls show that more and more people describe themselves as spiritual, not religious.

When I started this adventure, I had mixed feelings about the overlap between faith and forgiveness. Raised by a psychologist mother who meditated every morning and believed in reincarnation, and a physician father who prized science and tangible proof, my beliefs were an amalgam of the two. In my personal life I was open to forgiveness as a spiritual phenomenon, but in my professional life I was the objective reporter who watched and listened and wrote down the things I could see and hear—and only the things I could see and hear.

And yet, I had also been a seeker for as long as I could remember, as have most of the women in my family. My great-grandmother Blanche didn't so much seek as she was found. She was stricken by the Great Influenza of 1918, and her husband, a severe and imposing man named Luther, started seeing another woman while she was bedridden. This woman happened to be a devotee of Mary Baker Eddy, the founder of Christian Science, a religious movement that advocated healing through prayer. Through this mistress, Luther acquired a copy of Eddy's book, *Science and Health with Key to the Scriptures*, and gave it to his ailing wife. Soon after reading it, Blanche emerged from bed and went on to divorce Luther, remarry, and raise three children. She considered her healing an answer to prayer and raised my grandmother in the church of Religious Science, founded by Ernest Holmes in the 1920s and heavily influenced by Eddy.

My mother ascribed to prayer and the new age philosophy that "what you think about you bring about," while my father, a reform Jew, took me and my sister to synagogue. I was always fascinated by the differences and similarities between various religions, and by any attempt to seek answers to life's biggest questions. In addition to attending worship services with friends as a child, from Catholic mass to Baha'i meetings, I was also drawn to less mainstream practices. I read horoscopes. I researched the chakras. I watched documentaries about near-death experiences. While studying abroad in college, I paid to have my fortune told by a Chilean woman who "read" a handful of coca leaves and proclaimed that I would be "incredibly wealthy," an entertaining memory years later when I couldn't pay my electric bill. In my years of being the Skeptical Objective Journalist, I also took yoga and dabbled in meditation as a way to diffuse my natural perfectionism and anxiety. I was even known to take wildlife sightings as signals from the spirit world. While I wasn't quite as committed to this Native American tradition as a friend whose habit of "following the crows" once led her to a new job, I still feel comforted when I look up to see a red-tailed hawk soaring above me.

As I got to know Azim and Ples, both parts of me—the seeker and the skeptic—were spellbound in equal measure. I may have held conflicting beliefs, but I knew transcendence and enlightenment when I saw them. Somehow, these people had attained a higher level of humanity, whether strictly practical or imbued with an otherworldly spirit, as Alexander Pope suggested in his famous quotation, "To err is human, to forgive is divine."

As I studied forgiveness in practice, it struck me that the daily habits that facilitate forgiveness seem to especially overlap with Buddhist practices. Though the word "forgiveness" is rarely used in the tradition (because Buddhism is nondeistic, instead of requiring forgiveness from God it teaches that every action has a consequence, and that aggression and hate are born of suffering and only cause more suffering), the Buddhist tenets of detachment (accepting reality as it is instead of wishing it were different), nonjudgment (equanimity), and compassion are in many ways a map to forgiveness. And if those ideals are the map, meditation may be the vehicle. It's not merely belief, either: A large body of scientific research shows that regular meditation calms the brain mechanisms involved in stress and anxiety, rage, and depression.

For the past decade, the Dalai Lama has recruited experienced Buddhist monks to participate in scientific studies that evaluate how meditation influences the brain. Using control groups and fMRI scans, researchers such as Richard Davidson and Antoine Lutz at the Waisman Laboratory for Brain Imaging and Behavior at the University of Wisconsin–Madison have discovered that meditating alters the structure and function of the brain. Experienced meditators have more gray matter—and thus more ability—in the parts of the brain important for controlling attention, regulating emotion, and making choices based on all the information available. In turn, they have less gray matter in the amygdala, which as the brain's fight-or-flight "alarm system" plays a large role in anxiety, stress, and anger. In people suffering from insufficient levels of certain neurotransmitters or weak neuron function in other parts of the brain, the alerts of the amygdala tend to outweigh the cortex's ability to synthesize the alert with the rest of the information at hand. The result is getting stuck on the danger warning and reacting based on anger or fear. Meditation balances out this system, so that the alerts are more fluidly assessed with the information perceived by the senses, leading to calmer, more measured reactions.

Meditation can alleviate symptoms in novices in addition to veterans. This was recently confirmed when a team of Johns Hopkins University researchers sifted through nineteen thousand meditation studies to find forty-seven that met their rigorous scientific criteria, then reviewed them to conclude that meditation alleviates anxiety, depression, and pain. How? In addition to calming over-reactivity in the amygdala, meditation strengthens brain areas involved in positive mood and problem-solving. Davidson found that an eight-week mindfulness meditation course increased electronic activity in the left anterior side of the brain—which is linked to positive affect or mood—a boost still evident four months later. Even minor amounts of mindfulness meditation reduce anxiety in healthy people without anxiety disorders. In a 2013 study by researchers at Wake Forest Baptist Medical Center, fifteen people learned to meditate in four twenty-minute classes, their brains scanned and anxiety levels measured before and after. The majority reported less anxiety, and the post-meditation brain scans showed more activation in the anterior cingulate cortex, ventromedial prefrontal cortex, and anterior insula, parts of the brain involved in executive function and control of worrying.

These conclusions didn't surprise me. Since my visit to San Diego to meet Azim months earlier, I'd been trying to meditate every day. I usually only wound up doing it a few days a week, but I noticed a marked difference about those particular days. If I made a point to sit up in bed for twenty minutes in the morning, breathing deeply and noticing my thoughts and feelings, I found that I had more energy throughout the day. One of the goals of mindfulness meditation is cultivating mindfulness—intense awareness of the present moment—throughout one's daily life. This means tasting a peach when you're eating a peach, focusing only on the person you're talking to when you're talking to that person, and basically being where you are when you're there, as opposed to being swept up in the constant tide of thought that prevents us from focusing on the moment. On the days that I meditated, I found I was less distracted and more likely to notice the hawk perched above me on my walk by the river, or really taste my tea, or concentrate on what Anthony was telling me about his day. And I was less likely to be reactionary, whether about a higher-than-expected tax liability or the person next to me at Starbucks talking loudly on the phone while I was trying to write.

So, why would mindfulness meditation have these effects? Recent research by Matthew Lieberman, a psychology and neuroscience researcher at UCLA, holds a clue. When subjects in his lab were shown a picture of an angry face, electronic activity rose in their amygdala, preparing the body to respond to what seemed like a threat. Yet when people labeled the emotion they felt upon seeing the picture—"I feel angry," for instance—activity lessened in the amygdala and increased in another area, the right ventrolateral prefrontal cortex. Located behind the forehead, this area is associated with thinking in words about emotional experiences, processing emotions, and inhibiting behavior. This shows that simply noticing and labeling our emotions—the mainstay of mindfulness—turns down the amygdala alarm response that triggers negative feelings and adrenaline-fueled reactions. Even simply breathing deeply, another hallmark of meditation, has a calming effect on the body. Deep breathing signals the parasympathetic nervous system to increase blood flow to the brain, while lowering heart rate and blood pressure.

Lastly, in addition to regulating negative emotional reactions and enhancing positive mood and logical problem-solving, meditation can also heighten compassion and empathy. When Lutz and his colleagues compared two groups of meditators—one experienced in compassion meditation and the other not—he instructed both groups to generate a state of love and compassion by thinking about someone they cared about, extending those feelings to others, and feeling general love and compassion. As each of the participants meditated inside the fMRI brain scanners, they were occasionally interrupted by unexpected human sounds—such as a woman screaming—that would trigger feelings of concern. While all of the meditators showed emotional responses to the sounds, the experienced compassion meditators showed a larger brain response in areas important for processing physical sensations and emotional response, particularly to sounds of distress. The structural reason for this likely has to do with the anterior insular cortex, which plays a role in being able to understand and even feel the pain and suffering of others. In people who meditate, this area—considered the seat of empathy in the brain—is substantially thicker than in those who don't.

All of this science supports the commonsense theory the Buddha taught twenty-five hundred years ago: that focusing on the present, instead of ruminating about the past or worrying about the future, leads to greater happiness. It also increases performance. As I would discover in researching this chapter, practicing mindfulness-aided forgiveness of oneself and others as a daily habit enhances performance in multiple areas of life, from business and relationships to crisis response and sports. We'll explore that through one of the most famous, yet misunderstood, basketball stories of the twentieth century. But first, let's go to the Shambhala Mountain Center in Northern Colorado, where I went searching for answers to my questions

about how forgiveness can be practiced regularly by believers and secular-
ists alike.

I met Rose Sposito a few weeks after the Colorado floodwaters receded. She
was teaching a meditation class at the Shambhala Mountain Center, a Tibetan Buddhist retreat outside of Fort Collins. Founded in the seventies by
Tibetan Buddhist monk Chogyam Trungpa, the campus is set on six hundred acres of pine and juniper, in a Rocky Mountain river valley shadowed
by granite peaks. I visited to explore the links between mindfulness, meditation, and forgiveness. Sitting in one of the cabins by a crackling fire one
evening, Rose described the flood as a test that revealed just how important
her years of meditation had become. The hours she'd spent breathing
deeply, watching her sloshing thoughts and letting them go, had built a
pillar of equanimity that she could stand on when the world was dissolving
into chaos around her, letting her remain calm so she could focus on whatever was needed, and, if the time came, face death bravely.

One morning in a large, light-filled room surrounded by woods, Rose
led a group of about twenty of us in mindfulness meditation, the basic
practice of focusing on the breath, noticing sensations in the body, and
allowing thoughts to come and go without getting sucked into the "story
line." The ultimate goal is to be able to bring this sense of calm into your
daily life, so that you no longer react to the roller coaster of life like a pin-
ball in the machine, going ape shit or getting depressed when you don't get
what you want, or losing all reason when you find yourself surrounded by
floodwaters and worsening an already-dire situation.

We spent the day sitting in a circle on cushions near a large altar decorated with crystal bowls, incense, and framed photos of Trungpa sporting
orange robes and a peaceful smile. Across from me sat Jessica from Tulsa,
who stopped at the retreat while on a postdivorce road trip. Next to her was
Mary Ann, a software developer and mother of three from nearby Golden,
who began exploring meditation after noticing what felt like a spiritual void
in her daily life. Next to me were Donna and her coworker, Joe, who came

from Wyoming, where they managed construction crews installing technology centers for government contractors. On my other side sat two young women from Denver who had recently finished their MBAs.

Rose sat at the altar, her legs crossed and shoulders back. "Most of the time we're in a reaction to things and can't see a situation clearly," she said. "We go into the rabbit hole of blame and struggle, and it makes us miserable. Meditation gives us the opportunity to notice the thoughts flickering back and forth, our hearts beating, deep-held emotions coming to the surface. It's about developing friendliness toward yourself and the thoughts that come and go."

Over the past two weeks, I'd been skipping the daily meditation I started after meeting Azim. On deadline with multiple projects, I'd been leaping out of bed in near-panic, grabbing a cup of coffee, and running frantically to the computer to start working. Now, I focused on my breath, noticing what felt like a relaxing space at the end of each inhale and exhale, a peaceful silence that I could sink into. As I breathed, I noticed the sounds of people shifting position, and a little farther away, the calls of birds and pitter-patter steps of squirrels. Focusing on the ins and outs of my breath mingling with that palette of sound, I felt connected to the world around me in a way that I don't when I'm talking or thinking or going through the usual daily motions. My mind seemed totally still. *Wow, I'm really doing it! I'm not thinking at all!* Realizing the absurdity of this thought, I stifled a laugh. Random thoughts or not, it felt easier to shut out the chaos of the world here, with people who were also seeking to experience what Rose described as "the true nature of mind—steady, stable, open, and pure."

That evening, as we sat around the fire, Rose told us about how her decades of daily meditation helped her during the floods. "It allowed me to be present for my family and friends when we were surrounded by water with no way out," she said. That phrase—surrounded by water with no way out—is the perfect metaphor for what psychologists refer to as "flooding" in the brain: stress hormones like cortisol and adrenaline coursing through the lobes and neural pathways, temporarily incapacitating the prefrontal cortex and its powers of problem-solving and creativity. It's when we're flooded that we're likely to hide, say things we later regret, hurt ourselves or someone else, or fail to act in an emergency. Those responses of our ancient "lizard" brains aren't necessarily helpful when it comes to solving modern, complex problems. We may not literally be surrounded by water like Rose was that day in Lyons, but rage, self-loathing, and fear can be just as debilitating, preventing us from thinking clearly, having compassion for ourselves or others, or making the choice to forgive.

As I sat listening to Rose, relaxed after a full day of meditation and yoga, I thought about times when I'd become flooded. There were the early days after the breakup with Mike, when I'd recall The Play or our last conversation and suddenly find myself fantasizing about punching him in the face. There was the time, more recently, when Anthony's grandfather was diagnosed with cancer. We'd been together for nearly a year, and he briefly considered moving across the country to help care for the man who had helped raise him. While I was moved by his commitment to his family, I was terrified: What if he moved to Boston? I was a Western girl and felt claustrophobic in large cities. Would we break up? Would we try long-distance? These thoughts, circular and maddening and unanswerable, consumed me in a swirl of anxiety, briefly convincing me that he didn't care about me at all. I even considered breaking up with him in a fit of panicked fear.

Once I'd calmed down, we talked through our options and agreed that for now, he would visit his grandfather as much as possible until we knew how the treatment was progressing. Anthony assured me of his commitment, and I felt silly about jumping to conclusions. I decided to talk to a therapist about my anxiety. Anxiety and depression, or what my mother calls "anxious depression," run in my family. They tend to crop up in my life during big changes: a new job, a new city, a new relationship. I'd been on medication twice over the years, each time for several months (once after a friend died suddenly and once after starting a new job in a new city), but found I was able to manage my mood with regular exercise, time outdoors, and a nutritious diet. Now, I wanted to learn more about what was happening in my brain when I got anxious, and test new ways to change it.

I settled on a cheerful middle-aged psychologist with a sensible name

(Mary Margaret), a motherly mien, and a killer understanding of brain chemistry. When I told her about the occasional meltdowns that made me feel like Blanche DuBois, she explained the brain circuitry involved in anxiety and obsessive thinking. "It's a neurochemical storm," she told me. "It creates a sense of dread and doom that characterizes the thoughts, and it will pass. If you can learn to recognize the footprints of these neurochemical states on your thoughts, then you can realize it's not a reflection of a doomed reality and refrain from believing the content of these thoughts or acting on them."

In her cozy office filled with cushioned couches and books, she showed me a hardcover called *Brain Lock*, about how mindfulness practices combined with cognitive behavioral therapy have been successful at treating obsessive-compulsive disorder without medication. The book shows the brain scans of people before and after the treatment, and you can see the "neurochemical storms," in the form of overblown activity, visible in the lit-up caudate nucleus and amygdala, which fuel repetitive thoughts and a growing sense of dread. The after photos show much less activity in those parts of the brain. While I don't suffer from OCD, the lesser anxiety I periodically suffer likely involves a similar brain pattern, and the approach my therapist recommended was mindfulness. She recommended a book called *The 10 Best-Ever Anxiety Management Techniques*, in which psychologist Margaret Wehrenberg describes mindfulness practices that use the brain to change the brain.

"Instead of running with the content of the thoughts and trying to problem-solve when you're in the midst of the storm, notice it and get quiet and calm down," my therapist said. "We're talking about how human beings have monitored aggression for millennia, so you're not going to erase that immediately. Our brain doesn't evolve as quickly as our circumstances, but we do have this newer part of the brain, the prefrontal cortex, and that helps."

Tibetan Buddhists have an ancient word for the neurological storms my therapist described: *shenpa*. I learned about *shenpa* a few weeks before the Shambhala retreat, while driving from Denver to New Mexico to visit my family. An hour into the six-hour drive, I rummaged in my glove box and retrieved a poppy-colored CD called *Getting Unstuck,* by Pema Chödrön, who in addition to being a female Buddhist monk is also a celebrated author. As I coasted through sage-dotted foothills, Chödrön's warm voice filled the car, sounding more like a wise, funny, self-deprecating aunt than a spiritual icon. *Shenpa,* she explained, is translated as "attachment," but that doesn't fully capture what it is. "It's getting hooked," she says. "It's that feeling of not being okay. Like when someone says a mean word, and something in you tightens. That's the *shenpa.* It's almost preverbal. And then it spirals into blaming them, or poor self-esteem. It's a reaction that breeds thoughts, which in turn breed actions."

Unfortunately, the thoughts and actions that *shenpa* breeds tend not to lead us to live our best lives. They're fearful, angry, resentful, envious, self-loathing, and spiteful. "Mindlessly," Chödrön continued, "we get better at what we don't like about ourselves. Like our out-of-control anger or low self-esteem or fearfulness. The more we strengthen it, the more we do it. This is what we call the habituation of patterns that cause suffering." The answer? Learning to stay in the present moment. That means that when you meditate, you practice noticing the thoughts but not "getting hooked" by them. It means that when you have a *shenpa* attack, you sit with the feeling and avoid actually doing anything.

The natural impulse is to do something habitual to escape "this feeling of not being okay," whether drinking whiskey or driving by your ex's house again or taking some other action that seems right if you're listening to the *shenpa*-laden thoughts in your mind, but is really counterproductive. "The key is to stay with the unease, not turn away from it, to end the cycle," Chödrön explained. "Getting stuck means you disappear into the worry, the fear, the anger or fantasy of getting even. . . ." When you notice your thoughts and feelings, you're you, in the moment, noticing. It's when there ceases to be an "I" observing that the flood of thought takes you away.

Ironically, even as I heard Chödrön saying this, I drifted away into thoughts. An incredibly smart and accomplished journalist friend had recently secured a six-figure job writing speeches for a state politician, and out of nowhere, in the middle of the New Mexico desert, my mind clenched at this random thought with sharklike ferocity. *Will I ever make any money? Have I condemned myself to poverty and debt forever? I should look for more corporate writing jobs....* Then, for some reason my mind leapt at another thought: the recent lunch with Mike. While the anger and shame were gone, the *shenpa* apparently was not. As I drove, eyes on I-25, I wrinkled my nose, as if there were a rotting hamburger in the backseat. The thoughts that accompanied this *shenpa* were, shall we say, less than mature, focusing on how one of my best friends and her husband often spent time with Mike and his girlfriend. *Why do they have to invite them? Do they like them better than me and Anthony?! Are they more fun than we are?*

Then, as if stepping outside my mind, I noticed the thoughts. Struck by how juvenile they were, I laughed aloud. In noticing and laughing, I unhooked myself from the dark, sticky, unsettling feeling that I could now identify as jealous insecurity. I was back in my car, in the desert under a turquoise sky, hurtling toward home, toward the bright unknown future but firmly in the present moment. It was as if I'd returned from a dream, and was fully awake. I resisted the urge to berate myself for getting lost in thinking, or for feeling anything but absolute neutrality about my ex. I was human. I was alive. And it was okay.

What Chödrön said next, about the connection between meditation and compassion, struck me as resoundingly true: "The more you realize what humans are up against with that urge and drive and wish to move away [from the present], and how strong it is, once you experience that within yourself, then you begin to have enormous compassion for the crazy antics of other people. Because they're just up against what you're up against. They have this *shenpa* and these urges, and they probably have had no training. And even if they have, like you have, do you always do it right?"

Around the time of that drive through the desert, a few weeks before the Shambhala retreat, I attended a workshop led by psychologist Fred Luskin, the cofounder of the Stanford Forgiveness Project. It was a professional, not a spiritual, conference, but he weaved compassion meditation into his presentation. Wearing a worn purple polo shirt with khakis and Chaco sandals, his curly, grayish brown hair grazing his shoulders, Luskin looked the part of the laid-back Northern California academic, but he spoke bluntly, fixing his audience with a steely gaze.

"You *must* have a strong meditation practice and a strong gratitude practice. If you do, you at least have a chance," he said in the Denver conference room.

It sounded as if he were addressing armed peacekeepers or martial artists. In a sense, he was. They were mediators, and Luskin was advising them on how to broker agreement between feuding parties. The job, he said, is essentially adrenaline management. If you get sucked into your clients' drama, sharing in their flooding stress hormones, rising heart rates, and high blood pressure, you will fail at helping them reach consensus. Remaining calm and neutral in the face of flying chairs and insults requires both a Zen mind and granite-hard chutzpah. Today, he would lead his charges in a compassion meditation to help them achieve that.

He told the group of about thirty professional mediators that the key to helping their clients is to halt the adrenaline response and help opponents change the story they've been telling themselves about the "enemy." Since someone who's blaming someone has a physical, emotional, and mental response when they see their antagonist, he explained, you must help them make their internal storyline about the person less antagonizing. For instance, a man who's convinced that his brother intentionally ruined his life by securing more of their parents' inheritance could alter his perception by separating the facts (he got less money than he wanted) from his interpretation (his brother maliciously screwed him over).

Luskin explained that our brains often construct a story about reality that matches our biological fight-or-flight reaction (the anger of aggression or the fear of victimhood, usually), or one that evokes a past situation that provoked that reaction. That's why working to change both the adrenaline response and the story that fuels it is important. Yet attempting to accomplish anything when a client is "adrenalized" is counterproductive, Luskin said, recommending instructing clients to take a break before returning to the negotiating table. He also recommended rules, such as "If you yell, we're stopping the meeting."

A middle-aged woman with a bright scarf raised her hand. "Okay—but I can't tell them they should forgive each other," she said.

Luskin nodded. "No, but you can tell them it's possible to find ways to resolve the issues," he said. "You create the space. You don't want them creating the space with their smallness. I'm not interested in who's right and who's wrong, and I want them to tap into that part of themselves. We want people to be free from suffering—adrenaline wants them to be right."

Guiding people to a place of neutrality means living there yourself most of the time, knowing how to cultivate the neurological environment for compassion, empathy, and problem-solving. Luskin suggests taking a moment to look out the window and appreciate natural beauty. "Look at that beautiful sky," he said, gesturing out the window at the sunny Colorado day outside. "Sure, there's conflict, but there's also a beautiful world out there. It's beautiful, even if you were in an abusive relationship or enabled terrible behavior or didn't stand up for yourself. It's still beautiful. And we all live under that same sky." The enduring rhythms of nature can help provide perspective, or, as Luskin said, realize that "in fifty years, we'll all be dead and no one will give a shit about who did what to whom."

In the interest of strengthening the mediators' compassion muscles, Luskin led the group in a meditation called "Just Like Me." After a few minutes of silent breathing, he instructed them to imagine someone they'd been in a conflict with. "Just like me, they want to be happy," he said, instructing everyone to imagine that person as they heard the words. "Just like me, they want to have a good day. Just like me, they'll do almost anything to avoid suffering." He finished with another few minutes of deep breathing. Afterward, the mediators agreed that they felt calmer. They looked calmer, too. One man, whose arms were crossed tightly over his chest before, sat back slightly in his chair, arms relaxed at his sides.

Luskin told the mediators about the time in the midnineties when he led a group of women from Northern Ireland through a series of compassion meditations. Both Irish and Protestant, all the women had lost children to the Troubles. It seemed to him that after so many years of war, they didn't even know there was a response to their loss other than to remain furious. After the three-day workshop, all of the women reported higher feelings of goodwill, calm, and the ability to forgive. "They didn't know that part of themselves, and we helped them touch that place," Luskin said. "It's always there, it's just that adrenaline hides it."

As the workshop neared its end, he took one last question from a man in the front row: "Why is it that so many of the dramatic stories of forgiveness we hear come from people with strong religious backgrounds?" Luskin thought for a moment, then replied, "There are two things that usually allow people to forgive something huge: One, their suffering is so profound that they truly want it to end, and two, they experience what I like to call 'a touch of grace.' Something that opens their hearts. People who have a sincere religious or spiritual practice tend to have more access to that."

When Phil Jackson was playing for the New York Knicks, he began to practice Zen meditation off the court. Much like Tibetan mindfulness meditation, *zazen* involves noticing your thoughts as a way to return to the present. Almost immediately, Jackson began to notice his thoughts on the basketball court, too. There was self-interest (When I get the ball, I'm going for the hoop, no matter what), anger (That $%^* Wilt Chamberlain! Next time he's dead), and self-blame (What's wrong with you, Phil? A sixth-grader could make that shot). He also noticed in practice that when he covered Bill Bradley, the Knicks player who would go on to become a U.S. senator, if his mind wandered for a moment—distracted by a thought or judgment—Bradley would vanish and reappear on the other side of the court to make a shot. In his book *Sacred Hoops*, Jackson writes that his obsession with winning was often his undoing.

> *I was trying to force my body to cooperate, but when it didn't respond, my mind became even more insistent. . . . I discovered*

that I could be more effective by letting go and not thinking. . . .
The simple act of becoming mindful of the frenzied parade of
thoughts, paradoxically, began to quiet my mind.

Most people know Jackson, a six-foot-eight-inch forward from North Dakota, as the NBA's most legendary coach. He won a record-breaking eleven NBA titles as head coach for the Chicago Bulls and the Los Angeles Lakers, and holds the highest winning percentage of any coach in the league. What many people don't know is that Jackson attributes much of his success, as both a player and a coach, to mindfulness, along with other principles and practices from Eastern traditions and Native American spirituality. He taught the Chicago Bulls how to meditate. He invited a colleague of Jon Kabat-Zinn, founding executive director of the Center for Mindfulness in Medicine, Health Care, and Society at the University of Massachusetts Medical School (Kabat-Zinn created one of the most widely used forms of secular meditation, Mindfulness-Based Stress Reduction), to give the team a three-day mindfulness course during training camp. He decorated the Bulls' team room with sacred objects given to him by Lakota Sioux friends from his home state of North Dakota (an arrow with a tobacco pouch tied to it, a bear claw, and a painting of Crazy Horse).

Drawing from traditions that stress the importance of remaining calm amid chaos, Jackson worked to cultivate a team mind-set that hinged on focus, being present, and an egalitarian sense of teamwork. This was rare. As basketball became increasingly focused on star power in the decade of Michael Jordan and Dennis Rodman, meditation and Native American totems were not exactly common coaching tools. Yet the approach worked. When Jackson started coaching the Bulls in 1989, most of the players were intimidated by Jordan, either afraid to get near him and look bad in comparison, or else prone to stand around waiting for basketball's biggest star to save them. By using a unique lineup formation and teaching mindfulness principles that helped the players focus and become more attuned to one another's moves, along with instilling an ethic of individual sacrifice on behalf of the whole (distilled from Lakota and Asian warrior philosophies), Jackson led the team to win six NBA titles in nine years.

The conventional wisdom is that the team was primarily a one-man show, Jackson writes, Michael Jordan and the Jordanaires. But "the real reason the Bulls won three straight NBA championships from 1991 to '93 was that we plugged into the power of *oneness* instead of the power of one man, and transcended the divisive forces of the ego that have crippled far more gifted teams."

In addition to staying focused on the present instead of ruminating about the past, the practices that Jackson used to up his team's performance and remain calm himself amid the highs and lows of each game shared other similarities with habits that foster forgiveness: accepting what's happening without judgment, forgoing aggression, and being committed to something larger than oneself. Jackson reminded the players that the moment they got cocky or angry about a shot or pass, they were setting themselves up for a mistake. Indulging in mean-spirited aggression was equally counterproductive, he told them, which he learned in the seventies while playing for the Knicks. Jackson once shoved a hotheaded Baltimore forward—with the intention of luring the guy into a fight and getting him ejected. It worked (the player threw a punch and earned his sixth foul), but a year later, the same player retaliated by hitting Jackson while he was jumping for a shot, nearly seriously injuring him. As a coach, he recommended that when his players were fouled, they turn around and take a breath to stay focused on the goal: victory.

When we watch athletes and dancers perform the way Jackson helped the Bulls perform—with the smooth effortlessness that comes from constant practice and focus—we call them "graceful." I find it fascinating that "grace" is also used the way Luskin used it when he talked about people who forgive having "a touch of grace." In a religious context, grace describes God's favor or underserved mercy. The word "grace," like forgiveness, happens to have roots in the word "give." (Consider the term "grace period.") It's no coincidence that we use the word "graceful" to describe skilled athletes and performers whose nature seems to surpass human qualities and take on Godly ones. Their beauty could be seen as a gift to the audience, and their own experience of grace, of being in what the psychologist Mihaly Csikszentmihalyi calls "flow," is a gift of joy to themselves.

Csikszentmihalyi began studying artists, especially painters, who became so absorbed in their work that they lost track of time, even forgetting to eat or sleep. He later expanded his research to dancers, athletes, and professionals in various disciplines, describing "flow" as the state of being single-mindedly immersed in an activity, harnessing thought and emotion in service of a task. In a state of flow, you lose track of time and have a feeling of spontaneous joy, even rapture. You also lose a sense of being separate from your surroundings. As the mind becomes absorbed in an undertaking that is challenging enough but not too challenging, whether it's basketball or painting or software design, the result is a feeling of contentment and boundlessness in which the limits of time and self disappear into what Jackson would describe as oneness. This is similar to the emphasis in Buddhism and Taoism on the "action of inaction" and "doing without doing." While in flow, you're not thinking about yourself or thinking angry thoughts about the past or fearful thoughts about the future—you're totally in the moment, dedicating your focus, skills, and efforts in service of something larger than yourself.

In the people I interviewed about practicing forgiveness, this experience of belonging to or serving something larger was common. Some were religious, and others were not. But most were committed to something bigger than themselves, whether it was helping neighbors in crisis or being an example of survival and resilience for others. You don't have to be religious or even spiritual to forgive, I realized, or to use mindfulness and compassion to help you do so. The idea of belonging to something larger, and serving a larger purpose, is not limited to believing in God. It could be serving the vision of a world without youth violence, as it is for Azim, or rebuilding a harmonious family, as it is for Karen. It could even be something more abstract, such as peace of mind or robust health or love.

———

On my last day at the Shambhala Meditation Center, I hiked up to the Great Stupa of Dharmakaya, a temple built in the Tibetan tradition to honor the late Trungpa and to serve as a guiding meditative heart and home in his absence. From the main campus, you can see the stupa's gold dome towering over the forest, glinting in the sun. As with most houses of worship, every detail of the building is symbolic. The white details represent purity of awareness, and the gold, the enlightenment that stems from it. I made my way toward it on the snowy trail, breathing the crisp mountain air and watching ravens fly overhead.

After spending most of the weekend meditating, my awareness was sharp. I felt and heard each footstep crunch the snow. I heard the sounds of twigs breaking and a nearby stream flowing. The sky looked bluer than I remembered, the trees greener. I paused to admire a towering pine. It must have been at least two hundred years old. Its ruddy brown trunk stretched as wide as a Volkswagen Beetle, and midway up it bent over, askew, as if it had been hit by lightning. Yet above the bent place the branches and green needles continued to reach up toward the glowing sun. Imagining the network of deep roots that stretched below the earth to keep the tree strong, I felt a sense of being held steady by the ground myself.

I crossed the bridge and made my way up the steps, past an altar set with incense to symbolize a Phoenix-like mythical bird. In legend this bird never returns to the ground once it leaves its nest, which to the Buddhists signifies the ability to be invigorated by the constant change and impermanence of life. I paused at the entrance to take in the temple, with its multicolored swirls and arches, the palette unlike anything you normally see in the United States. The blue entrance symbolizes loving-kindness and compassion, or as a guide had described it earlier, "leaving the confusion of the mind to arrive at the awakened heart." Mindfulness, I thought, allows us to explore and know our own suffering, wandering its halls and running our fingers down its walls, to eventually arrive at the gilded room that is compassion for everyone, including ourselves. I thought about how the people I knew who were the most compassionate—Azim and Rebecca, for instance—had suffered the most.

I went into the temple and sat down on a cushion before the twenty-foot-tall golden statue of the Buddha. The small, round room was empty, and I could hear each of my breaths. As I quieted my mind, I felt grateful. I felt grateful for this journey of discovery, for the peace I was increasingly able to find, for my health, and for all of the love in my life. Every few minutes, a worry or judgment crept in—*When will I get that check? Do I really want kids or not?* After that came the fear. I was leaving for Rwanda in only a few weeks.

I wanted to see just how far forgiveness can reach by looking for it in the aftermath of the worst possible thing people can do to one another: genocide. Is forgiveness possible after such a horrific series of crimes on such a vast scale? In search of answers about what role forgiveness can play after genocide, if any, I would spend a month in Rwanda, interviewing survivors and perpetrators of the bloodbath that consumed the country in 1994. It had been more than three years since I'd left the country alone to report a story, and the last one was about a competitive memory championship in London, not murder or war. I'd spent weeks in Mexico reporting on migrants fleeing violence and poverty in Central America by riding dangerous freight trains to reach the United States, but that was five years earlier. I was nervous about traveling alone in an unknown place, being away from Anthony, and finding the right sources for the chapter.

I recalled Rose saying, "To be fearless, you have to face and know fear. Give it some attention and care from the big, compassionate mind, that part of ourselves that is stable, profound, and always available."

I resisted the familiar urge to berate myself for having worries or fears or judgmental thoughts, but I also resisted the urge to follow them onto the hamster wheel or try to fix them. (*Maybe I should go to law school! Or freeze my eggs! Or decide that I'm not having kids and move on! Or cancel the trip to Africa . . .*) Instead, I acknowledged the thoughts and feelings like a mother notices her four-year-old getting antsy in the backseat of the car, with loving patience. Sure enough, they dissipated like smoke.

After another few minutes, I rose to leave. As I emerged into the midday sunshine, I thought of something Chödrön said about accepting the present moment and being prepared for anything: "It's about opening to the unknown future as thrilling, rather than threat." And it was thrilling, wasn't it? Anthony would move into my apartment in a few weeks, along with Stella. I was on the verge of traveling to Africa and exploring which societal habits and practices make forgiveness more likely in communities and institutions, and then sitting down to write this book, chronicling all that I discovered during this adventure in forgiveness. I didn't know how any of it would turn out. But that wasn't the point. Not knowing was what made it thrilling.

I made my way back toward my car along the snowy trail, which ran along the stream for a few yards. Something caught my eye near the water. It was a jagged line of coyote tracks. They led into the water and disappeared. I glanced into the woods across the stream, wondering where the creature went, but saw only pine trees. It was out there somewhere, as mysterious and thrilling as the unknown future.

7

The Survivor: How One Woman Forgave the "Unforgivable" in Rwanda

One warm, overcast afternoon, Chantal Nimugire took me to the place where she almost died. The clearing, roughly the size of a football field, was nestled amid hillsides in Kicukiro, a suburb of Kigali, the Rwandan capital. On one side of the clearing was patchy grass and red dirt framed by tall eucalyptus trees, and on the other was a two-story cement building painted pink. It was constructed to commemorate the 1994 massacre of some three thousand men, women, and children during the genocide that claimed the lives of more than one million people in just three months. Only an estimated fifty people survived the massacre, and Chantal, now thirty-five, was one of them.

For today's visit she wore a brilliant peacock-blue dress and a delicate silver cross necklace. Her cheekbones were prominent, her eyes clear. When she smiled, her whole face opened up, lit by a wide, megawatt grin that made her eyes twinkle and angle upward. But as we walked toward the building, she grew serious, a faraway expression settling onto her face. Inside, we met Adelite Mukamana, a staff psychologist for IBUKA, an umbrella group of organizations that help genocide survivors. Adelite's office was in the building, and she had agreed to take us on a tour of the site. Unlike the main genocide memorial center in Kigali, which encompasses multiple rooms with exhibits starting with precolonial history and ending with the prosecutions of *genocidaires*, this memorial is smaller and simpler.

We went back outside and stood alongside rows of large mass graves topped with cement. Chantal explained to the psychologist, a cherub-faced woman with braids, that I was writing a book and that she had survived the massacre here in 1994. Adelite flashed her a look of understanding. While most of those buried here were killed throughout the larger vicinity, Adelite explained, some three thousand were part of the group that sought sanctuary at a nearby school guarded by Belgian peacekeepers, but were left defenseless when the troops left. Chantal told her that she was among those who fled the school and wound up here. "Then you know there weren't many survivors," Adelite said. "It was a small group, with serious injuries."

Chantal stood with her arms crossed. I studied the thick, raised scar from a machete wound that snaked along the length of her left forearm and transfigured the shape of her bone at the deepest part. Another scar was visible on her face, just below her mouth. Looking at her, I recalled her telling me how she often felt strange walking down the street, because "people know who you are, that you survived—it's hard to describe how that feels." Since my arrival in Rwanda, I'd seen more than a few people with similar-looking scars, and others without hands, arms, or legs. On one bus trip, during a stop a middle-aged man holding a begging bowl in his right hand approached and thrust through my window what should have been his left hand but was instead a weathered stump. I froze, looking at the mangled limb, unable to speak or determine whether to dig for change, until the man gave up and moved on.

Adelite was pointing at a ten-by-twenty-foot wall behind us, across the walkway from the mass graves. Seven columns of names were engraved in the wall's cement. "There are only some names listed—you can't know exactly who is here because only some have been identified," she said. She turned back to the graves, which held the remains of some ten thousand people. "This site is evidence of how the international community didn't care about what was happening here and did nothing to stop it," she said. I juggled my camera and notebook, jotting down her words.

"Yes," Chantal said. "When we were at the school, people explained to the Belgian peacekeepers that we would die if they left. They knew. But they left, anyway."

The actions of the United Nations during the Rwandan Genocide are an education in just how selective the international community can be when it comes to defending the rights outlined in the Geneva Conventions. Along with the well-known film *Hotel Rwanda*, perhaps the most haunting account of the UN's failure came from the mission's commander in Rwanda at the time, Canadian lieutenant general Roméo Dallaire. In *Shake Hands with the Devil*, which he wrote after suffering a mental breakdown in the wake of the genocide, Dallaire tells of being alerted by a Rwandan army informant of detailed plans by Hutu extremists to exterminate every Tutsi in the country. Dallaire sent repeated messages to UN headquarters describing not only the intelligence, but also his troops' confirmation of arms caches that the man had described. He was ignored. When, over the following weeks, he told his higher-ups about the large-scale massacres of men, women, and children happening across the country, insisting that he could stop it with just five thousand well-armed troops authorized to use force, he was refused. He would have to do what he could with a small force that had no authorization to use weapons unless fired upon. (Most of the killing was being done with machetes and clubs, not guns.)

While Rwandan families were being chopped into small pieces and thrown into pit latrines, the Clinton administration attempted to justify inaction by declaring that it was unclear whether what was unfolding in Rwanda satisfied the requirements for genocide. In the years since, President Bill Clinton, former UN secretary general Kofi Annan, and former U.S. secretary of state Madeleine Albright all apologized for not doing more while one million innocent people were slaughtered. Unlike the former Yugoslavia, where the UN and the U.S. military intervened to stop genocide, Rwanda was of little geopolitical importance. And, just months before genocide began in Rwanda, eighteen U.S. Army Rangers were killed by militants in nearby Somalia, their bodies dismembered and paraded through the streets of Mogadishu in an international spectacle of defeat and humiliation. The United States had little taste for sending soldiers into the fray in another faraway African nation that boasted no natural resources or strategic significance. The genocide was finally stopped by the invading Rwandan Patriotic Front, an army of Tutsi refugees led by today's president, Paul Kagame.

Standing at the memorial, I said to Adelite and Chantal, "If I were Rwandan, I would be so angry—I think I would hate the UN." They considered what I said, then replied.

"It's more a feeling of helplessness than hate," Adelite said. "Because what are you going to do with hate? It's more helpful to express the feelings, and then focus on healing and moving forward."

For Chantal, forgiveness has been a crucial way to move forward. She calls forgiveness "the key to healing a broken heart." Even so, she and Adelite agreed that it's important for people to find forgiveness in their own ways, and in their own time.

"Some people tell victims, 'Forgive! Forgive!'" Adelite said, wagging a sanctimonious finger in imitation. "But no—if someone is not ready to forgive, that is okay. Everyone has her own process. You can't force forgiveness." She surveyed the graves next to us, which were in the process of being equipped with shade structures for the upcoming twentieth anniversary commemoration events. "Anger," she said, "refusing to forgive—that's a defense mechanism, and it serves a purpose."

Chantal smiled in agreement. "That's right! Otherwise, you'd just stay in your bed, not eating, not sleeping, and die!" she said, tipping her head back and laughing, marveling at the brilliance of our coping mechanisms. Then her face grew somber. "Yes. It took me years to even think about forgiveness."

I found Chantal by chance. She had briefly worked for a nonprofit I contacted, and the director put us in touch. *If you're interested in forgiveness*, he wrote, *you must talk to Chantal.*

I met her on a Sunday afternoon at the four-star Umubano Hotel in Kigali, where men in suits and women in dresses were having a pleasant brunch. Set back from a wide, tree-lined boulevard, the hotel lobby opened onto a large patio with outdoor seating and a stage, where a four-piece band played the blues. Behind the musicians in the pool area, families frolicked and iridescent-plumed birds flitted amid stands of trees with glossy leaves.

While visitors and upscale locals relaxed at the hotel, outside, "The Land of One Thousand Hills" bustled with activity: Land Cruisers and taxi motos sped along, children walked hand in hand, women in colorful traditional *kitenge* dresses carried bundles atop their heads. Above it all, the sun beamed in a bluebird sky.

Visiting now, it was difficult to imagine that twenty years ago, the city was gripped by one of history's darkest chapters. In April 1994, hundreds of thousands of people across this tiny Central African nation picked up machetes and clubs and proceeded to butcher more than one million of their neighbors. The meticulously planned genocide executed against Rwanda's ethnic Tutsi minority, and any Hutus who stood in the way, was horrifically efficient: For one hundred days, more than 10,000 men, women and children were killed each day—that's 417 per hour and 7 per minute. To try to wrap your mind around the sheer scale of this slaughter, compare that to the Holocaust, in which the Nazis, with their advanced killing technology, murdered at a much slower rate—roughly 2,500 per day, 106 per hour, 2 per minute. While the Nazis utilized mechanized gas ovens for their "final solution," Rwanda's genocidaires used a sustained propaganda campaign over a period of years, even decades, to dehumanize their targets and mobilize the mostly illiterate and obedient masses to kill. Neighbors massacred neighbors, doctors and nurses murdered patients, teachers killed pupils, and priests led congregations to their deaths. One priest actually bulldozed a crowd of his own parishioners, while two nuns doused a church with gasoline so the people seeking refuge inside could be torched.

This swift, widespread killing featured mass rape, too, with an estimated half-million women sexually assaulted and many intentionally infected with HIV. Also widespread were forms of torture that beggar the imagination. People slowly dismembered, women raped with tree branches, babies smashed against stones, entire families tossed alive into pit latrines. As someone who has been outraged by humanity's capacity for cruelty for as long as I can remember, I relate to what Philip Gourevitch writes in his seminal book about the genocide, *We Wish to Inform You That Tomorrow We Will Be Killed with Our Families*:

The best reason I have come up with for looking closely into Rwanda's stories is that ignoring them makes me even more uncomfortable with existence and my place in it. The horror, as horror, interests me only insofar as a precise memory of the offense is necessary to understand its legacy.

I went to Rwanda because I wanted to explore that legacy, and because I wondered: Is it possible to forgive violence on this extreme scale, violence that most people would consider unforgivable?

Since the late nineties, Rwanda has been at peace. When I visited in 2014, the country was preparing for the Twentieth Annual Genocide Commemoration, during which Rwandans would reflect on this bloody history, honor the dead, and share testimonials. One of the most unique aspects of postgenocide Rwanda is that, unlike in many other postconflict societies, Hutus and Tutsis don't live in segregation. Hardly two separate tribes to begin with (they have long shared the same land, religion, and language), they live and work together in villages and neighborhoods, hospitals and schools, churches and companies. I wondered: How are Rwandans coexisting after the most extreme genocide of the modern era claimed an eighth of the population? How are victims living across the street from their perpetrators, and children of survivors marrying children of killers?

Chantal had suggested the Hotel Umubano, since it was easy for her to reach by cab and was a well-known landmark. I would be able to find it on foot. (There aren't addresses in most of Kigali, so when giving directions, people say things like "take the first left after the president's office," or "take the alley next to the market with fresh eggs outside.") I'd only communicated with Chantal online, but as I entered the hotel with my bag filled with pens, notebooks, and a digital recorder, I spotted her immediately. She wore a brownish-orange skirt suit and pumps, her hair closely cropped.

We served ourselves at the buffet and sat on the patio, eating vegetables and roasted goat while chatting amiably about her husband, David, and their three children, and my boyfriend, Anthony, and our dog. We discovered we were the same age—thirty-five, born just six weeks apart. We were sixteen in 1994. I was a high school junior, spending my weekends skiing, attending parties at friends' houses, and writing college application essays. Chantal's sixteenth year couldn't have been more different. She wanted to tell me about it, and how it took her almost twenty years to forgive, in the hopes that her story might help others. As she said to me, "I think sometimes God sends you down a certain path so you can tell others, 'Hey, watch out, there are lions down there!' Or 'Look! There's safe passage that way!'"

Early on the morning of April 6, 1994, Chantal awoke to find her aunt Joseline (her relatives' names have been changed) listening to the radio, terrified. "We're dead," she kept saying. "The people who did this will make sure we die."

"Who is?" Chantal asked. "What are you talking about?"

Since Rwanda's independence from Belgium in 1959, the Hutu-led government had been taking revenge upon the Tutsi minority. The Belgians arrived in Rwanda after World War I to discover that the land of lush hilltops was populated by two groups that appeared to be distinct: the Tutsi, who seemed to be taller, with "finer" features and bridged noses, and who mostly worked as herdsmen, and the Hutu, whom the Belgians described as shorter and stockier, with "coarser" features and a more "savage" look, and who tended to be farmers. Though the Belgians regarded all Africans as subhuman creatures placed on the earth to serve whites, the colonialists bestowed privilege upon the Tutsi and made them the overlords over their Hutu compatriots. The Belgian masters had the Tutsi driving and whipping the Hutu slaves into building roads, bridges, and buildings, and they instituted ID cards that denoted who was Hutu and who was Tutsi, even though there had been intermarriage for generations and the distinction was not always clear. When the Hutu government took the reins of power after independence, they continued the ID card policy and launched a campaign of radio propaganda that described Tutsis as cockroaches and blamed them for every misfortune the country faced. Massacres of Tutsi families began in 1959 and occurred periodically until the nineties.

When Chantal was growing up in the eighties, Tutsis were frequently denied an education and were barred from government jobs. They were often robbed of their property and possessions by roving bands of armed men. Chantal's mother, Vivienne, was born to a Hutu woman and Tutsi man, but since her male lineage was Tutsi, that's what she was labeled. She caused scandal in her village in South Province when, at eighteen, she had an affair with a Tutsi married man who was a family friend, and became pregnant with Chantal. After Vivienne gave birth, she left the infant with her mother and proceeded to have four more children, all with different men. She was considered a shame to the family. Chantal's grandmother sent Chantal to live with Vivienne's sister, Joseline, in Kigali. It wasn't until Chantal was about eight and living with Aunt Joseline and her husband, Jean-Marc, a Hutu, that Chantal learned that she was considered Tutsi. In primary school, the teachers would highlight the difference by saying, "Hutus, stand up!" And then, "Tutsis, stand up!" Often, they did this so that the Hutu children could laugh at the Tutsi children. "I didn't really know what was going on when they told us to stand," Chantal told me, "But my friends did. They said, 'Chantal, stand up! You're Tutsi.'"

On the morning Chantal awoke to find her aunt in a panic over the radio news, she had only a vague awareness of what had been happening over the past few years. She was a serious, quiet girl, avoiding boys and frivolity so she wouldn't end up like her mother. She went to school, did dishes and errands when she returned home, and then did her homework. She knew that in 1990, a band of Tutsi refugees had invaded Rwanda because the Hutu government refused to allow them to return to the country. She knew also that it was dangerous to associate with these refugees-turned-rebels, the Rwandan Patriotic Front, for risk of being jailed for aiding the enemy. But, since she and her family had nothing to do with them, she didn't understand her aunt's fear.

It turned out that the president's plane had been shot down over the city. Aunt Joseline knew that those responsible most likely belonged to a group of extremists who called themselves Hutu Power. They also ran the main radio station, and already they were blaming the president's death on the Tutsi. Aunt Joseline also knew that after months of ratcheting up their call for a solution to the "Tutsi problem," the president's death was the opportunity Hutu Power had been waiting for—or the one they manufactured themselves. Joseline's husband, Jean-Marc, worked for the government as a truck driver and was out of town for work. Joseline likely hoped that her marriage would save them, but she must have known that she couldn't count on it. She and Chantal remained inside the house, hearing explosions outside. On the second day, they got word from neighbors that a Tutsi woman who lived across the street had been killed.

Aunt Joseline told Chantal and her cousin Ariella, who was visiting from out of town, to quickly gather some clothes and food. They left the house and walked toward a nearby school, where they knew a contingent of Belgian UN soldiers was stationed. The women saw groups of armed men manning checkpoints. The men were Interahamwe, which means "those who stand together," and they had been organized by the Hutu Power government as local militias, training in combat, killing, and torture. They'd been preparing for this day by stockpiling munitions caches, distributing machetes to Hutu males, and compiling regional lists of Tutsi families to be exterminated.

Chantal and her aunt and cousin spent three days in the school, cramped among the desks and tables with several thousand other people seeking refuge. Newly arrived refugees told them that Interahamwe had surrounded the school outside and were killing people attempting to get in. The peacekeepers had no authorization to use force, and no power to patrol the outside of the building to protect people.

Chantal paused for a moment before continuing her story. "'We're in good hands,' we told one another, 'they won't come to kill us here,'" she said. She let out a harsh laugh, the long lens of hindsight highlighting the tragic irony of that hope.

On the third morning at the school, they saw the Belgian soldiers talking on their radios. The peacekeepers then began to pack their things, throwing rucksacks into their trucks and four-by-fours. Unbeknownst to those seeking refuge there, ten Belgian peacekeepers had been murdered in another part of the city, and the remaining soldiers were getting orders to leave. If the peacekeepers gave any explanation for what was happening, Chantal wasn't aware of it. She just remembers watching, a pit in her stomach, as the blue helmets disappeared into the vehicles and the caravan drove away. At this point, Chantal's memories cease to contain many feelings or sensations; to review them is at some points like clicking through someone else's macabre slideshow. They climbed the wall and ran as the killers spilled into the now unguarded school. "We had no time to think where, we were just running," she told me. "We were in a large group, hundreds of people, and some people chased us, yelling, 'Tutsis! They're getting away! Get them!'" The group emerged near the main road that leads to the airport and were surrounded by trucks filled with soldiers carrying guns and Interahamwe wielding crude clubs and machetes.

"They made us march," she said. "I was confused. I'd heard on the radio the announcer saying all Tutsis were collaborators [in the president's death], but I didn't get it because I didn't have any contact with relatives outside the country." The new Hutu Power government was pinning the blame for the president's assassination on the RPF, and declared that any Tutsi in Rwanda was associated with the resistance—even women and children.

"Auntie, where are they taking us?" Chantal asked Joseline.

"Chantal," her aunt replied, "you can't see they are taking us to be killed?"

To be killed. To be killed. The words bounced around in her head, like phrases in a foreign tongue. *To be killed? How? Why?*

The armed men yelled at them, saying, "Our president did so much for you and you killed him! We're going to kill you and bury him on top of you."

As they marched, Chantal looked at the buildings she passed every day on the way to school. Describing this to me, for a moment it seemed as if she stepped into the memory, feeling the feelings, remembering what it was like to be there. She crossed her arms tight across her chest as her eyes filled. "I thought, this is the last time I will ever see this." She looked away for a long quiet moment before continuing.

By the time the group of some three thousand Tutsis crested a hill and found themselves in a field, it was nearly dusk. Rain descended like a gray shroud. A man yelled, "Let us run—let us die running." As they ran, the soldiers started shooting. Chantal hit the ground. She felt other people fall alongside and on top of her. When the shots stopped, the explosions began. Grenades. She felt one graze her foot, burning it. After a while, the explosions stopped. The soldiers ordered the Interahamwe to "use whatever you have to make sure they're all dead." This meant it was time for the machetes.

In the fading light, the rain fell harder. Face in the mud, eyes closed, and nose filled with smoke, Chantal heard screaming and wailing. As the earth ran with rain and blood around her, she thought: *We are going to die—but how?* She could hear people pleading with the killers, offering them gold or cash if they would only use a bullet. The killers would take the money but cut them up anyway. "No, we won't shoot you," she heard them say. "You'll die slowly." When the killers seemed farther off, Chantal and those lying around her would whisper updates. The neighbor boy nearby had been shot and lay dead. A young mother with a baby whom they'd met at the school was also dead. Aunt Joseline had a large leg wound from a grenade and a deep gash on her head. She was bleeding profusely and said she wouldn't last long.

After what seemed like forever, Chantal heard the men yell in the wet dark, "Who's still alive?"

It seems a ridiculous question. Why would those who were still alive announce their presence, and why would the killers expect them to? To the second question, the explanation is likely the same reason that Hutu peasants were persuaded to murder their neighbors in the first place, and why most Tutsis did not fight back: Rwandans were accustomed to following the orders of kings, then colonialists, then an authoritarian government— obedience had been a way of life for generations. As to why any survivors would announce their presence, what Chantal told me next cleared up my confusion.

"Me and my cousin agreed to cry out so they would kill us," she said. "We wanted to die. Who wants to live like this, especially since we figured everyone we knew was gone?"

She and Ariella, still on the ground, yelled at the killers. "We are here!"

A couple of men made their way over in the dark, climbing over piles of bodies. Chantal could barely see them, though she was now faceup, but they moved slowly and seemed tired. After all, they had been busy killing for hours now, and killing with machetes is not easy. "They gave us a couple of machete blows to the head and arm," Chantal told me. "Hit us with clubs. Then they left." She and her cousin were amazed—and disappointed—to find that though they were bleeding from various wounds, they were still alive. Her accented English cut through the pleasant afternoon at the hotel, "We wanted to die—but we missed!"

Chantal heard the killers planning to leave and return in the morning to "finish" their work. After grabbing jewelry and other belongings from the bodies, they disappeared into the night. Aunt Joseline, her strength ebbing, gave the girls her keys and told them to try to make it back to the house. "Please go," she said. "You're young, and they can take you and rape you when they return. Leave at once."

As she told me this, Chantal wore a faraway expression, her face impassive. She was watching the slides inside her mind, knowing where they were headed. "We ran into the forest," she said. "Ariella was losing lots of blood from a head wound. I tried to cover her with my clothes, but they were drenched in mud and blood."

"What were you feeling or thinking?" I asked.

She shook her head. "Nothing," she said. "To sleep is impossible, to think is impossible. You are just there."

During our visit to the massacre memorial in Kicukiro, Chantal and I talked to Adelite, the psychologist, about the difficult task of providing mental health services for genocide survivors. Adelite leads weekly group therapy sessions for women survivors, many of whom lost their entire families and were sexually assaulted. When the killing stopped, Rwanda was virtually destroyed. After the destructive actions of Hutu Power, the war between the regime and the invading rebel army, and the looters who destroyed homes and buildings as they fled the country into bordering nations, there was little left. Those who remained, led by the new government, were starting from zero. A Rwandan friend, who at eleven became the only surviving member of her entire extended family, told me that one reason the annual commemoration is so important is because "We need an appointed time to stop and be still to remember and reflect. We had to rebuild an entire nation in twenty years, so we've been very busy." On the mental health front, the largely poor, underdeveloped country had a massive population suffering from post-traumatic stress disorder with virtually no mental health care system to speak of. The few psychologists who existed in the first place were either dead or abroad.

This lack was acutely felt in 2004, when Rwanda began what the genocide memorial center describes as a "unique experiment in post-genocide justice." Since roughly half the country's population either actively participated or facilitated the genocide in some way, there was no way to traditionally prosecute every single suspect. The government resurrected an ancient tribal network of community courts called Gacaca. Prisoners were given the option of confessing, telling whom and how they killed and where they disposed of bodies (important information for victims' families in order to find some sort of closure), and then apologize to their victims or victims' families in exchange for reduced sentences or freedom. These proceedings were attended by the entire community. Not surprisingly, listening to perpetrators explain the details of their atrocities was traumatizing for many survivors. It was common for observers to faint or weep uncontrollably as the stories triggered memories and a range of trauma symptoms.

IBUKA and other survivors' groups saw the need for trauma specialists. They trained more than six hundred community leaders in recognizing signs of trauma, simple ways to support victims, and how to refer people to clinics or organizations for help. AVEGA, a widows' support organization that belongs to IBUKA, now employs thirty-eight full-time psychologists nationwide. That's not nearly enough, Adelite told me. "There is only about one for each district," she said. "We have group therapy to reach the largest number of people, but we are so few, and there are so many who need help."

"That's important," Chantal said. "Because to see people hurt and killed is one thing. But to endure that and also be raped is another. It's the worst."

"Yes," Adelite agreed. When I asked what is most helpful for these women about therapy, she said, "The most important thing is to find a space where it is quiet and they can talk, because family is so important, and usually they don't have anyone left. The group is like a container where they can let go of it all, a container that can hold those emotions and memories of unspeakable horrors."

One thing that can damage the feeling of safety and the processing of trauma and grief, Adelite said, is when people tell survivors that they must forgive and try to push them into it. There have been many efforts on the part of the government, nonprofits, and church leaders to foster forgiveness and reconciliation, and some have been successful. (We'll explore one remarkable effort in the next chapter.) Yet many critics say that perpetrators often apologize merely to get lighter prison sentences, and that survivors have been pressured to forgive.

Unfortunately, pressured and forced forgiveness has been used against victims not only in Rwanda, but around the world. Sometimes it's just a well-meaning person who wants someone to heal but unwittingly rushes them along, like the oblivious relative who says to a grieving loved one a year after someone's death, "But it's been *a year*. Isn't it time to move on?" As if there were a tidy, scheduled way to grieve or a deadline for forgiveness. There is not. In worse examples, religious leaders have pressured victims of sexual assault to "forgive" their assailants, which in their verbiage means to ignore their pain, get on with it, and drop any expectation of justice. This is not forgiveness at all, and it turns what can be a healing and freeing process into an abomination used as one more bludgeon against people who

have suffered enough. Take the appalling series of mass rapes in a Menno-
nite community in Bolivia.

In an excellent story in *Vice* magazine called "The Ghost Rapes of
Bolivia," Jean Friedman-Rudovsky details how, for at least four years, a
group of nine local men in an isolated, self-governed community called
Manitoba Colony would break into homes, gas entire families with a spray
made from a chemical used to anesthetize cows, and rape the women and
girls while they were unconscious. During the 2011 trial, the men, teenaged
through middle-aged members of the colony, admitted there were at least
130 victims, aged three to sixty-five. In her many visits to Manitoba Colony
after the trial, Friedman-Rudovsky determined that even though those
men were in prison, the rapes were still happening. The town has no police
force and is ruled by male "ministers" who turn a blind eye and enjoy lecturing victims about forgiveness. When Friedman-Rudovsky noticed that
most victims, though they'd never received counseling and still suffered
trauma symptoms, insisted they'd forgiven their rapists, she asked one of
the ruling ministers about it. If a woman didn't want to forgive, he told her,
she would have been visited by the town's bishop and highest authority, and
"he would have simply explained to her that if she didn't forgive, then God
wouldn't forgive her."

Even in less egregious situations, telling people that they "should" forgive, as if it's another item on a to-do list on which they are currently falling
short, sends the message that if what you're feeling is other than blissful,
Christlike peace, there is something wrong with you. This is the last thing
people who are suffering need to hear. Constance, a woman I met in Kigali
who lost her husband and one son during the genocide, was then taken as
"a wife" by her husband's murderer for two months. After Constance described to me the incomprehensible nightmare that was sleeping with her
husband's killer in order to survive and care for her remaining four children, she revealed two more horrific events: In 2005, she grew ill and discovered that the man who raped her had given her HIV. Then, the following
year, after starting antiretroviral drugs, she returned to her home village to
see if she could reclaim the land that was stolen by the Interahamwe in

1994. There was an ex-militant living at her former home, and when he saw her, he attacked her with a machete, cutting her on her arm and neck and leaving her for dead. This solid rock of a woman survived and reported him, and he spent a few years in prison. He's now free, however, and though she has made a life in Kigali, the government is telling her that to keep her monthly survivor's stipend, she must return to her home village—where this man lives.

When I asked Constance about her thoughts on forgiveness, here's what she told me through tears: "It's hard to even talk about forgiveness, because the people who killed my husband and raped me, then hurt me again in 2006—no one has come to seek my forgiveness. No one has apologized. I lost so much, I had to leave my home and start over. To me, it seems like they won."

Constance's experience confirms just how important certain factors are in order for survivors to truly forgive: There must be some basic level of safety, and it helps immensely if perpetrators have faced justice and show remorse. In the absence of safety and remorse, forgiveness is difficult. And yet, therapeutic interventions in Rwanda that include forgiveness, but don't attempt to force survivors into it, have shown promise.

It took two days of walking by night and hiding by day for Chantal and Ariella to reach Aunt Joseline's home in Kicukiro. The house was destroyed, with no doors, windows, or furniture left intact, so they tried the neighbor's, which wasn't as bad off. There, in a bed that had been left behind by looters, they slept. They awoke to footsteps and yelling. Since Chantal assumed they were neighbors, she went outside first. There were about thirty people, many of whom she recognized and several of whom carried clubs and machetes. "Why have you left the house?" one man demanded, referring to the curfew. "You must be Tutsi!" Some wanted to kill the girls, while others argued that Jean-Marc, Chantal's uncle, had come by the other day and said if any of his family were alive to tell him and he'd come for them. Probably because her uncle was a Hutu who worked for the government perpetrating the genocide, the mention of him seemed to appease the group. One couple told Chantal and Ariella to come stay with them.

The couple was Hutu, and Chantal noticed a few of her family's belongings in their home, but she kept silent. Yet they showed the girls only kindness. The woman bathed them, shaved their heads, and cleaned and dressed the oozing wounds on their scalps. She then hid them in a back room. She even took the pair to a nearby clinic, where nurses gave them antibiotic ointment and oral medication for their infected cuts. On the third treatment, though, one of the clinic staffers said, "Don't come back. They're coming through and killing injured survivors."

After a few weeks, the battle between the Hutu Power government and Kagame's RPF rebel army was intensifying in Kigali. The shelling and mortar fire grew dangerously close to the neighborhood, and Chantal's hosts decided to flee. "We weren't sure what to do," she told me. "There were some educated Hutus who didn't kill, but they didn't intervene, either. We weren't sure if we could trust them or not, but what were our options?"

Chantal and her cousin joined the couple and a river of fleeing people headed out of the city. It was chaos, with families carrying loads and dragging animals, women balancing large bundles on their heads and some children trailing alone, either orphans or left behind by their parents. As Chantal was running through a roadblock, a member of the Interahamwe stopped her. As he eyed her, she watched Ariella continue down the road. Before she disappeared, Ariella turned her head and strained to look back at her younger cousin. "I thought, *this is surely my last day*," Chantal told me.

A government soldier appeared and told the Interahamwe, "I know this girl and her father." Chantal didn't recognize the soldier but assumed he was talking about her uncle. The Interahamwe said, "Okay, but we can't let her go just like this." The two men whispered for a few moments. Then the Interahamwe, holding his machete, led her and the soldier into a nearby house. The inside was stripped of everything save a few beds. They forced her to lie down and then took turns raping her.

"All these things turned in my head," she told me. "How I had worked so hard to not be with men, to not do that, to not be like my mother. And this was my destination? I could not speak. I was like a dead person."

After they let her go, Chantal figured her only option was to return to the house. If she got killed, fine. Better to be dead than alive with these memories, especially since now she might have HIV or be pregnant. On her way, she heard someone calling her name. It was a boy she knew, a Hutu who had worked as a housekeeper for her aunt. "I'm going to help you," he said. He persuaded her to come with him to the house where he was staying with relatives. She agreed. After a few days, the boy declared, "You have to be my wife." She told him no. He grew angry. The next day, four Intera-hamwe with guns and grenades knocked on the door. "We need the young girl you are hiding," they told the boy's uncle and aunt. The couple came to Chantal in the other room and told her to leave. She went.

"I saw everyone as my killer—I decided to do everything I could to get them to kill me," Chantal said. "Insult them. Refuse to do what they wanted." The men took her to a complex of houses where they were staying as the battle for Kigali raged. It was filled with things they'd taken from Tutsi houses, and they had plenty of food—meat, spaghetti, rice. "One man was not married, so they said I would be his wife," Chantal told me. "I said to myself, 'Okay, I'll do my best so that he kills me.'" They slept in the same room, but when the man tried to touch her, she recoiled and refused. "I can't sleep with you," she'd say. "I'm sick. I have these cuts. And I have them because I'm Tutsi. And you're hiding me. Are you crazy?" He just looked at her, silent. But he did not rape or kill her. As she told this part of the story, Chantal wiped her tears and again said, "I tried to be killed, but I missed."

Several weeks passed, as bombing and shooting continued to rage out-side. Then word arrived that the RPF was closing in on their sector of the city, and government forces were fleeing the country. The militia men packed their belongings—including Chantal and some other Tutsi women—and headed out of town in a convoy of trucks. Soon after, a government truck pulled up to the convoy and they all stopped. Chantal recognized the man talking to the Interahamwe in charge. It was her uncle, Jean-Marc. She was flooded with relief. She had never been fond of Jean-Marc—he was gruff and distant, he made her go to the bar to buy banana beer every day after school, and once when she went to a friend's house instead, he beat her with a stick, but he and Joseline had legally adopted her. And now he was here in his government truck to pick her up. *Thank God*, she thought. *He will protect me.*

Jean-Marc brought her south to Gitarama, where his family had a home and where the government was still in control. He would leave her there and tell her to stay inside while he left to transport supplies to the army and Interahamwe. One day he told her that he'd gone by her grandparents' home, and that they, and Chantal's mother, were all dead. "I'm sorry," he said. Chantal wept. Now, any reason for living she may have had was gone. Later that night, Jean-Marc came into the room where she was sleeping. "Chantal," he said, "you're not related to me, and I know you're not a virgin. You were a wife of those Interahamwe." Her stomach was gripped with nauseous dread as he continued. "You must be my wife. Or I will not keep you in my house."

"What?" she replied, incredulous. "Your wife? Do you know the age difference between us? You've known me since I was four. What are you saying?"

At this point in the story, my third day of interviewing Chantal, we had made tea at the home where I was renting a room. We sat at the dining room table as the sun sank low, holding our cooling cups in silence. Chantal looked exhausted. I was drained just from hearing it. Over the past few days, I'd attempted to describe Chantal's story in e-mails home to Anthony and my parents, but I soon gave up, overwhelmed by the magnitude of what she'd gone through, and the fact that hers was one story out of millions. All I wound up telling them in my e-mails was what I concluded after spending a week with Chantal: If she could somehow find forgiveness after all she went through, don't the rest of us at least have a moral obligation to try? At the table opposite her, I finished my black tea with milk and asked if she wanted to break and resume the next day. She shook her head and took a sip of water. "He got angry," she said. "He said, I'll do what I'll do. And he did. And from that time I just kept quiet."

At dusk I walked with Chantal to find a taxi. The sun looked like an egg yolk spreading slowly in a frying pan, its golden yellow light spilling down onto the tin roofs and whitewashed walls and making the reddish dirt look richer than usual. As we passed shopkeepers, mothers leading children, and men out for an evening run, I couldn't help but stare at every-one of a certain age and wonder: Where were they in 1994? Did they kill? Statistically, I knew most of them were Hutu. (Hundreds of thousands of Tutsi refugees returned to Rwanda after the genocide, many of whom had been gone for decades, but they remain a minority.)

As if reading my mind, Chantal said, "Many of those who killed live in neighboring countries. Others are here, among us." She spread her hands to indicate the crowds walking the dirt road. "One of the hardest things was to see how quickly people changed. People you thought you knew. Cousins, friends, uncles. In a conflict, everything changes, and sometimes only then do you see who people really are."

When the RPF routed the Hutu Power government in August 1994, the extremists set up shop in the massive refugee camps in neighboring Congo, continuing to launch attacks on Rwandan Tutsis from the safe haven of aid tents supported by the international powers that had abandoned Rwanda to its genocide. Eventually, after several years of frequent massacres, the camps were shut down and many refugees returned to Rwanda. The new RPF-led government declared itself not a Tutsi regime but a Rwandan gov-ernment for all, free of past divisions. The new leaders stressed that all Rwandans were welcome home and began rebuilding the country.

For months, Chantal lived like a prisoner of her abusive uncle, first at his home in Gitarama, then in the old, restored house in Kigali. She en-dured not only sexual abuse but also constant verbal abuse and the occa-sional beating. She eventually found out that some distant relatives had survived, as had her father. Before the genocide, her mother, Vivienne, had visited Aunt Joseline and Chantal in Kigali. Chantal asked her repeatedly for information about her father, and her mother acquiesced. He was a teacher, and still married. Chantal contacted him, hoping he could help her attend school in South Province. His wife was not enthusiastic about him being in touch with the child born of his affair, but he helped Chantal with her school applications and arranged for her to stay with him temporarily, and later with relatives while she finished school. One day while her uncle was away from the house, she quickly packed a bag and left. He didn't follow her.

Seeking God, and driven by a desperate need to know why she was spared while everyone she cared about had died, Chantal visited many churches in search of a spiritual home. I thought perhaps she would have been angry with God (I know I would have been—my immediate reaction when circumstances take a turn for the tragic has often been to wonder why a benevolent God would allow such things), but she told me, "I was confused. I could not be angry at God because he was all I had. I would ask, *Why? Why?* I felt only God could explain it." At one church, a group of Christian women welcomed Chantal and became her first true friends and confidantes. Also at this church, she met a serious, devout young man named David. He was also a genocide survivor, though he'd lost his family before that for different reasons: His Muslim father disowned him and kicked him out of the house because David became Christian. He was living among the banana trees when the genocide started, and he sheltered a group of fellow Tutsis there in his makeshift camp. He and Chantal became friends at church, began dating, and eventually married.

By the time I met Chantal in 2014, she had borne three children and worked as a teacher, loan officer, and nonprofit administrator. Her fourteen-year-old son had a severe vision problem that doctors said would require treatment abroad, so she and David, a pastor, were trying to raise the money and get visas. It was stressful, she said, but nothing compared to what she endured as a teen. Chantal never went to a therapist to work through that trauma. Even now, the idea of seeing a counselor is a fairly new concept in Rwanda, and for years, most people didn't have access to medical care, much less mental health care. So instead of sitting on a therapist's couch, she spent hours writing in journals and praying to God.

Like all of the Rwandans I interviewed who had transformative forgiveness experiences, Chantal found forgiveness through God. In one of the most devoutly Christian countries in Africa—mostly Catholic, though the evangelical population is growing—most people's concept and experience of healing, whether physical or emotional, is profoundly spiritual. A Colorado-based doctor who frequently trains physicians in Rwanda told me, "I tell my students that while we in the U.S. have this mechanistic, strictly scientific view of medicine, in Rwanda people view health and healing through a very spiritual lens. If you ignore that, you will miss a lot." Chantal puts it this way: "Jesus was my counselor."

In 2012, Chantal was reading a Christian book that described blame and resentment as ways to keep yourself down, remaining a bitter prisoner to a victim mentality that makes you miserable. She had to agree. She was struggling with blame, but not for Hutus generally, or even the killers she encountered. When I expressed surprise at this, she shrugged and said, "When you look at the history, when you know the extent of the propaganda and fear . . . Maybe if you or I were in their position, we would have done the same. Besides, I would hate to be them, having to live with the things they did." What about the soldier and Interahamwe who raped her? "I didn't know them; same with the men who cut my head and killed all those people," she replied. "I wasn't as angry with them—it was more about my own family."

Most of her suffering over the years was related to her abusive uncle, as well as her father and stepmother. She had always yearned for love and recognition from her father, and for acceptance from her stepmother. Yet the older woman all but ignored her, and since an argument shortly after her wedding, Chantal hadn't talked to either one of them for thirteen years. Her husband didn't understand why she wanted a relationship with them, but she did. They were among her only living relatives, and she had begun thinking about forgiving them. What did it mean? What must she do? "One day on the way to church," she told me, "God told me to call my father." She still had his phone number. She didn't particularly want to call. The thought of it made her perspire, her heart quicken. But she dialed his number.

"As the words, 'I love you, Dad,' came out, I found they were true," she told me. "I did love him." Her father, shocked and delighted, began calling regularly and asked when they could visit. "It was like I opened the door and realized that he'd been standing there, too," she told me. When they reunited, they talked for hours, and he told her things she never knew about his childhood and about his relationship with her mother. Months later, her stepbrothers told Chantal that he'd been drinking heavily and that he stopped after they reconciled.

Chantal wasn't sure how to approach her stepmother, Irene. She prayed, and in her prayer, an inner conversation began, initiated by a voice that Chantal ascribes to God: *It's not your problem to fix, it is your mother's.*

But she's dead!

She may not be present but you are, and you're part of their story. You can apologize on her behalf.

I must have looked shocked as she described this to me, because Chantal said, "I know—I didn't want to. But God asked me, *How would you feel if another woman was with your husband and she had his baby?* For the first time, I understood how she must have felt."

Soon after, Chantal visited her stepmother. They sat outside on the patio. Chantal began by saying that she wasn't angry about anything in the past and apologized for anything she may have done to offend her. This captured Irene's attention. Suddenly, all of the feigned disinterest and scorn disappeared, and she focused intently on Chantal, who took a deep breath and tried to steady her voice. "On behalf of my mother," she said, "I apologize for what she did with my father—for how she hurt you. I understand now because I'm a wife, too. I'm sorry. If she were alive I would have brought her here with me." Without thinking about it, she kneeled and said, "I wasn't there, and it was the fault of my mother and father, but I'm sorry." Silence. Then Irene began to weep. After what seemed like a long time, she wiped her tears and hugged Chantal. "All these years," she said, "I was sick over what happened. Seeing you made me think of it over and over again. But now I will be able to move on." Later, Irene told Chantal that this conversation enabled her to finally forgive her husband for straying.

Chantal saved the hardest for last: her uncle. The Hutu adoptive father who became her worst betrayer and abuser. She'd heard about him over the years, learning through the grapevine that he'd contracted AIDS, his second wife and son died of the disease, and he'd lost his home. But while learning of these events gave her some satisfaction, it did not give her peace. Anytime she heard his name or even heard a voice that reminded her of his, she felt all of the old hatred, hurt, and shame rise in her. "If I happened to pass him on the street, it would ruin my day," she told me. "So, I asked God, How do I talk to him?" Like many victims of sexual abuse and incest, Chantal was not interested in renewing their relationship, and she didn't feel safe around him, so she decided that writing him a letter was the best option.

> *It's been eighteen years since the genocide, and in all that time I didn't forgive you for what you did. Now I make the decision to forgive you. And I bless you. I know you have had a lot of troubles, and I think it was because of what you did. But I know that God is good, and that He can forgive you as I have.*

She didn't expect a response, and she didn't get one. But she immediately felt different. "I felt so free, so good, so happy," she told me. She no longer found herself ruminating about her family. She also had a newfound freedom to talk about what happened to her, which is rare among victims of sexual abuse anywhere, especially in Africa. "For eighteen years I was healing and having memories of genocide, but after I forgave, I began to share my story and become passionate about advocating for women who have suffered rape and sexual abuse," she told me. She recently began speaking to groups of widows through AVEGA, making an effort to inspire and support women who lost their husbands and children in the genocide. She's determined to take a stand against rape as a tool of war, whether in nearby Congo and Sudan or around the world. "We have to stand up and speak out," she told me. "We have to demand a better world."

8

Chain Reaction: The Institutional Habits That Spread Forgiveness in Schools and Communities

On April 20, 1999, Craig Scott was applying hair gel when his older sister, Rachel, called to him from the kitchen: "C'mon! We're going to be late!" As they climbed into her red Acura and headed to Columbine High School, their annoyance was mutual. The siblings loved each other but were . . . different. Craig was sixteen, an athlete who tried to fit in with the cool kids. He was often late. Rachel, seventeen, loved her church youth group and was always punctual. When she tuned the radio to a Christian station, Craig abruptly changed it to rock, and as they arrived at school, he slammed the car door without saying goodbye.

Several hours later Craig was studying in the library when teacher Patti Nielson ran in, shouting, "Get under the tables, kids!" Everyone looked around at first, suspecting a prank. Just then, a student stumbled through the doors and collapsed. Craig and his friends Isaiah Shoels and Matt Kechter clambered under a table. He heard Nielson talking on a school telephone, telling emergency dispatchers there was a shooter roaming the halls. Then he heard the doors open. "Oh God," the teacher said. "He's right there, he's in the room." The "he" was actually them: Eric Harris and Dylan Klebold.

When Craig, a wrestler, heard Klebold and Harris talking about targeting anyone with the white hats often worn by athletes, he shoved his baseball cap under his shirt. Amid the echoing gunfire and the whimpering of other students, he squeezed his eyes shut and prayed as one of the gunmen drew near and yelled, "We have a nigger over here," referring to Shoels. They fired off more racial slurs and then shot both of Craig's friends to death. Possibly because he appeared dead, they left Craig unharmed. He soon fled the library, where ten victims had been killed, and emerged to horrific news: Rachel had been the first student murdered. She was eating lunch outside when the killers approached the school building and shot her on their way in.

After the shootings, Rachel's bedroom became a place for reflection. For months, some members of Rachel's family—she left behind a mother and stepfather, father and stepmother, and four siblings between the ages of fourteen and twenty-three—would wander into her room at her mother's house to think about her, talk about her, or simply to cry. One afternoon, Rachel's father, Darrell Scott, and Bethanee, her oldest sister, found a graded essay called "My Ethics, My Code of Life" tucked under her mattress. *I have this theory that if one person can go out of their way to show compassion, then it will start a chain reaction of the same*, she wrote. *People will never know how far a little kindness will go.*

The family eventually found a half-dozen more journals, including two that were in her backpack when she died. Many of them were filled with prayers expressing a fervent desire for her life to somehow help others, and several passages were hauntingly prescient: *This will be my last year, Lord. I have gotten what I can. Thank you*, read one entry from May 1998. Rachel's sister Dana, then twenty-two, recalled Rachel once mentioning that she thought she would die young, but Dana wrote it off as a comment made by a theater-loving teenager with a flair for drama.

The Scotts started to hear stories about Rachel from her friends. One girl told them how Rachel invited new kids to sit with her and her friends at lunch; a special education student described the time Rachel stopped some boys from mocking him. During this time, Darrell gave media interviews about Columbine and spoke publicly about the ordeal; his talks always focused on Rachel's essay, on kindness and compassion starting a ripple effect. The more he told his story, the more requests he received, primarily from colleges and youth organizations. But he soon realized the best way to memorialize Rachel and prevent the kind of violence that took her life would be to focus on schools.

Darrell founded Rachel's Challenge in 2000 as an educational non-profit. He delivered his first presentations to students in El Paso, Texas, where he knew people involved with the local school system. Soon he was telling school assemblies across the country about Rachel's life, death, and writings. Today, Rachel's Challenge has become the largest school assembly program in the United States. More than fifty full- and part-time present-ers use anecdotes and video clips to remember the Columbine shootings and share Rachel's message that selfless acts such as reaching out to lonely peers, reconciling with estranged friends, or refusing to be a bully can pre-vent violence and suffering.

The organization supplements the assemblies with twenty-seven pro-grams that include exercises designed to combat low self-esteem and help students see what they share instead of what separates them. Scores of schools have also started Friends of Rachel Clubs, which conduct every-thing from graffiti cleanup and hurricane relief efforts to recognition days for teachers, janitors, and librarians. (Dana, now thirty-six, is a Friends of Rachel Coach.) Most recently, Darrell has begun training teachers in the new programs. "Rachel is the heart of our organization," Dana says, "but my father has been the head and hands."

The results are impressive. Participating schools have reported sub-stantial declines in disciplinary actions such as suspensions and expul-sions. Rachel's Challenge has received more than five hundred unsolicited e-mails from students who say they were considering suicide until they heard Rachel's story. Organization staffers also say there have been at least six school shootings that were averted following assemblies, often because students overheard peers discussing violent plans and alerted school au-thorities.

Craig, a longtime presenter for Rachel's Challenge, recalls an espe-cially chilling experience after one assembly in Texas. During his presen-tation, he'd noticed an angry-looking teenager dressed in black in the audience. He told himself, *If I can reach that kid, I'll reach everybody.* Afterward, the teen approached Craig and handed him a hit list. "You just saved a lot of people," the boy said before turning himself in to school authorities.

Institutional Practices: "We Shape Our Houses, and Then They Shape Us."

Exercises like those led by Rachel's Challenge bring out what we identified in chapter 2 as the instinct for forgiveness. Because we are evolutionally hardwired and psychologically disposed toward both conflict and cooperation, vengeance and forgiveness, it is our environment that often determines which impulse is expressed. And our environment includes our culture and societal practices (practice is defined as the application or use of an idea or method). In many communities, especially impoverished urban areas or conflict zones, people live in what Mike McCullough and other evolutionary biologists call "cultures of honor," where amid rampant violence and insufficient security, revenge is used to wield power, gain protection, and regulate behavior. In such an environment, forgiveness is rarely presented as an option. Uninterrupted, it's difficult to see how such cycles of violence could ever change. Improved education and increased employment would of course make a huge difference, but so would emotional and interpersonal healing.

In the past decade, watershed discoveries about the brain and neuroplasticity have made it clear that while nature and nurture both contribute to forming human behavior, our behavior can change our brains and our biology. Today's leading psychologists and neuroscience researchers have shown that from new thoughts, feelings, and actions spring new neural pathways that alter our actions and experience. Winston Churchill said, "We shape our houses, and then they shape us." The American founders believed that institutions can do the same thing. And what are institutions but sums of their methods, the customs—the collective habits and practices—that they use? Our institutions shape us through those customs and practices, and so what could be more important than examining them to ensure they're shaping us in the ways we want to be shaped? If we would like to see a more peaceful and harmonious world, we would do well to examine the wave of new customs that are creating more forgiving habits throughout the world.

Like Azim Khamisa in San Diego and the Scott family in Denver, a growing number of people are creating interventions that facilitate forgiveness for every level of society: from individuals and families to schools and conflict-gripped groups. Led by different people in a variety of places, they all include the following critical elements: developing empathy and understanding, raising awareness about the consequences of one's actions and the importance of taking responsibility, and setting an intention for inner and outer peace. In this chapter we'll explore the "restorative circles" that have nearly eliminated fights and suspensions in an inner-city Baltimore school and the mediation program that reduced bullying in suburban New Jersey, and in the next chapter, we'll examine a unique class in Rwanda that unites genocide victims and perpetrators, and a summer camp that brings Israeli and Palestinian girls to the United States to get to know each other.

Many of these efforts are led by people like the Scotts, who have suffered the effects of violence and found that forgiveness was critical to their recovery. While Azim tells the story of his murdered son to students in San Diego, across the country in Pensacola, Florida, Renee Napier talks to children, too—with help from the man who killed her daughter. In 2002, Eric Smallridge got into his Jeep after a night of partying and smashed into a Mazda carrying two twenty-year-old friends, Meagan Napier and Lisa Dickson. They were both killed instantly. Smallridge, a recent college graduate at the time of the crash, was sentenced to twenty-two years in prison. Like a growing number of bereaved parents, Meagan's mother felt that she wouldn't be able to recover without forgiving. She wrote to Eric offering her forgiveness, and he in turn apologized.

When Napier founded the Meagan Napier Foundation to raise awareness about the risks of drinking and driving, she asked Smallridge to collaborate via writing and video. He agreed. In a letter posted on the foundation's Web site, he wrote about his remorse and regret:

> I had a great life full of opportunity and promise, a wonderful family, lots of friends, a beautiful girlfriend and I had just received my bachelor's degree in Management Information Systems. In a split second, everything changed . . . If only I could trade places with [Meagan and Lisa] so they could realize the great lives they should have had, but I can't and they can't and I will live with that reality every single day of the rest of my life.

In addition to Darrell Scott, other parents who lost children to mass shootings are leading efforts to prevent violence and facilitate forgiveness. Scarlet Lewis, who lost her seven-year-old son, Jesse, to the massacre at Sandy Hook Elementary School in December 2012, has been developing school curriculum based on compassion and forgiveness. In her book, *Nurturing Healing Love*, named after a note Jesse scribbled on a chalkboard at home before he died, Lewis writes about how she and Jesse's teenaged brother forgave the shooter, Adam Lanza, and managed to heal. One turning point came when a therapist she knew mentioned that he'd worked with orphans of the Rwandan genocide and recommended that her son, JT, talk to them via Skype. JT became so inspired by the orphans' stories of fortitude and forgiveness that he raised money for them and their families. "It's already happened to them and they got over it and were able to forgive," JT told NPR one year after his brother's death at Sandy Hook. "So to hear it from them—and they've gone through something much worse than what we've gone through—it was comforting."

It's not surprising that forgiveness has been part of these people's healing, or that they are committed to helping others by sharing their stories. Acceptance is the final phase of grief according to most psychologists, and forgiveness—not only relinquishing any expectation of a different past, but also giving up resentment—is intimately tied to acceptance. They are part of the same process. And just as forgiving helps people to accept what has happened and move forward, so does helping others. Humanistic psychologists such as Viktor Frankl, a Holocaust survivor and author of the classic book *Man's Search for Meaning*, identified purpose—often through altruism—as the antidote to suffering. Recent research on the health and mood impacts of generosity confirms that giving to others is good for your health.

As it turns out, then, the expression "Forgiveness is a gift you give yourself" is merely a starting point. When followed through to its fullest expression, forgiveness can be a gift that benefits everyone.

Inner-City Baltimore

On a Thursday morning at City Springs School, a twelve-year-old named Antonio stood wailing and hollering in the hallway. Brendan Lee, the school's "restorative practices" facilitator, calmly pinned the child's flailing arms to his sides. Antonio, whose school file said he suffered from "severe ADHD," strained against him, attempting to kick a nearby trash can. The boy's tear-streaked features were knitted in a knot of fury, and his uniform—a navy shirt with khaki shorts—was disheveled.

"Hey," Lee said, "I'm on your side. I want to help you. Calm down."

"I wanna leave!" Antonio screamed.

"Let's go upstairs. We can play some cards, or go to the gym and play basketball," Lee said.

Antonio let Lee lead him to the gym to shoot baskets.

Ten minutes earlier, Antonio's sixth-grade teacher had come to Lee for help. "I need you to talk to Antonio," he said. "He's banging on the walls. I can't control him." The teacher's creased face glistened with sweat above his graying mustache; he looked exasperated and drained, like a new mother who hasn't slept in days and is on the verge of tears—or booking a flight out of town.

Upstairs in his office, Lee set up a circle of chairs and asked Antonio to sit down.

The idea of using "peace circles" to resolve conflict is an offshoot of "restorative justice." With the goal of repairing crime's harm to communities, healing victims, and rehabilitating criminals, restorative justice originated not in the punitive model descended from English Common Law, but from tribal customs practiced by native cultures throughout the world (the original Gacaca community courts in Rwanda are one of many examples). Over the past half century, some of those age-old customs have been adopted by modern justice systems. In the criminal justice setting, they often include victim-perpetrator meetings. In schools, the approach has become known as "restorative practices." When conflict erupts, those involved are typically brought to a meeting with community leaders and witnesses. Each is asked to share her version of what happened and how she feels about it. If one student hurt another, that student must listen to the consequences of his actions and ultimately agree to repair the damage.

City Springs principal Rhonda Richetta has spent the past five years integrating restorative circles into the daily fabric of the school's life, with stunning results. Situated northeast of Baltimore's touristy Inner Harbor, the school sits at the center of several large public housing projects that have long been home to the sort of gang violence dramatized in the television series *The Wire*. City Springs' student body of about seven hundred is nearly 100 percent black, and well over 90 percent qualify for free breakfast at school, which means they live below the poverty line (as of 2013, less than $23,500 for a family of four, according to the U.S. Census). Most of the kids come from single-parent families and many were born to teen parents.

When Richetta became principal, the school was listed as "failing" academically, and the daily environment was chaos. A petite fifty-six-year-old with shoulder-length brown hair, a determinedly set square jaw, and a wardrobe that mostly features purple, the school color (including her manicured nails, which are usually painted the same shade), Richetta would find herself sprinting through the hallway each day to arrive at the same scene: students standing outside classrooms, shifting their weight and whispering, while inside children hurled insults and brawled.

In 2008, desperate for anything to alleviate the squabbles and gang clashes, Richetta attended a workshop at the International Institute for Restorative Practices (IIRP) in nearby Pennsylvania. They taught her how to do "reactive circles" after an incident, which use the following basic script: *What happened? What were your thoughts and feelings about what happened? What are your thoughts and feelings now? What can be done to repair the harm/make things better?* Since Richetta has trained teachers, students, and parents in what she learned, fighting has nearly disappeared and suspensions plummeted from eighty-three in 2008 to just eighteen in 2013—a 78 percent decrease.

Richetta had known Brendan Lee for a decade when she named him the restorative practices facilitator. She met him while teaching at the alternative high school he wound up in after getting kicked out of half a dozen traditional schools for fighting. Lee grew up just blocks from City Springs, and when his hard-drinking, abusive father died the year Lee turned twelve, he became a "corner boy" for local drug dealers in order to support his mother, grandmother, and two sisters. He sold baggies of cocaine, crack, and marijuana and turned the cash over to his mother for rent. At sixteen, he joined the Bloods.

Richetta, an aspiring administrator, saw something in young Lee. Something pure, something she couldn't exactly identify at the time but followed on instinct. In spite of his tough-guy street persona and sagging pants, she would talk to him in the halls and outside the school. She got on his case about the red bandannas he wore tucked into his pockets. "You're better than that," she'd tell him. Her colleagues thought she was nuts. "You'd better stop talking to him," they would tell her. "You're going to come out one day to find your tires slashed, or worse." Richetta ignored them. When Lee graduated, she gave him her number. "Call me if you need anything," she told him.

Soon after, Lee got into a physical fight with his stepfather because the older man didn't approve of him holding Bloods meetings in his mother's backyard. Lee wound up in jail facing assault charges, and his mother testified against him. When he saw her tell the judge that she was afraid of her own son, something crossed over in Lee. He broke down. He'd been blind to the ways his choices affected his mom. He swore he would never again do anything illegal, and the judge let him go with time served. Afterward, Lee enrolled in community college and got a temporary job handing out fliers for a congressional campaign. One day he ran into his former principal. "Ms. Richetta is looking for you!" she told him. "She has a job for you." A job? For him? By then he'd lost Richetta's number, but the principal wrote it down for him on a slip of paper.

Richetta was now principal of City Springs, an elementary and middle school, and she needed a kindergarten teaching aide. Lee's face kept popping into her mind. He had an assuring way about him, a gentle strength, and if she could just get him into a job she thought he'd soar. It was a risk, but she persuaded her superintendent to sign off on the idea. When Lee called her after running into the former principal, she felt it was meant to be. He excelled teaching kindergarten and soon noticed that the boys in higher grades were struggling with the same problems he had as a kid—abusive dads, no dads, murdered dads. He started a lunchtime mentorship group for them. Some days, he taught them how to put on ties. Others, he had them write letters to their fathers. Most of the letters followed a similar refrain: *I wish you would come to my ball games; I could be a good son to you if you'd just come by sometimes.* Soon, when the adolescent boys were sent to the front office for misbehaving, Richetta started sending them to Lee.

Lee says he wasn't sure about the circles at first. "It was real bubblegummish," he says. "Like, sitting down middle school students and asking what their favorite color is. Maybe that would work out in the country, but it's not gonna work in Baltimore City in the middle of the projects. Sitting them in a circle and saying, 'What's your favorite color?' No." Once he learned the basics of the various types of circles, he began to tailor them to their student body, using topics and questions they could relate to. It worked.

At City Springs, circles are not only held when there's a fight or a discipline problem. They're done every day, in every classroom, week in and week out. They do circles to get to know each other at the start of the year and to reconnect at the start of a new week. At the first whiff of conflict, students, teachers, and even parents request a reactive circle. "You should have seen this place in the beginning, five years ago," Lee tells me one afternoon. "I wouldn't have been able to talk to you like this, because it was just constant. I was getting three to four calls every minute instead of three to four calls every day. It was just one circle after another, trying to get kids to stop arguing and disrupting class, to stop walking out. It was *off the hook*. But as everyone got on board and the teachers realized there's no magic wand to this, that they can do it themselves, I watched things calm down and saw suspensions go from like one hundred and fifty per year to about five last year."

When I told Anthony about City Springs' success, he said, "I wish they'd had that at my schools growing up—they would have been completely different places." Brawls were commonplace for him starting at age eight, when he was riding his skateboard home with a gallon of milk for his mother and a group of older boys attacked him, stealing both the milk and his baseball hat. A few years later he was visiting his grandmother at the school where she taught, and as he walked out of her office a kid he'd never seen before punched him in the face. (Anthony took the boy to the ground, hitting him in the face until his grandmother walked outside and pulled him off.) He learned to fight early, because he had to. The only option was to be prepared and willing to dish out punches so people didn't think you were an easy target—even if you risked suspension. Thinking about circles, he asked me, "The thing is, how do you get kids to do them when they might think they're dumb or cheesy?"

The key to City Springs' strategy is making circles, and the kind of conversations they prompt, habitual from a young age. The week I visited, I watched kindergarteners circle up to sing a song about friendship, first-graders pass a fuzzy flower talking stick around to announce their favorite foods, and third-graders take turns discussing the most influential people in their lives. That might seem trivial, but over time they help kids to understand each other and see what they have in common.

On that Thursday morning, as Lee sat down with Antonio, he showed the even-keeled sense of safety and stability that leads students to relax when they see him. He seems much older and wiser than his twenty-six years, and if you removed the dreadlocks that he keeps pulled back in a ponytail, he would look exactly—and I mean exactly—like the Rev. Martin Luther King Jr. The kids notice the resemblance as soon as they learn about the civil rights icon. Lee asked Antonio what upset him. Antonio stared at the floor and said in a small voice that Mr. Blackwell said something bad about his father. It sounded like the teacher, frustrated over Antonio's lack of attention or respect, said that he was tired of them rebelling as if he were their father.

"Both of you were angry," Lee started. "Mr. Blackwell, you were angry with behavior you've seen from Antonio, and he was angry about a comment that was made about his father. But one thing I know is that you two have a great relationship. Just like anyone, we're human. We get into an argument and say some things and do some things to make each other angry. But the main focus of this circle is to let each other know we care about each other and to resolve this."

He handed the boy a round glass paperweight from his desk, which would serve as the "talking stick," and asked him what happened.

"He said he don't wanna be like my father," Antonio said, barely above a whisper.

"Mr. Blackwell, what's your response to Antonio?" Lee asked, passing the paperweight.

"Antonio, your behavior has been terrible; for what reason I don't know," the teacher said, his eyes flashing behind his spectacles. "I'm not supposed to be addressed as 'dummy,' 'faggot,' or anything else. I'm just like you are; I don't want somebody calling me something other than my name. I don't like it. How many times have we talked about the things you're supposed to do so we get along all day?"

Antonio stared at the floor, but he was still and seemed to be listening.

"Every day, I get up and come in here because I want to see you and all the others be successful," his teacher continued. "Jordan, Cory, DaShawn, Dante, Antonio, DiMarco, Joseph, Keante, Terrell. I go through the same thing with all ten of you every day. I don't come in here every day to be verbally abused the way you've been doing for the last ten days."

"So, Mr. Blackwell," Lee asked, "how do you feel when he calls you names?"

"I get very angry," the older man replied. "I have to walk away. That's when I hear you, Mr. Lee, in my head—and I have to walk away so I don't do anything that hurts him or me."

Lee turned to Antonio. "Do you understand how your words affect Mr. Blackwell?"

Antonio nodded.

"Mr. Blackwell, do you understand how comments about his father impact Antonio?"

The teacher explained that he was merely saying that the students shouldn't rebel against him as if he were their father.

Lee nodded, making a note to remind the middle-aged teacher, whose father was a Tuskegee airman, teacher, and family man, that because Antonio and most of his peers don't have fathers involved in their lives, comments about fathers can set them off. Looking back at the duo, he said, "I'm hearing that you both care about each other but things were said that made both of you angry. What needs to happen for both of you to feel comfortable in class?"

"When he acts up, when I act up, eventually I go apologize to him, and he comes and apologizes to me," Blackwell said.

"So, do you feel like this is one of these times for you to apologize and let some things go?" Lee asked. Teacher and student nodded and apologized to each other. They also agreed that when Antonio gets upset, they'll walk the halls together for a few minutes to cool off.

"I need you to do more of that," Lee said. "Antonio, when you get agitated and upset, I need you to ask Mr. Blackwell, 'Can we take that walk?' Because I don't want to see you like this. I don't want to see you make the wrong decisions when you're upset. Okay?"

"Okay," Antonio replied. His face was still serious, but he looked calm. He and Blackwell headed back to their classroom, and Lee returned to his to-do list for the day—the next parent to call, the next circle to plan.

The Origins of Restorative Justice and Restorative Practices

In the late seventies, word of a curious process made its way to police offi-cers in West Auckland, New Zealand. When teenagers from the Maori tribe got in trouble with authorities for misdemeanor crimes like vandalism or petty theft, their families sent them to the Te Whanau Awhina, a group of Maori who ran a special kind of meeting at the local high school. In ac-cordance with Maori and Aboriginal traditions, they'd unite the victim and the victim's family, the offender and the offender's family, and a panel of elders and other community members. All of them would sit, often in a circle, and each person would give a brief speech that expressed respect for the other participants. Then, a facilitator would call for accounts of the crime.

In keeping with the Maori proverb "Let shame be the punishment," most offenders admitted their crimes and apologized to the victims. The group would determine, by consensus, the reparation required (such as repayment for robbery) and means of rehabilitating the offender (counsel-ing, for instance). What struck local police was that the kids who went through this process rarely reoffended. Officers, then judges, began refer-ring young people to the group even if they weren't part of the Maori tribe, and by the midnineties the "Family Group Conferences" became the heart of New Zealand's revamped juvenile justice system. As the resulting dips in incarceration and recidivism rates became public, the experiment spread to other countries.

The idea of focusing more on accountability, reparation, and forgive-ness rather than merely punishment has become increasingly common around the world, especially in Australia, Canada, and the United King-dom. Studies have shown that it's effective. A literature review of nearly eight hundred cases by Lawrence Sherman, a professor at the University of Cambridge, found that crime victims who participate in conferences with offenders who robbed or assaulted them are 23 times as likely as other crime victims to feel that they've received a sincere apology from their offenders, 4 times less likely to experience lingering desire for revenge, and 2.6 times more likely to report forgiving their offenders. The review also determined that restorative justice reduces reoffending—especially with violent crimes—and lessens PTSD symptoms in victims (through the opportunity to reprocess the traumatic experience and to be heard and understood). The United States is still largely committed to a strictly punitive justice system, but based on our soaring recidivism rates—which range from 70 to 90 percent depending on which study you reference—it's horribly ineffective.

The restorative model spread to schools as a way to diffuse conflict and prevent crime from happening in the first place. Over the past two decades, organizations like the International Institute for Restorative Practices in Pennsylvania have trained administrators and teachers in restorative practices throughout the United States, focusing primarily on schools in inner cities plagued by high violent crime and low graduation rates. Meanwhile, across the Atlantic, the port town of Hull, England, is aiming to make itself into "the world's first restorative city." The city's street fighting and overall crime rose as shipping declined, and the dwindling financial security of blue-collar families began to manifest in behavioral problems at local schools. A principal named Estelle MacDonald learned of the IIRP and began using circles. Fighting plummeted, just as it did at City Springs, and learning and test scores rose. Today, Hull trains every citizen under eighteen in restorative justice practices, and all public employees learn them, too, from teachers and police officers to investigators, prosecutors, and judges.

If you're thinking this sounds like one of those cheesy team-building exercises your company forces on staffers for naught, think again. Remember McCullough's forgiveness instinct, and the factors crafted through natural selection to foster reconciliation so that primates and ancestral humans could preserve valuable relationships to retain evolutionary fitness. People are more likely to forgive, and by extension reconcile with, people whom they care about and whose presence in their lives is valuable, usually family and friends. The closer students are, and the more empathy they have for one another, the more likely they are to maintain and repair relationships through the seeking and granting of forgiveness.

Parents can use restorative tools at home, too. Some of the most effective practices with children—at home or at school—include "affective statements" that express your feelings, such as "When you yell when I'm talking I feel disrespected and angry," instead of using merely punitive ones like "If you don't stop yelling you're never playing that video game again!" Devita Basu, City Springs' assistant principal and a married mother of two daughters, is one of several staffers who says she uses restorative tools at home with great results. If, instead of telling her seven-year-old to get her toys off the floor, she says, "Mommy works really hard and it hurts Mommy's feelings to come home and find it so messy in here," her daughter complies more quickly. Other ways to use the habits at home include having children engaged in conflict share with each other the consequences of the actions on both sides (feeling excluded, for instance, or upset over the loss of a favorite toy). I made a personal note of this, since Anthony and I were talking about having a family, and musing about which values we would want to cultivate with our kids. Empathy and compassion were high on the list.

"We find that we have to teach empathy, and restorative practice really does teach that, because one of the restorative questions is, 'How has your behavior impacted others?'" Richetta told me. "Once we teach them that, they start to do it naturally. And when you have empathy it's much easier to forgive."

Postconflict, people are also more likely to forgive and reconcile with transgressors who they perceive as safe, either because the transgressor says the offense was unintentional or because he or she is contrite and has changed, signaling that the offense will not be repeated. When compensation is offered by an offender in an attempt to repair harm, forgiveness and reconciliation become incredibly likely. Granted, resolving minor issues such as student-teacher tension over homework is not the same as restoring harmony after a violent assault, but making the former common practice among younger generations could prevent disagreements and behavior problems from escalating to the point of violence in the first place.

When it comes to preventing and resolving conflict, empathy must flow both ways, of course. One crucial aspect of circles and restorative conferences features questions that increase awareness of how one's behavior affects others. Most people, the occasional sadist excluded, don't set out to hurt others, nor do they enjoy doing it. So usually, when a child hears a classmate she hurt describe how he feels, it enables her to understand the effects of her behavior, while also developing empathy. It's why Lee, upon hearing how his gang activities made his mother feel terrified (as opposed to just hearing her yell at him), decided to give up his "street life" and begin anew.

Jean Stracy, an adjunct professor at Denver's Regis University who has designed mediation and restorative justice programs for the past thirty years, says that the lofty goals of forgiveness and reconciliation, if they're reached at all, must come after a much more basic goal is reached: understanding. She recalls one conference she facilitated with two middle schoolers who broke into a Chicago home and stole a man's television. The man, understandably angry, merely wanted to be paid his insurance deductible in restitution. Once they got into the conference and he met the kids and learned about their deplorable home lives, though, what he wanted changed. He wanted them to pay the deductible, but he also wanted them to graduate high school, attend college, and lead productive lives. The resulting agreement: The boys would maintain a B average and send him their grades each semester. They would also get after-school jobs when they were old enough and make monthly payments toward his deductible. They did, and as they repaid the $1,200, the man kept it in a savings account, to be returned to the boys with interest to go toward community college.

"That sort of thing happens all the time," Stracy says. "People start out saying, 'I don't even know if I can be in the same room with this person, much less talk to him,' and then things change when we get in the conference—because they see this is a person and not the gorilla they were picturing."

Lee has had the same experience at City Springs. "I'd say that ninety-nine percent of every circle that I've ever done ended with an apology and the people forgave each other. I've done circles with parents, with gangsters when we were having real problems with the Bloods and Crips, when they couldn't even be in the same class because of the colors they wore. We put them in one room and did a circle, and eventually at the end they apologized to each other and we didn't have problems with them after that."

To McCullough, restorative practices are an ideal way to shape our environment so that it brings out humans' hardwired tendencies toward forgiveness, apology, and collaboration. "Although the restorative justice movement was created without reference to the principles of evolutionary psychology," he writes, "no evolutionary psychologist could do much to improve upon this combination of ingredients for making forgiveness happen."

Suburban New Jersey

Restorative practices aren't only effective in crime-prone urban areas and schools. Anyone who has attended middle or high school in a suburban setting knows that conflict is just as prevalent, but often in different ways. In 2006, I visited Franklinville, a Philadelphia bedroom community in southern New Jersey, because the town was leading the national charge in anti-bullying efforts. When someone at Delsea Middle School was punched in the face, or a flurry of nasty notes was passed, or a rumor was spread, the kids involved were sent into a classroom to face two fellow seventh- or eighth-graders trained in conflict resolution. In an approach similar to a circle, teen mediators guided the "disputants" through a process that ended with a signed agreement. While talking to one group of girls who went through the process, I felt as if I were talking to a middle-school version of myself.

It all started on a chilly November day, as the seventh-grade girls filed through the lunch line at Delsea, loading their trays with super pretzels. One by one, they carried their trays into the large dining hall full of long gray tables and sat down. On that day, their table seemed especially full. Elbows knocked and sauce spilled as the girls jostled to squeeze in.

One of them had an idea. Someone would have to leave, and they would take a vote to decide which girl it should be. Alison, a skinny twelve-year-old with sandy brown hair who wore baggy sweatshirts and basketball jerseys, went around the table and asked each girl to whisper into her ear.

"Who do you want off the table?" she asked each of them. Brittney, a petite, quiet girl with long, wavy red hair, blue eyes, and thick glasses, just looked at her and shook her head.

"I'm not voting," she said.

Alison returned to her seat and announced the results: four for Dina, five for Brittney. "Brittney," she said, "you got the most votes, you have to leave."

Brittney remained silent.

"Come on, Brittney," a couple of the other girls said, "you have to leave, we voted you off."

But Brittney didn't move. "I'm not leaving," she said.

After a moment, the girls resumed their chatting, picking at nachos and cheese and drinking Snapple. But whenever Brittney tried to join in, they ignored her. They offered each other food and passed plates over her while she sat quietly, eating her ham and cheese sandwich.

A few days later, one of the girls threatened to hit Brittney with a backpack if she didn't give up her seat in the lunchroom. Again, she refused. Then several of the girls began making fun of her clothes.

"Hey, Brittney, have you gone shopping lately?" one asked.

Brittney, feeling her classmates' stares, put her head down on the table and cried.

When Alisa and Alison received notices to report to the classroom of Frank Myers, the language arts teacher who ran the mediation program, they were nervous. "I was like, I hope I'm not in trouble," Alisa said. They went into the classroom one by one. Alisa, as the acknowledged leader of the group, went first. When she came out, Alison wanted to ask her what had happened, but Myers made sure they didn't talk. He'd found out about the incident after Brittney told the vice principal. About 70 percent of mediations happened after students reported an incident to administrators,

Myers told me, while the remaining 30 percent were reported directly to him by students or teachers.

Alison walked into the classroom and saw that four desks had been pushed together in a T. The mediators were seated across from one another, and there was one empty desk—across from Brittney. Alison sat down.

"I was scared," she told me.

Using what they'd learned from the scripts Myers prints out, the mediators introduced themselves and assured her that whatever she said would be completely confidential, unless it involved drugs, weapons, or anything life-threatening. They listed the ground rules: Be willing to solve the conflict, tell the truth, listen without interrupting, show respect, and carry out your agreement. They asked what had happened, and listened as Brittney and Alison recounted the lunchroom vote. Brittney was asked to tell her classmate how it made her feel.

"I felt really sad and left out, like a piece of garbage thrown away," she said.

Alison didn't know what to say. She'd known Brittney since the third grade, and she immediately regretted taking part in the vote.

"Sorry," she told Brittney. "I didn't mean to hurt you like that."

Myers said that if there was another incident, Alison would get detention. As Alisa had before her, she signed an agreement to welcome Brittney at the lunch table and treat her with respect.

Afterward, Brittney thought the girls might be angry with her and ask why she told on them. Instead, a few days later, they gave her a card. On the cover was a drawing of Brittney, and inside, a message that read, "We're really sorry, Brittney. Please forgive us." Below were the signatures of all of the girls at the table.

"We're friends now," Brittney told me.

I wondered if the other girls felt the same. Alisa, playing with her long brown hair, her large, beaded earrings dangling, claimed she did.

"When we actually got to know [Brittney] more, we realized she's really nice," she said. "She's not like the popular type—" She caught herself and quickly added, "But that's okay."

These practices, from restorative circles to mediation, create precisely the kind of environments that trigger people's hardwired propensity to seek and grant forgiveness, whether they choose to reconcile and carry on relationships or merely share a school or a community peacefully without antagonizing one another. Like Anthony, as I learned about these behavioral innovations, I wondered what it would have been like if we'd had such habits ingrained into our schools and institutions growing up. Most likely, my sixth-grade bullying would have been intercepted and I would have been forced to face the consequences of my behavior much earlier. Just as Churchill said that our houses shape us, our institutions shape us, too. The more we devise institutional habits that make seeking and granting forgiveness a more natural response in our communities, the more harmonious our lives will be.

Next, I wanted to examine the possibility of such collective practices in societies that have been locked in intergroup conflict and war for generations. Do such restorative practices exist? If so, how do they work?

9

Living Peace: How Innovative International Programs Are Setting the Stage for Forgiveness Between Longtime Adversaries

On a clear summer day in northern New Mexico, my mother and I visited a large, private adobe home nestled in the Pecos Mountains. This week, it was being used for an annual summer camp called Creativity for Peace, which brings Israeli and Palestinian girls to the United States with the goal of helping them get to know one another outside of their militantly separate and tension-filled lives in the Middle East. Creativity for Peace unites the young women for two weeks each summer through a series of art projects and group conversations led by Israeli and Palestinian facilitators trained in conflict resolution, then continues with programming in their home countries throughout the year.

It was almost lunchtime when we arrived, and the girls had just finished their morning session of intense discussion about their lives back home. Now, in the home where the Jewish and Palestinian girls were sharing bedrooms and doing chores together, a few girls in the kitchen prepared a Mediterranean lunch of hummus, baba ghanoush, and salad, while others lounged on the porch or talked on couches in the living room. Most of the young women participating in camp this year for the first time said they rarely had much contact with members of the "other side" back home. They lived alongside one another, yet had to travel more than seven thousand miles to have any meaningful interaction.

"Forgiveness" is not a word used at Creativity for Peace, or in other places where people are contending with blazing, unresolved conflicts. As my psychologist friend told me months earlier, when someone is standing on your toe, you don't forgive them, you ask them to get off your foot. And yet, there are aspects of the forgiveness process that can be utilized to help warring groups diffuse hostilities and arrive at some sort of agreement. When it comes to groups that have been locked in cycles of resentment for generations, the challenge is immense. That's why Creativity for Peace and other camps like it take young people out of their usual environments.

Researchers have coined a term in recent years called "competitive victimhood," which refers to a phenomenon that exacerbates and perpetuates intergroup hatred and violence. Competitive victimhood means that two groups that have been mired in conflict become entrenched in a competition over which group has suffered more, steeping new generations in the idea that their own group has suffered more than the other and is therefore entitled to act in certain ways. Dr. Masi Noor, of Liverpool John Moores University in the United Kingdom, has studied the phenomenon extensively, and says it can be applied to conflicts in places like Northern Ireland, Rwanda, and Israel-Palestine.

Competitive victimhood depends on the historical narrative that groups tell about themselves and each other. Especially when groups are separated and have little contact with the opponent, there is scarce hope of understanding the perspective or experience of their enemy. In recent years, programs designed to change this have become increasingly common. For Creativity for Peace, the goal is for the girls to get to know one another through storytelling, examining their differences, and discovering what they share. The group's motto: "An enemy is a person whose story you haven't heard."

I met the fourteen Palestinian and Israeli teens attending the 2013 camp, along with a half dozen counselors who had already been through the program and continued to attend ongoing social and leadership training events at home in Israel and in the West Bank (since 2003, more than two hundred young women have participated), at a fund-raising dinner, where they arrived for a Mediterranean buffet and live music and dancing.

Yuval Dadoosh, an Israeli with long, shiny chestnut hair and almond-shaped eyes, described the transformation she underwent since 2007, when she first attended camp: "I came like a book of answers and facts, ready to shoot a fact at any Arab like an arrow," she said. "Once I started talking to Arab women, I realized I didn't know anything about what was happening on the other side."

Majdal Natshe, a Palestinian from Ramallah with raven hair and eyes to match, told me of her unlikely friendship with Ya'ara Tal, an Israeli with a round freckled face usually lit up by a smile. "When I came here in 2008, all I knew about the other side was the military—I'd been through a lot of bombings and attacks," Majdal said. "But over the past five years, I became very close to Ya'ara. All of my Palestinian friends know I have a Jewish friend, and they're shocked."

The two kept in touch through Ya'ara's compulsory service with the Israeli army, which they both say was difficult. Ya'ara, assigned to patrol a border post along the Gaza Strip, worried that her friends might be among the long lines of Palestinians waiting to get through the checkpoint and feared having to shoot at them if something happened. At one point, they were able to get Majdal permission to visit Ya'ara and her family at their kibbutz six miles from Gaza, and she reflected upon the visit with joy and wonder. "I kept thinking, 'There's a girl from Ramallah sleeping in my house!'" she told me, laughing.

All of them acknowledged that while getting to know "the other side" had enriched their life and expanded their perspective, it was also extremely difficult. The conversations led by facilitators during the program, which are closed to observers because camp leaders worry their presence would make the girls wary of sharing, are designed to address the conflict head-on, but through personal experience. "Camp always starts with blaming, blaming, blaming," Yuval said. "It's 'You occupied me,' and 'You bombed us,' et cetera, et cetera. It's complicated, but it's about realizing that we didn't do this—we were born into it."

Frances Salles, the Creativity for Peace operations director, said the dialogue helps the girls to see each other as human beings who are all suffering amid the conflict. "We address the conflict not through politics but through personal stories. If you have an Israeli girl saying she lost five family members to suicide bombers, you can't dispute that. Or a woman from the West Bank saying her father died from a heart attack because they couldn't get through the checkpoint. It's the shared tears of compassion that form the basis for the friendships."

The young women have a powerful example in their two middle-aged housemothers—Itaf, a school administrator with olive-toned skin, and Yasmin, a blond therapist with electric blue eyes. While Itaf is a Palestinian Muslim and Yasmin is a Jew of European descent, both live near the northern Israeli city of Haifa, and they became friends years ago. Once, when Yasmin invited Itaf to stay with her family while she attended a local conference, Yasmin's daughter objected, asking with raised eyebrows, "You're inviting an Arab to stay with us?" Yasmin replied, "I'm inviting a *friend*."

I felt inspired just to be in these women's presence, watching the affectionate banter that comes with decades of friendship, and the relationships they're helping to build among young women of the new generation. "This is living peace," Itaf told me. "Not just talking about it."

Victims and Perpetrators Help Each Other Heal in Rwanda

In his office in Western Rwanda, Father Ubald Rurirangoga keeps a sepia-toned photo in a simple wooden frame. Unlike the beatific images of Jesus and the Virgin Mary gracing the walls nearby, there's no transcendent joy in this one. It shows the priest, younger and wearing a dark coat, walking alongside a mountain of corpses.

"Those were my people, my parishioners," he told me one January evening, gazing mournfully at the macabre tableau that he keeps as evidence of what happened in Rwanda in 1994, and as a reminder of why he works to ensure it will never happen again. Among the estimated one million Tutsis and moderate Hutus murdered during the genocide were Father Ubald's mother and siblings, along with an estimated 45,000 of his parishioners. "I escaped miraculously," he said. "I heard the mob was coming for me and hid at the bishop's house, then fled into Congo and on to Europe until it was over."

Before arriving in Rwanda, I'd read that here in Cyangugu, a network of farming hamlets nestled in lush, hill-studded terrain near the Congolese border, Father Ubald brought Rwandan genocide survivors and perpetrators together in a reconciliation program that ended in some sort of forgiveness ceremony. To find out more, I set out for the Western province. Since outside the capital most people spoke only Kinyarwandan fluently, I brought along Solange, a Rwandan interpreter about my age whom I met through a journalist friend. During a six-hour bus ride from Kigali that wound through Africa's highest protected mountain rain forest, Nyungwe National Park, we dialed the priest's cell number repeatedly to let him know when we'd be arriving. No answer. Solange wasn't surprised. "He's very famous in Rwanda," she told me. "Tens of thousands of people travel from far away just to see him give Mass."

Finally, Solange reached him as the bus pulled into the depot, and he arrived to pick us up a short time later. Father Ubald stepped down from a Land Cruiser to shake our hands and load our luggage. I was blinded by white: Long, Catholic vestments cloaked his medium-sized frame, and a huge, toothy smile beamed from his face, which was the shade of rich soil. A pair of stylish, merlot-toned Ray-Bans set off his thick, caterpillar eyebrows and gave him a sophisticated look. He chatted amiably about the Mass he'd just given as we rolled on rutted reddish dirt roads through brilliant, emerald-green countryside filled with rice fields, banana plants, and the occasional troupe of ambling cows or goats.

Soon we arrived at the Cyangugu Pastoral Center, a collection of brick buildings that sits atop a hill overlooking Lake Kivu, one of the African great lakes. The gray-blue water shimmered under the sinking sun. "Beautiful," I said as we pulled into the parking lot. Even so, I couldn't help thinking about the thousands of corpses dumped in these waters twenty years ago. They washed up on the shores of Congo for months.

"Tomorrow we'll talk with survivors and perpetrators who are now friends," Father Ubald said, "You won't believe it. But now you rest, and I need to go to the bank. You see, my daughter is here."

Daughter? A priest?

"Well, she's practically my daughter," he explained. "Her father killed my mother and I forgave him, and then I took care of her and her brothers and sisters while he's been in prison. She is here because she's on her way to medical school in Burundi and has come for school fees."

My head swam. Though I'd spent months talking to people who had forgiven in extraordinary circumstances, his breezy mention of how he helped raise the children of his mother's killer strained my mind. That evening he showed me the black-and-white photo of the dead, and the following day he told me how and why he came to create an in-depth program to facilitate reconciliation among genocide victims and perpetrators.

Within months of escaping with his life and losing his family and parishioners, he told me, he made a pilgrimage to the shrine at Lourdes, France. While he prayed, grief-stricken and inconsolable, he had a revelation: the only way such a monstrous wound could be healed, and such horrific crimes could be prevented, was through true forgiveness and apology. He began preaching about reconciliation in the late nineties, even visiting prisons to talk to the hundreds of thousands of genocide convicts about how to repent, forgive themselves, and apologize to their victims' families.

During a 2005 prison visit, a man approached the priest. "He said, 'Father, I have something to tell you: I killed your mother,'" Father Ubald said. The prisoner wept and begged for the priest's forgiveness. For a moment, he felt shock and anger pin him in place. But then he thought of his epiphany at Lourdes, his promise to be merciful, and Jesus' exhortation to love your enemies. He took a deep breath and embraced the man.

Later, Father Ubald would get to know this man and find that his wife had died of an illness, his eldest son was getting bullied at school for being the son of a murderer, and the children were languishing with distant relatives who didn't have enough money to support them. That's when Father

Ubald stepped in to pay their school fees and mentor them. He's now help-ing the daughter, Gisele, to attend medical school in neighboring Burundi.

Around that time, the government resurrected the traditional commu-nity Gacaca courts to process genocide cases. The courts featured testimony from perpetrators, victims, and witnesses before their communities, and allowed perpetrators reduced sentences if they confessed and apologized. While the community courts were a somewhat efficient way to process mil-lions of murder cases in just a few years, most Rwandans acknowledge their flaws, from retraumatizing victims to setting perpetrators free after insin-cere apologies and pressuring survivors to forgive without sufficient mental health support. "The Gacaca courts weren't enough," Father Ubald told me, "The people still had to be reintegrated." In 2009, he began a formal six-month program on repentance, apology, and forgiveness. While repentance and apology both broadly mean showing remorse, apology refers to seeking forgiveness of one's victims, while repentance is the process of showing re-morse before God and seeking absolution—or, according to *Merriam-Webster's*, to "turn from sin and dedicate oneself to the amendment of one's life." This is how Father Ubald and most Christians view repentance, and it is one of the first steps for perpetrators in his program, which meets twice weekly and is led by sixteen parish facilitators.

Many survivors do the six-month program with the people who killed their relatives, and there is a lot of sharing and deep listening. The gradua-tion is a ceremony in which perpetrators kneel, survivors pray for them, and they hug in a gesture of peace. "If people are not ready, they repeat the whole process," Father Ubald says. "It's very deep reflection and learning."

Dialogue and Cooperation

I would discover that the Mushaka program founded by Father Ubald hap-pens to be a model embodiment of research-tested practices that experts say facilitate intergroup forgiveness. Dr. Ervin Staub, a professor at the Uni-

versity of Massachusetts at Amherst, has spent decades studying mass violence around the world, as well as ways to diffuse and prevent it. In a 2013
research review in *American Psychologist*, he highlights the importance of
developing more positive attitudes toward "the other," through meaningful
contact and collaboration. "The depth and quality of contact matters," he
writes, pointing out that most effective is when people collaborate on joint
goals. Many rescuers of Jews during the Holocaust, for example, grew up
in families that had positive relations with people outside the dominant
"Aryan" group. "Through deep contact and joint projects, people can develop relationships and see the other's humanity," Staub writes. "Deep contact can also lead people to see themselves and others as part of a common
in-group."

The Robbers Cave experiment showed this concept in action back in
1954. University of Oklahoma researchers selected twenty-two adolescent
boys from similar backgrounds (lower-middle-class Protestant), divided
them into two groups, and brought them to the Boy Scouts of America
camp at Robbers Cave State Park. The two groups were at first kept separate
and encouraged to bond within their own group through various activities.
One group named itself the Rattlers, the other, the Eagles. The two groups
soon grew competitive and began calling each other names in the cafeteria
and singing derogatory songs about each other. At one point they nearly
came to blows.

When the researchers introduced events intended to be conciliatory,
like joint movie nights and a Fourth of July firecracker celebration, the
tensions remained. Yet when they introduced a different type of activity—
a goal that both groups needed or wanted to reach but could not be reached
by one group alone—the results changed dramatically. The camp staff announced that the water supply, housed in a reservoir atop a nearby hill, had
failed after being vandalized, for instance. The boys, in one large group,
made their way to the reservoir and investigated. Upon finding an outlet
faucet stuffed with a sack, they worked as one team to clear it, voicing suggestions and taking turns without regard to who was a Rattler or an Eagle.
After forty-five minutes, the pipe was cleared, and the Rattler-Eagle divi-

sion had fallen away. They rejoiced as one large group. The results were similarly cooperative when the researchers introduced a stuck vehicle that had to be mobilized in order to deliver camp food provisions.

More recently, studies in classroom settings have shown that children from different racial, ethnic, and socioeconomic groups who work on shared tasks in cooperative learning environments developed more positive attitudes toward each other.

The science of cooperation has become well-publicized in various areas of research, from the classroom to the boardroom, and it harkens back to McCullough's theory about why forgiveness is a hardwired evolutionary response in the first place: it aids cooperation that leads to thriving communities. But must forgiveness always come first, as the handmaiden of cooperation? The Robbers Cave experiment and subsequent classroom research seems to suggest that cooperation toward a shared goal can lead to forgiveness by taking precedence over past disputes and uniting separate groups.

While collaboration on a shared need is especially effective, even mere positive contact has the power to change groups' perceptions of one another. A 2009 study found that merely guiding people to envision a sequence of positive interactions with a member of another group led to more positive attitudes toward that group, and a 2005 study in Sri Lanka found that when Sinhalese and Tamils spent four days together doing educational activities, their attitudes were still more positive a year later compared to a control group.

Another way to help groups discover what they share is through educational curriculum and media. Staub developed a radio drama in Rwanda that explored themes of intergroup violence and reconciliation in a fictional show about two imaginary towns. When the broadcast of "New Dawn" began, he had six groups of people agree to listen to it regularly, while another six groups agreed to listen to a different, unrelated program. When he surveyed both groups a year later, he found that the people who listened to his drama had improved views toward the other group, unlike the control group. One village even reported that after listening to "New

Dawn," they approached a neighboring village where they had killed people during the genocide. They apologized, asked for forgiveness, and helped these neighbors work their land.

In educational settings, students exposed to learning about both sides of faraway conflicts are more likely to understand the perspective of an opposing group closer to home. A 2004 study found that Israelis who studied both sides of the Northern Ireland conflict were better able to see the Palestinian perspective.

One of the most powerful ways to increase groups' mutual empathy is through the sharing of testimonials and what therapists call "empathic listening." Since the South African Truth and Reconciliation Commission began the tradition of using victim and witness testimony to determine what happened and establish "historic memory," such testimonials have become a hallmark of subsequent efforts to reconcile opposing groups. Hearing and sharing such testimonials can trigger trauma symptoms for survivors, but it still alters people's views of "the other."

Rwandan survivors and perpetrators assessed before and after participating in the Gacaca courts suffered great emotional upset and retriggered trauma symptoms while giving and hearing testimony, but they also showed less negative views about each other afterward. Similarly, when white South Africans learned through testimonies and education about the inhumane practices of the apartheid government, they developed more conciliatory attitudes toward blacks.

The end goal of all of these efforts is to help groups relate to one another and see themselves as one common, unified group (humans). After all, as McCullough and other social scientists have pointed out, one environmental factor that makes forgiveness more likely is being interdependent and belonging to the same group. What if we expanded the "group" to include everyone? Jews, for instance, were much more likely to forgive Germans for the Holocaust when presented with historical narratives that identified the Nazis as human beings more than merely as Germans.

People who belong to the same family group, or "tribe," experience higher production of the brain chemical oxytocin when they're together.

Oxytocin is often referred to as the "bonding hormone" because it plays a large role in sex and falling in love, childbirth and breast feeding, among other relationship-building activities. Research also shows that it plays a role in empathy. In one study, half of the participants—their oxytocin levels measured at the outset—watched an emotional scene, while the other half watched a non-emotional scene. They rated their emotional reactions, then played a game involving monetary awards. Those who had empathetic reactions to the scene they watched showed increased oxytocin levels while those of the control group remained static, and also proved more generous during the game. Another study indicates that just as empathy raises oxytocin levels—and generosity—administering doses of oxytocin can in turn increase people's empathy and generosity, even toward people who aren't necessarily part of the family or "tribe." The group that took doses of oxytocin, when presented with a decision about how to split a sum of money with a stranger, offered 80 percent more money than the group that took the placebo.

Okay, so if higher oxytocin levels make for more empathetic, generous people, maybe they also increase the likelihood of sharing and consensus, even with opponents. Even if that's true, though, it would be difficult to go around forcing oxytocin nasal spray on warring groups. What we can do, though, is ingrain mediation-building mechanisms throughout institutions and in conflict-ridden areas. In that sense, activities that increase mutual understanding and empathy, and facilitate cooperation toward shared goals, could serve as a sort of behavioral oxytocin that moves formerly warring groups closer to becoming one.

On our second day in Cyangugu, Solange and I met around 20 of the 300 survivors and perpetrators who'd graduated from the class that Father Ubald started in 2009. Sitting in a small brick classroom near the Mushaka church, they described how the sixteen course facilitators provided a forum for a sort of group therapy experience grounded in sharing and empathic listening. Victims, who often do the course with the perpetrators who hurt them or killed their family members, have the opportunity to ask unanswered questions about how their loves ones died so they can have closure, while perpetrators listen to victims talk about the impact of the violence. Ultimately, they apologize and provide some sort of restitution.

"It's not just about words, it's about action," said facilitator Aloys Unemeyimana, a Hutu who saved 122 Tutsis during the slaughter by hiding them in his parish room and guiding them over the border at night. Some perpetrators help their victims cultivate crops, while others give them goats or other valuable animals.

In addition to the one-on-one reconciliation process, every graduating class at the Mushaka parish creates a joint development project, the most recent being a communal vegetable garden. Graduates told us that the process helped them to heal and get along with their neighbors, a meaningful accomplishment in a country where genocide convicts are continuously completing sentences and being returned to their communities.

Standing with her twenty-year-old son, a petite forty-year-old woman named Jeanne Mukantwal told of how her husband was killed by a friend while she was four weeks pregnant. The killer, a tall, lanky man with broad facial features and sand-colored skin named Innocent Gashema, stood beside her. He explained that when he saw Jeanne's husband, Emile, whom he knew to be Tutsi, walking through town already badly wounded by other Hutus, he approached him with his machete to finish him off. Emile begged Gashema to kill him at home. The other man obliged, and Jeanne, hiding nearby, saw his mutilated body. "I threw his body in a latrine," Gashema told us, stone-faced. "By the time I got back here from Congo a few months later, I felt guilty and turned myself in. I was haunted by what I'd done."

When he finished his ten-year prison sentence and returned to Mushaka, he sought Jeanne out in the banana fields. At first, she ignored him. "It was very hard because we were recently married, still in the honeymoon phase, when my husband was killed," she told me, "To see what he went through, seeing his body—I had a headache for seven years. When Gashema returned from prison and I saw him around town, I felt just as bad as when it happened. Seeing him alive and healthy, walking around,

when I would never see my husband again . . . I wanted him to die in jail."
But Gashema kept showing up and insisting on helping her in the field. "I
said, 'I'm sorry,'" Gashema told me. "'I was his friend.'" Jeanne just wept.

Around this time, Jeanne heard Father Ubald preaching about forgiveness, and she decided to try the program, inviting Gashema to do it with
her. During the class, Jeanne told me, Gashema helped her son by telling
him how his father died and apologizing for killing him. She hadn't told her
son exactly what happened to Emile, wanting to protect him, but not knowing proved damaging. The boy had struggled with depression and dropped
out of school. After learning the truth from Gashema, he returned to his
studies and passed the standardized test for his grade level. "I was so happy
to see my son focusing and less upset," Jeanne said. She said she eventually
forgave the man who murdered her son's father. "It helped me a lot," she
told me.

Jeanne's son remained silent, his body as tightly wound as a spool of
thread and his mouth a straight line. He, his mother, and Gashema posed
for a photo together, holding hands, and for a fraction of a second, I saw a
smile flicker across his face. Before I bid them farewell, Gashema said, "I do
my best to support them by working the field and helping grow food—I will
never do what I did again. No matter who, or what government, told me to
do it, I would not."

Another perpetrator, Nicola Nikuze, a tiny middle-aged man with
kind, sad eyes and a collared shirt, told of how he came to apologize to his
victims. "During the genocide I became a different person. I killed people.
One day I led an attack and we killed a man named John. He was my neighbor." Why? I asked. And how did he feel afterward? "I was trained to do it
by the government," he said. "What was in my mind was to kill Tutsi—that
is all. We thought we would just take their properties, that there wouldn't
be consequences because the government told us to do it—we weren't
thinking ahead."

After killing John, Nicola and his comrades drank beer and celebrated
the land and belongings they'd pillaged. "I felt nothing until jail," he said.
"Then I began to feel guilty—to wonder, why did I do that?" His mournful

eyes widened and welled up. It was difficult to imagine this tearful man, at roughly my age, hacking people up with machetes and toasting to stealing their belongings. He explained that in prison, he heard Father Ubald preaching about taking responsibility and apologizing. "The government people told us that if we told our crimes to the Gacaca court we could go free, but I didn't trust that," he said. "It seemed like a trick."

Nicola was the first of several perpetrators who told me this. They felt the government was saying that they killed through no fault of their own, as mere puppets of an evil regime with no free will, and it struck them as insulting and false. "We didn't trust the Truth and Reconciliation Commission because they said, 'It wasn't your fault,'" a man named Teresphore told me. "But we did it, we were guilty. Why would they say it wasn't our fault? Father Ubald told us that we are all created in God's image and that hurting others is sinning against God. That made a lot more sense. Father Ubald said that first, we had to repent before God and forgive ourselves. Then, we would think about others and seeking their forgiveness."

Nicola, moved by Father Ubald to confess and apologize, was terrified to face the people whose relatives he killed. "How could I face them, speak to them after what I did?" he told me. Yet he confessed before the Gacaca court proceeding. "I humbly begged for forgiveness," he said. "I believed and felt deeply all that I said, and I was lucky that the family believed I was sincere."

After he was freed he visited John's widow to apologize again, and again, she forgave him. Then they attended the priest's program together. When one of the widows' children voiced anger at this, Nicola told us, the woman held a family meeting and requested her son listen to Nicola apologize. This resistant son eventually invited Nicola to his wedding and asked him to be the godfather of his children. "Now, we all live peacefully as friends—I help the widow gather firewood and fix things at the house," he told me. "My calling is to lead former Interahamwe to take responsibility for what they did and repair the damage however possible."

Listening to these stories of perpetrators seeking forgiveness and survivors offering it, I thought about an example of the opposite. Jean-Baptiste

Ntakirutimana, a Tutsi man whom I'd met in Kigali, had sought out the Hutu neighbor who killed his mother and visited him in prison. Only after Jean-Baptiste showed the prisoner compassion and willingness to forgive did the killer show remorse and apologize. An educated man who has worked within international development organizations and the United Nations, Jean-Baptiste is average-sized, but his presence makes him seem much taller. I met him through a British colleague, and he invited me to the attractive home he shares with his wife in a Kigali suburb. At his dining room table over tea, he told me that he managed to be evacuated from Kigali during the genocide with a Canadian teacher friend. He didn't know what was happening to his large family in a village several hours away near Butare, but when he returned months later, he found out they were all dead.

The remaining townspeople told him that most of the area's Tutsis had been killed in the local stadium, but that no one wanted to kill his mother, Generosa, since she was a respected elder from a family with a farm, and known to feed the town's poorer residents. They recalled that finally, one man agreed to "do the job." His name was Innocent—not a rare name in Rwanda—and Jean-Baptiste remembered him as a young neighbor who had often eaten at his parents' table. After he learned the identity of his mother's killer, Jean-Baptiste couldn't stop thinking about him.

This neighbor whom he hadn't seen in years and who was now in prison became the focal point for Jean-Baptiste's profound sadness and anger at having lost more than sixty family members and being left alone in the world. "Most of us here in Rwanda," he told me, "are walking upon the ruins of our lives." His ruins were haunted by images and thoughts of Innocent. "I could only sleep a few hours each week, and when I did I'd have nightmares. He was in them," Jean-Baptiste told me. "He was in my mind . . . I wanted him out of my mind."

Jean-Baptiste grew older, and as he pursued a master's degree in international development in England, he became an increasingly devout Christian. He was raised Catholic but gravitated toward the evangelical teachings about Jesus. Like Chantal and Father Ubald, he spoke not of a conceptual Christ, but of a direct relationship with God. Eventually, after months of intensive prayer, the epiphany he attributes to God directed him to pray and fast and purify himself of all negativity, including anger, division, and bitterness. As he prayed, he began to think more and more about visiting Innocent in prison, with the intention of forgiving him.

After two forty-day periods of praying and eating only one meal per day, Jean-Baptiste felt ready to visit Innocent. Sentenced to twenty-eight years for killing multiple people, Innocent was at Mpanga International Prison in Nyanza District, where many of the facility's eight thousand prisoners are genocide convicts. Jean-Baptiste brought a friend for support. When they found themselves face-to-face with Innocent, the three of them seated on a bench in a hallway, they were enveloped by a tense silence. Jean-Baptiste could hear his own heart hammering. Glancing sideways at Innocent, he noticed the man's lips were trembling. "I wasn't there, Innocent," he began. "Please tell me what happened." Innocent began on the day the president's plane was shot down and the genocide began, telling how he gathered with a group of other men and went on a killing spree. Once he started, the words poured out, as if he'd been waiting years for someone to ask him.

When Innocent got to the day when he killed Generosa, Jean-Baptiste swallowed hard and told him to go on. At the description of the first machete blow, he told me, "I went off, far away, as if I were flying." He wept. Silently, he told God he was going mad. Immediately, he said, he felt a soft breeze sweep down over his head, "as if it were untying knots in my neck and brain. My chest, which felt tight and numb as a rock, began to relax." When I said some people might have a hard time believing that, he shrugged. "Forgiveness is not human," he told me. "I didn't have the power to meet Innocent and forgive him—that power did not come from me."

Jean-Baptiste asked Innocent what he would tell his mother if she were there. "I would ask her for food," the man replied, seemingly oblivious to how this would sound to the man whose mother he murdered. Food? I had actually seen a brief interview with both Jean-Baptiste and Innocent in a documentary called *Beyond Right and Wrong*, and Innocent acknowledged in the film that this was his response. I was floored by this. Jean-

Baptiste told me that he was surprised and disappointed, but maintained his composure and did his best to be compassionate.

"I told him I had some cash and could give him some," he said. Then he asked again, what would he say to her if she were here?

Innocent said he'd ask her to come visit him, because his wife and children were ashamed of him and stopped visiting two years prior.

Jean-Baptiste's friend, unable to contain himself, burst out, "Can't you apologize and ask for forgiveness?!" I would have said, or at least felt, the same thing. Yet Innocent's reply was revealing.

"Ask for forgiveness?" he said. "How could I? She fed me along with her own children, and I killed her. How do you expect me to apologize and ask forgiveness for that?" At this, the stone wall of his face cracked and emotion spilled out. His eyes welled. He looked miserable. "I'm so sorry." Jean-Baptiste told him that he forgave him.

Looking back, Jean-Baptiste says seeing that Innocent's pain was real was the turning point for him. "If you don't feel someone's hurt, you can't truly forgive," he said, "Only when you have been united in suffering can you find reconciliation." Seeing Innocent's tears and shame changed everything for Jean-Baptiste. And yet it seems like Innocent wouldn't have shown his true emotions, were it not for the extraordinary patience and understanding that Jean-Baptiste showed him. Still troubled by Innocent's initial lack of remorse, I asked about it again. "Shame," Jean-Baptiste said. "Think about when you were a kid and you stayed out past your curfew. You were ashamed and probably didn't apologize, right? And we're talking about someone who killed babies, mothers, children. Can you imagine the shame?"

At the end of their meeting, Jean-Baptiste said, Innocent was smiling. Jean-Baptiste felt, as he put it, "incredibly light." Because he had told Innocent he would, Jean-Baptiste later visited the man's wife and children. He told Innocent's wife about his prison visit, and soon after, she brought the children to see their father at Mpango. "It's like I'm a family member now," Jean-Baptiste told me. "Whenever I'm in that area she's the first to come visit." In April 2011, Jean-Baptiste had his mother's remains exhumed from where they lay after the genocide. With the help of local villagers, some of whom had killed in 1994, he reburied her in a commemoration ceremony. At the memorial, Innocent's wife spoke publicly, saying she was sorry for what her husband did and grateful for Jean-Baptiste's reaching out to her family. Jean-Baptiste has since founded an organization dedicated to helping people take responsibility for their actions and forgive.

On my last day in Cyangugu, I stood with thousands of people in a rural village near the Congolese border to hear Father Ubald deliver one of his famous masses. Between the midmorning sun and the multicolored *kitenge* skirts worn by many of the women near me, I had to shade my eyes. Dressed in his white robes, Father Ubald stood on an outdoor stage with several other priests and a chorus. Below, the people sang and held their hands aloft, waving back and forth like reeds in the wind. Some held umbrellas to shade themselves from the sun; others sat on stumps or rocks on the edge of the crowd.

Unlike most church leaders in Rwanda, Father Ubald wove the genocide—and the challenge of healing—throughout Bible stories about Jesus. He told the crowd how even now, he wondered if there was anything he could have done to prevent what happened in 1994. "Afterward I cried all the time, I couldn't think," he said. "The way to heal and move on—the only way—is forgiveness." The people grew quiet and somber then. The dancing and clapping and swaying had stopped, and I noticed many people looking down and shifting their feet. "I have done what I am asking you all to do," Father Ubald continued, telling them the story of the daughter of the man who killed his mother. "She is my daughter," he said. "I take care of her." Surprised murmurs rustled through the crowd.

"We must have empathy for each other," he told them, and mentioned a new government initiative promoting national solidarity. "In this 'I am Rwandan' campaign, we are celebrating being Rwandan. This is not a country only for Hutus or only for Tutsis, this is a country for us all. We are all Rwandan."

Next came songs, prayers, and communion. Afterward, Father Ubald stood center stage and spread out his arms. "Who is ready for forgiveness?"

A long silence. And then, a middle-aged woman in a red *kitenge* approached the stage, took the mic, and announced that she was now ready to forgive the people who killed her husband. "Even if they don't seek forgiveness," she told the crowd, "I am ready." The throngs stirred and parted to reveal a man. He came forward to stand next to the woman, who now openly wept. He helped kill her husband, he admitted, and turned toward her. "I am sorry for what I did. I beg your pardon." They shook hands, and he turned to the audience. "I also apologize to the community, to all of you," he said. He and the woman embraced.

The colorful parade of loving-kindness continued into the afternoon, as the sun sank lower and grew hotter. A young woman said she was ready to forgive the killer of her brother. A man said he forgave the man who stole his property and then tried to kill him when he returned to claim it. On and on it went. Overwhelmed and exhausted by the emotion, the crowds, and the beating sun, I looked up, as if I could get more air if I searched for it above the masses. High in the grayish-blue sky, two African hawks soared over the church steeple and its collage of stained glass. As the birds floated through the air, their wings seemed to part a lingering haze of clouds, clearing the sky to leave it all the more blue, all the more vast, and as blank as a fresh canvas.

The peace-building practices featured in this chapter utilize the crucial process of sharing and being heard, grieving and letting go, and for communities, they harness the development of empathy, interdependence, and mutual value, as well as apology and behavior modification that decreases hostile words and acts. If such systems were more widespread in families and institutions across cultures and societies, I concluded, we would live in a different world.

The stories of people like the Mushaka graduates, and Majdal and Ya'ara, are a reminder that just as humans are capable of extreme meanness and violence, from bullying and parental abuse to genocide, we also have the capacity for incredible healing, profound love, and feats of reconciliation and collaboration. I didn't always see it that way. I remember once, when I was living in Central America in my early twenties, despairing the world's violence and inequality, my editor at the local economic and political newsletter where I worked chided me for being so negative. "Sure, all of that bad stuff is true," he told me as we sat sipping coffee on his porch, perched atop a hill overlooking the outskirts of Guatemala City. "But a lot of other things are true, too." He gestured at his ten-year-old daughter, Pilar, playing in the front yard, and beyond her, the rolling emerald hills and majestic volcano rising to meet the sky above them. "When you get upset, just look at Pilar, or at the view, or at how people help each other and love each other in spite of it all."

He was right. In my explorations of the nature of forgiveness, I realized that in many ways, forgiveness is the willingness to place more attention on the good than on the bad. It means taking on a view of life, and a practice of living it, that enables you to experience more joy and love while also giving more joy and love to others. When I find myself clutched in the grip of anger or blame, I think of people like Azim and Chantal. If Azim can forgive and see the beauty in life after losing his son, and Chantal can do it after surviving a massacre and sexual slavery, I believe the rest of us can at least do our best to follow their lead.

10

Orange-Yellow Streams of Light: A Forgiveness Ceremony

On a crisp Colorado afternoon, I drove into the heart of White River National Forest. The snowy peaks of the Collegiate Range swung into view against the azure sky, the sun bathing the ridges and valleys in bright golden light. The edges of everything looked sharp and clean, as if rain had scrubbed the wilderness of any residue, clouds, or softness. I felt about as washed clean as the view looked, with the same sharp edges. I'd just attended a funeral and delivered a eulogy for a woman named Nicole, whom I'd written about two years prior. We'd grown close over the months that I followed her treatment for breast cancer, with which she'd been diagnosed at twenty-five, while pregnant with her first child. She was twenty-nine when she died. Her daughter was four. Having cried for most of the morning, I had no tears left. In their place was a clear, hollowed-out calm.

I drove my Subaru through a ranch gate and parked near a compound of wooden cabins, where a retreat was being held by a mentoring organization named Colorado Youth at Risk. The group pairs adult mentors with teens living in poverty and grappling with the effects of urban violence. When I arrived, the teens and mentors were on the ropes course in a wide forest clearing. They sported helmets and cheered each other on as they scaled walls, did trust falls, and leapt off the top of what looked like a telephone pole in an attempt to grab a trapeze overhead. Behind it all was the notion that just as violence, poverty, and neglect were obstacles for these young people, so were fear and hopelessness, hatred and resentment. One of the activities designed to help free them from emotionally crippling patterns was the reason I'd come: a forgiveness ceremony.

It was held in a large common room attached to the dining hall in the main log cabin. While outside the sun sank over the ridge and blanketed the forest with a dim violet glow, I helped the mentors stack chairs and clear the hardwood floor. Blazes were lit in both of the room's large fireplaces. The lights were dimmed; small tables were set with lit candles. Colorado Youth at Risk is not a religious organization, but the intention for the evening was clearly to create an atmosphere that felt sacred. Shortly after dark, mentors quietly led groups of teenagers into the room. During the course of the weekend, these young people had confided stories of abuse and gang rivalries, of parents who'd been deported, and babies they'd had at fourteen. Tonight, they would confront those stories in an entirely new way. They brought blankets and sleeping bags, and each small group of mentors and mentees settled into a cozy circle on the floor.

Two girls wearing hoodies and fluffy slippers made room for me in one of the groups, and I settled into the circle. Up front, Patrick Kraus, a middle-aged retreat facilitator with piercing blue eyes and a booming voice, sat in a director's chair. The group listened as Patrick described how his father used to get drunk, yell, and hit him with sticks. He spoke of the time his father stole Patrick's van from the high school parking lot. "That was it," Patrick said. "I refused to speak to him. I tore up his letters. I didn't give a shit."

Ten years later, Patrick said his mother called to say that his father had died. At the funeral, all the rage rushed back. "I was so angry at him, even in the casket," he told the students and mentors. "My wife did something brave. She said, 'Honey, you have to deal with this. I know he was shitty, but look at you.' I said, 'What do you want me to do, forgive him?'" There was incredulity in his voice, and looking around, I could see the teenagers shared it. But Patrick told them that he couldn't get his wife's suggestion out of his mind, and he ultimately decided to forgive his father. "I looked up at the ceiling and said, Dad, what you did hurt me. And I miss you. And I forgive you."

"I was still upset," he said, "but my love for my father began to return.

As it did, I started to wonder why my father behaved the way he did." He asked around. His aunts told him how their father, Patrick's grandfather, was an alcoholic, too, and used to punch Patrick's father in the face while drunk. His aunts also said that Patrick's dad had eczema as a kid, and their parents were so disgusted by the weeping sores that they made him eat meals outside, alone. Retelling these discoveries and reliving the shame of not having known them before his father died, Patrick's voice broke. "It was too late," he said. "I beat myself up for never having the courage to sit him down and talk to him like a man." After a while, though, he said he realized that if he could forgive his father, then maybe he could forgive himself, too.

"Forgiving him didn't mean he won or that his actions were right," he said, leaning in toward the teenagers. "It allowed me to move on with my life. I can love freely, I can be a father. I'm afraid of what kind of father I would have been if I didn't go through this process." In the silence, the fire cracked and popped, and people shifted their weight. Patrick slowly scanned the room, locking eyes as he went. "No one can make you forgive," he said. "But you see what's possible if and when you do." At that point, the mentors, who would also participate in the ceremony, handed out blank sheets of paper and pens, and he gave instructions: "Write one letter to the one person you know you need to write to move on, and one letter to yourself. A lot of you are carrying around a lot of regret and shame. So write your letters, and then take them over to the fires and let the fires help you forgive."

In the silence of the log cabin during the forgiveness ceremony, I stared at the two sheets of blank paper in my lap. Most of the teens and mentors were bent over their papers, writing. I spotted Tre, a tall, skinny fifteen-year-old known for his jokes and wisecracks. He'd expected the retreat to be "a load of crap," he would later tell me, but now he sat quietly, genuinely moved by Patrick's story of forgiving his father. Based on the number of people who'd disappointed him, Tre could have written a lot of letters: His mother was in prison for unlawfully carrying a concealed weapon and possessing narcotics, and had been behind bars for most of her son's life; he hadn't seen his father in years ("The only thing he ever gave me was his sperm and a football," Tre would tell me); and his great-grandmother beat him with belts, switches, and butter knives when he didn't do his chores.

Tre decided to begin his letter with what was troubling him most. He and his ex-girlfriend had conceived a child, and after they discovered the sex (male) and discussed names, she got an abortion without telling him. He had dreamed of being a good father, and though he knew he wasn't anywhere near ready to have a child, he was devastated. When he saw his friends buying diapers and talking about their baby mamas, he felt bereft. And guilty. He wrote to this unborn son and asked for forgiveness for summoning him to the world too early and finding out he was gone too late. Then he forgave himself. In that quiet, dimly lit room, he felt as if he were stepping out of time and space into some alternate universe, where he could communicate with this son he'd imagined, at once meeting him and letting him go.

Emily, twenty-one, a petite blond college student and mentor with sapphire eyes, knew exactly whom she would write. Her father. She had adored him until the year she turned ten and he was arrested and convicted of operating a meth lab from their basement. As she wrote her letter, Emily felt the hatred and shame she'd felt for her father ever since he was busted. She also realized how strongly connected that experience was with the self-loathing she began to experience around the same time. As children so often do, she had linked his behavior with her worth (*Why wasn't I good enough for him to stop?*). This self-loathing led to an eating disorder, from which she had only recently recovered. She still felt angry as she wrote, but there was something cathartic about it, telling her father how she felt with the intention of forgiving him.

Nearby, Jason St. Julien, thirty-one, a strapping black attorney and mentor, sat reliving one of his earliest and most vicious experiences of racism. As an eighth grader in Louisiana, he was kissing his white girlfriend at a house party when the host's father discovered them. This man, white and burly and loud, became enraged. He screamed in Jason's face. He called him a monkey over and over again at the top of his lungs. During the ceremony, Jason imagined that red-faced white man who yelled at him in the eighth grade. *Mr. Smith,* he wrote, *I forgive you for calling me a monkey. I forgive you for believing I was any less of a man because I'm black . . . I understand that at that time you were doing the best you could, but your best was wrong and I was just a kid. I forgive you for everything you did. You no longer have any power over my life. I'm free.*

Crying openly for the first time in his life, Jason flipped the paper over and addressed himself. *I forgive you for believing the lies.* He wrote this over and over again. As he did, he saw in his mind's eye the subsequent insults or slurs that had previously confirmed his belief that he wasn't worthy because he was black. (At a football tailgate party during law school, where he was the only black man in his graduating class, a jubilant and clueless white guy said to him, "We're cool, right? You're my nigger!") Other memories came rushing back, too, and he was surprised to realize that his buying into the lie that his color made him inadequate may have caused him to suspect racism where it didn't exist. (When a girl asked him to a dance, for instance, he wondered if it was only to show charity to the token black kid, not because she actually liked him.) As he finished his letter to himself, he felt a sense of what he would later call "total newness, like there was a weight off my chest and I could finally breathe."

As those around me wrote feverishly, some already rising to take their letters to the fires, I stared at my still-blank pages. To whom would I write? My ex-boyfriend? I didn't think of him much these days, but I wasn't thrilled to see him at social gatherings. I didn't feel like writing to him. I didn't feel like writing to anyone. I'd spent half the day at a funeral, and I was exhausted. I imagined slipping out and going to bed. But when my eyes flicked toward the door, they rested on the facilitator who'd told me earlier, "Don't miss the opportunity to do the exercise—it's worth it."

I started with Mike. I wrote that I forgave him for getting drunk on stage and embarrassing himself and me in the Play. Mostly, though, I forgave him for not being the right person for me, nor I for him. After all, I was the one who tried to continue a relationship that I didn't even feel good about, probably out of some antiquated fear of winding up ancient and alone surrounded by dusty books and exotic pets. He wasn't a devil, he was just a guy. Then I broadened my scope. I forgave the past employers who couldn't afford to pay me more and the publishing executives who told me I wasn't right for a job. I forgave the magazine owner who still owed me $1,200 for a story I did two years earlier, and I forgave the countless editors who rejected story ideas that I found important and compelling. Silly as it may sound, I also forgave the Great Recession and the collapse of journalism, which had gone from being a profession in which you could make a living into more of an artistic pursuit that doesn't necessarily pay the bills.

In my second letter, I forgave myself for betraying Liz back in the sixth grade. I forgave myself for the harsh comments I was sometimes guilty of spitting at Anthony while in a foul mood. I forgave myself for not making more money and for not owning a house and for not having published the books or having the children I thought I should have by age thirty-five. And then I thought about the funeral I'd just attended, and the tears I thought I'd exhausted returned, pouring onto the page and smudging the words. Months earlier, I found out through Facebook that Nicole's terminal cancer—temporarily halted by chemo—had reappeared in the form of brain and spinal cord tumors. I texted her once, but I never called. I told myself that I didn't want to intrude, and that was partly true. But also true was that I hated the idea of her dying, of her not being around to parent her daughter or smile and give people pep talks while she was the one getting chemo. I didn't want to see it, and I didn't want to hear it. But now, just as Patrick had said of his father, it was too late. Nicole, just months shy of her thirtieth birthday, had been robbed of the opportunity to see her daughter grow up, and I had robbed myself of the opportunity to say goodbye.

As I wept, I realized that my forgiveness—just like my pain and disappointment and anger—wasn't as small as one breakup or one rejection letter or even one death. It was so much bigger and wider and deeper than that. It was as big as forgiving the world, as forgiving life itself. Growing up, I heard the phrase "Life isn't fair" as much as anyone else, and I thought I knew what it meant. I did not. I convinced myself that if I was nice enough and smart enough and worked hard enough, everything would turn out exactly the way I wanted it to. As a young adult and even into my thirties, I would have denied this, of course. I would have said, "Life is a mystery and a risk and you never know what might happen." But I would have been lying, even to myself. I was still trying desperately to prove my childish belief that if you are good and work hard, you'll hit every goal you dream you'll hit by your own personal deadline, with grace and ease and whipped cream on top. Whenever that didn't happen, I blamed myself, and anyone else who appeared to be responsible. I spent a lot of my time sad and bitter because, contrary to what I may have assumed, this vast, chaotic, mysterious planet does not spin on its axis merely to please me, or you, or anyone else.

Sitting on the floor with my smudged letters, I thought of that Ernest Hemingway line from *A Farewell to Arms*: "The world breaks everyone and afterward many are strong at the broken places." I wrote it down, twice: *The world breaks everyone and afterward many are strong at the broken places.*

Sometimes, our lives don't turn out as we hoped they might, and it's okay to adjust our plans without dismissing ourselves as failures. Sometimes, devastatingly awful things happen to great people, and it doesn't mean they did something wrong or that circumstances arranged themselves into a deliberate assault on their happiness. When you trust people, they often disappoint you, but that doesn't mean love is hopeless. And when the economy tanks and your industry becomes a sick shade of its former self, it's not personal, it just means you have to be creative and work within the constraints of the new reality. There is nothing wrong with being sad or angry and grieving whatever losses are lined up for us to grieve along our particular path of life. We have to do that. But we can only live fully and walk toward a better future when we're free of bitterness and finished once and for all with the futile habit of wishing the past were different.

I thought back to the conversation I had with Azim, when he told me about how someone asked him whether, if he could turn back the clock and bring back his son, he would do it. "Of course I would want Tariq back," he told me. "But if he hadn't died, I wouldn't be doing what I'm doing now."

How did that apply to my own life? If I'd had a plum journalism job, I would never have profiled Azim for a magazine and I wouldn't be writing this book. If things had worked out with any of my exes, I wouldn't have the fulfilling relationship I have with Anthony. Seeing all of this clearly, I laughed. Then I cried some more. I promised myself that I would never again take myself so seriously or punish myself or others so severely when things didn't turn out the way I wanted them to. And when I slipped up, as I likely would, I promised to forgive myself again.

I rose and walked with my folded letters to the nearest fireplace. I passed a boy sitting on the ground, hands covering his face, while a friend laid a hand on his back. On my left, a girl with a high-swept bun wept on the shoulder of an older woman. I neared the flames and felt their heat press against my face and hands. Stepping into it, I breathed in the warmth and felt it spread through me. I felt the fierce sense of awe and belonging that I always found in nature and its elements. Leaning forward, I dropped my letters into the fire and watched as the white paper dissolved into orange-yellow streams of light.

Levels of Forgiveness

As I began writing about what I'd learned in my year of travel and research, friends and colleagues reacted in various ways when they found out I was writing about forgiveness. Many asked me if forgiveness meant forgoing legal action, excusing damaging behavior, or letting yourself be mistreated. No wonder so many people, including me, associated forgiveness with weakness. I would explain that no, giving up resentment does not rule out justice or self-protection. And as for being weak, I'd come to understand what Gandhi said about forgiveness. He described it as "the ornament of the brave." It takes courage and great strength to forgive. It might even be the hardest thing you ever do, but it will bring a new sense of liberation that nothing else could ever touch.

Another common misconception about forgiveness concerns how

long it takes. "Is it a one-time thing?" people would ask me. "Do you do it and then it's done?" There's no one answer to this, of course, since the process varies from person to person. But most of those I profiled indicated that far from being a single, earth-shattering accomplishment with an end point, forgiveness is more like a regular habit or practice, like being optimistic or mindful or patient. Sure, when it comes to forgiving someone for spilling their coffee on you at Starbucks, it might be over in a moment. But for the bone-rattling, soul-injuring wounds for which forgiveness is most important, it is a process that ebbs and flows, one that may feel complete one day and begin yet again the next.

One especially thorny issue for me—and for many others, I discovered—was this: Does forgiveness require reconciliation? And does it imply that you must feel warm and fuzzy and loving toward your former enemy? Researchers and therapists are divided on this, with some saying that neutrality is sufficient, while others argue that forgiving must literally mean loving your enemies. I concluded that from a certain perspective, both views are true. Neutrality, after all, allows someone to live peacefully, and it allows the forgiver to live peacefully, too. I would even argue that neutrality is its own category of love. When you're neutral, you're doing no harm and you're letting someone be. And letting someone be, free of your judgments or blame or rage, implies a certain level of respect, an acceptance that that person, whoever she may be and whatever she may have done, is worthy of being here, on this brutal and beautiful planet, just like you are. Isn't that love?

Accepting someone's intrinsic human worthiness, even when you may not like the person or want to spend holidays with him, certainly dovetails with the concept of agape, the type of love that in ancient Greek referred to a love extended to all people, whether strangers or family members. The Greek word was translated into Latin as *caritas*, the origin of the English word "charity." In Buddhism, the idea of *metta*, or "universal loving-kindness," is similar to agape.

For practical purposes, I suggest thinking about forgiveness as containing levels. When I was in Rwanda, listening to Jean-Baptiste talk about extending love to the man who killed his mother, I was awed. But I also wondered: Is it necessary for everyone to take this process so far? To not only forgive but also reconcile and even befriend an offender? Sam, the family friend and psychologist I'd talked to at the start of this project, had told me that he didn't think people should force forgiveness or even attempt it if they're not ready, much less reach out to whomever hurt them to reconcile. But he also said something that kept echoing in my mind as Truth the deeper I got into my research. The Jewish philosopher Maimonides said there were levels of giving. Well, so it is with forgiveness. The highest level of forgiveness just might be reconciliation, and even the kind of love one feels for a family member or cherished friend.

To Jean-Baptiste, forgiving merely as a gift to yourself, a way to unburden yourself of pain, is a lower level of forgiveness. "It keeps you separated in two worlds," he told me. "I live in my world and you live in yours, with a wall between. True forgiveness means restoring relationship, recognizing that it is one world. That is what allows us to pool resources and work together. Until we can all recognize our common humanity, not live as right and wrong or black and white or Rwandan and Congolese, but as humans who share so much—there will not be peace. Forgiveness is a personal process. It's heart to heart, person to person. But on a broader global level, you can't have reconciliation without forgiveness."

Six months after I burned my letters in the fire at the mountain retreat, Anthony and I took a trip to La Jolla for his birthday. My mother, who lives in New Mexico, was meeting us there since we were staying with her sister, my aunt, whom she often visits. Anthony was looking forward to surfing and I was looking forward to walking on the beach. The second morning we were there, my mom and I played tennis, and I noticed that I was feeling extremely nauseated. I'd felt the same way the day before, on the way to the airport, and figured it was just car sickness. Now I was concerned. I never felt sick.

Suddenly, I thought about the diaphragm I'd recently purchased. I'd wanted to be hormone-free after fifteen years on the birth control pill, just to make sure everything was working the way it should in case we wanted to start a family in the next couple of years. That was a nice thought, but the round piece of rubber had remained in its plastic pink box for 98 percent of the time it had spent in our apartment. I should take a pregnancy test, I thought, so I could at least rule that out and then see the doctor to find out what was really going on. An ulcer, maybe? After tennis I went to the store and bought a test with two sticks. Back at my aunt's house, the first one came out positive. No way. I gave it another try. The second one came out positive, too, even brighter than the first. *My God.* I was elated. I was shocked. I was scared. I was excited. All at once. I decided not to tell Anthony, since this was supposed to be a trip in honor of him and his birthday. What if he was upset? Also, I told myself that I'd probably get my period any moment, so why create needless drama?

A few hours later, Anthony returned from surfing and we got ready for dinner. We were meeting my aunt Judy, my mother, and my cousin Sebastien at the house and then heading down to our favorite restaurant, Barbarella's, near the beach. When everyone arrived, Anthony said, "Let's take some pictures outside, by the view." Thinking nothing of it, I walked out the screen door into the backyard, admiring the sunset sweeping over the ocean. Anthony and I posed while my mother and cousin took pictures. Then Anthony turned to me. "Megan, will you marry me?"

I froze. A full minute of silence seemed to pass. "Is this for real?" I blurted. We'd been discussing houses and babies and marriage, but he'd thrown me off by making comments about how he thought finding a house should take precedent over a wedding. Yet here he was, kneeling on the patio and holding a blue box.

"Yes, it's for real," he laughed. "So?"

"Yes, of course," I said, still incredulous. Surprises, just like secrets, were not common in my family, since we basically tell each other everything.

Anthony opened the box to reveal three rings. All were family heirlooms. I immediately grabbed the most delicate, understated one, a retro forties-style band with a diamond in a square setting. It turned out to have belonged to my great-grandmother Blanche, whom I loved as a child and whose story I prized as a tale of perseverance and faith. She was the one who'd purportedly recovered from the Spanish influenza pandemic of 1918 after discovering the power of prayer.

We all enjoyed a celebratory dinner at Barbarella's, where I found out that months earlier, while I was out of town, Anthony drove down to New Mexico from Denver to ask for my father's blessing in person. (He tried to coordinate a meeting with my mom, too, but she was out of town so he called her instead.) His ruse was that he wanted my dad and my stepmother to meet him in Santa Fe to check out a painting that he'd fallen in love with the last time we were there. It was a scene of charging Native American warriors, blazing forward in a dynamic wash of reds and blues, their weapons held high. It wasn't until the three of them were standing before the painting, my father suggesting that they "go splitsies" on it, that Anthony explained why he was really there. "My jaw just dropped," my dad would tell me later. "I completely thought it was all about the painting—I must be the daftest dad in the world!"

I was shocked that my close-knit family managed to keep the proposal plans under wraps. Somehow, I hid my own secret throughout dinner, too, barely touching the champagne. Anthony ended up pulling the news out of me the following morning while we were walking down the hill to the beach. Ever in tune with my peculiar moods and idiosyncrasies, he said, "Are you okay? What is going on? You are acting so weird."

I took a deep breath. "Well, I took a pregnancy test," I said, marveling at my own words as they came out, "and it was positive."

"Really? Wow." He stopped walking. Surprise turned to joy. He hugged and kissed me. "I had a feeling, actually. When you said you were sick to your stomach."

Over the following days, we felt alternately shocked, excited, and terrified. When we got home we scheduled doctor's appointments, spent hours talking about money and spending habits, and decided to get legally married now and plan a wedding celebration for two years later, when our child would be eighteen months old. I began looking for full-time jobs in digital content marketing, which I'd started doing a year earlier on a contract basis to pay my bills. I had mixed feelings about taking a job that was not journalism, but for the first time in my life, my priorities were no longer just about myself and my own needs and wants. I was looking forward to being able to help provide for our family, and to learning a new, growing business. During this time, sometimes when I watched Anthony sleeping before I turned out the light, I'd find myself moved to tears with gratitude.

One weekend we took a road trip to New Mexico to look at wedding spots. As we were driving down the hill from Santa Fe toward Albuquerque, I had a flood of memories, scenes and images I hadn't thought about in decades. One was skiing with a guy named Rich, a racer for the Santa Fe Ski Team who was two years my senior. We dated for a while, and my sophomore year he asked me to go to prom with him in Santa Fe. (My parents said no, as it was an hour away and they didn't want me staying the night there.) The next image was the events sign in the driveway of my high school. On one particular fall morning, its black, block letters read, "Megan, will you go to homecoming with me?" It was from Oscar, a kind-hearted senior I knew through mutual friends. I went to that one, a double date with Oscar's best friend and his longtime girlfriend, and we had a great time.

The funny thing is, these were old, dusty, hazy memories. They weren't half as clear, half as well-worn and well-used, as the other track of memories: getting stood up for prom by a tennis player named Ollie the following year and going stag with a friend and her boyfriend, humiliated and mascara-streaked; standing around at parties feeling awkward and out of place; the boyfriend in college who broke up with me and called me selfish; my first "real" love who broke my heart in my early twenties. All of those things happened, but despite the fact that lots of other, more positive things also happened, the awful memories were the ones that formed the dominant narrative of my romantic life.

As I sat there in the passenger seat of Anthony's Honda Accord, the lights of my hometown blinking into view up ahead, I thought of Dr. Fred

Luskin of the Stanford Forgiveness Project and his theory of the grievance story. This was certainly one of mine. I'd convinced myself that the men I wanted always left me, and that I couldn't ever have what I wanted in love. And that storyline made me cold and aloof, or else embarrassingly needy. The truth was, I dated people who weren't the right match, just like most other people do until they find the right one and get married. But when Mike turned out not to be "the one," my "I'm a victim" alarm went off. I had blocked out those good memories about Rich, and Oscar, and a whole host of other pleasant relationships I'd had in my twenties, because they didn't fit my victim story, just like the people I interviewed earlier in the book blocked out the good memories of their parents until they began to forgive them. I felt a rush of gratitude. I was no longer the aloof and fearful girl, the one who thought she'd never find companionship. I was no longer bitter.

Gratitude and forgiveness, I realized, have a symbiotic relationship—they feed and strengthen each other. It seemed so simple. Almost too simple. But there it was. The more you focus on the warm memories and appreciate them, the less power the painful ones have. And the more you look for what you like in people, the less you blame them for your own disappointments or failings. I made a mental note to make gratitude not just a habit in my own life, but in my family's. We could make gratitude lists weekly or nightly before bed. I thought about the other practices I would take with me into the future: remaining vigilant about grievance stories and dismantling them as much as I could, examining my own role in problematic situations when tempted to place all of the blame on someone else, practicing empathetic listening with others and with myself, doing mindful meditation daily, having the courage to share my feelings with Anthony without blaming him for them, and writing letters of forgiveness to people against whom I hold grudges, including myself.

A few days later, I awoke to a rainy Colorado morning—a rare gift. I was sixteen weeks pregnant and just starting to show. A day earlier, I'd accepted a new job at a digital marketing firm, and I was relieved that they were supportive of my pregnancy, even though I would go on leave just four months after starting work. It wasn't journalism, but I would be writing, learning a dynamic, cutting-edge business and making the first decent salary of my life. I fastened Stella's harness, put on my favorite rain jacket, and headed out the door and down the steps. As we walked onto the bike path that runs along the Platte River, the rain began falling hard. It made everything greener and slicker and brighter—the grassy hill on our left, the cottonwood trees along the river, the brilliant yellow and purple wildflowers peeking out from the reeds. And the gray-brown river, swollen with rain, rushed past it all. Tumbling and churning forward, always forward.

I led Stella with one hand and placed the other on my swelling belly. Then I looked up at the gray sky and the water that poured from it. As my tears mixed with the rain and streamed down my cheeks, I said, simply, "Thank you."

ACKNOWLEDGMENTS

Thank you to Azim Khamisa, whose courage and tenacity first led me to this exploration of forgiveness, and whose gentle encouragement helped me along the way. Thank you to Jay Heinrichs, the magazine guru and guardian angel who flew into my life and helped me see that this could be a book. He provided invaluable insight, inspiration, and editing, and he and his wife, Dorothy, generously hosted me at their wonderful home in the New Hampshire woods while I bushwhacked my way through thickets of thought and research and philosophy.

Thank you to Caroline Sutton, my editor at Avery, who took a chance on me and my crazy adventure, and provided thoughtful edits throughout. Thank you to Brittney Ross at Avery, for her feedback and for expertly ushering the book through production, and thank you to Lavina Lee for her careful copyediting. Thank you to my intrepid, supportive agent, Larry Weissman, and to his partner-in-crime Sascha Alper, for finding a home for this book and for nourishing the project as it developed.

Thank you to my writer friends, Emily Brady, Catherine Elton, and Jesse Hyde, for reading drafts and providing encouragement, insight, and laughter, and thank you to author and writing teacher Lisa Jones and our troupe of lady-writers, who offered up their hearts every time we sat down to write together.

Thank you to my mother, Dr. Gail Carr Feldman, for providing a constant and generous stream of encouragement, proofreading, and psychological insight. Thank you to my father, Dr. Bruce Feldman, for always believing that I can do what I set my mind to and supporting me even as I flail like a five-year-old learning to ski, and thank you to my sister, Niki Feldman, for her love, laughter, and top-notch massages.

To my husband, Anthony Bettencourt, thank you for coming into my life when you did, thank you for loving me so thoroughly and unreservedly and thank you for supporting my work and always helping me to laugh and take myself less seriously. I love you. To our son, Santiago Wolf Bettencourt, thank you for choosing me to be your mother and for stretching my mind and heart in so many ways already, when your journey on this earth has scarcely just begun.

I am grateful to all of the friends who provided indispensable love, encouragement, and good times while I reported and wrote this book, particularly Stephany Arroyo Jones, Lara Mullin Morgan, Leslee Balten, Rachael Tracy, Mary Butler Harpin, Jim Rubin, and Courtney Tudi. Thank you to my luminous, enterprising, and ever-supportive "Lunar Ladies," Jami Duffy and Emily Andrews, for magical monthly conversations that combine spiritual, emotional, and intellectual sustenance to create a badass brew that makes me feel unstoppable. And for wisdom, guidance, and companionship, I thank my friend and former roommate Rachel Davis. I am beyond grateful for my "Denver family."

Thank you to all of the generous souls who helped make my travels possible by providing donations and contacts, especially Dr. Edward and Jane Feldman, Kateri Garcia and Drew Johnson, Chris Zook, Sandy Buffet, Jamie Van Leeuwen, Judy DePhillips, Jina Moore, Lars Christian Hvidberg, Marina Cantacuzino, Solange Impano, Sara Hakansson, and Annie O'Brien. And for his guidance and cheering from afar, I thank author and professor Stephen Fried.

Thank you to the incredible TEDx Boulder team and my fellow 2014 speakers, whose camaraderie and insight enabled me to share some of my findings and my story with a crowd of two thousand people without passing out or humiliating myself.

Finally, an eternal thank-you to the bright shining stars who were brave and generous enough to share their stories with me so that I could share them with others. Without their courage, this book would not have been possible. I thank everyone who took time to sit down and talk to me, whether to share an experience that contributed to the heart of this book, or to explain the research that provided its intellectual backbone. Thank you also to the academic researchers whose hard work informed my conclusions. I am forever grateful.

APPENDIX

Forgiveness Practices

I. Noticing

1. Sit down in a quiet, private place and set aside about half an hour.
2. Think for a moment about someone whom you've been blaming. When you think of feeling angry or resentful, who comes to mind?
3. Write down what happened. All of it. Don't hold back or self-edit, just let it flow. What did they do and say? What did you do and say?
4. How did you feel when it happened? How do you feel when you think about it now?
5. If you feel angry or resentful, where do you notice the sensations in your body? What sensations do you feel?
6. What thoughts go through your mind?
7. How have you dealt with your anger, and how have you avoided dealing with it?
8. How does your anger, frustration, or resentment influence your daily life currently?
9. Consider how it might be helpful if you were to forgive this person. How would you feel? What would you think? Would it free up energy to direct at more meaningful and productive pursuits? Would you be more present in every moment? What might that be like? What do you think it might make possible in your life?
10. Set the intention to forgive. Write, "I, _____, intend to forgive _____." Then date it.
11. Over the following days and weeks, make a habit of noticing when and how your anger toward this person comes up. Just be aware of it. How does it influence your day? Your mood? Also make a habit of thinking about forgiving the person. How might that work? What might it entail? Allow yourself to consider how your life might be different if you forgave. And then, without forcing anything, just pay attention and see what happens.

II. Finding the Impersonal in the Hurt

Developed by Dr. Fred Luskin of the Stanford Forgiveness Project, this exercise entails examining what was personal about a painful event, and what was not. You can't, of course, get into an offender's head, but you can use your powers of observation, your intuition, and your knowledge of human nature to speculate about this.

1. What was personal about the hurtful action? Was the person doing it intentionally to hurt you? (Usually there are both personal and impersonal aspects to an offense.)
2. What was impersonal about the action? What drove or compelled the person to

take the hurtful action, do you think? What were the circumstances of the action? What was the person's state of mind at the time?

III. Developing Empathy

You may have very little in common with whoever hurt you. And yet, that person is human, just as you are. Use what you know about the person to try to step into his shoes for a moment.

1. What is this person's childhood background? Did he grow up loved and adored? Excluded and rejected? Somewhere in between?
2. What are the factors that may have contributed to this person hurting you? Which circumstances led to the act? They could be mental, emotional, physical, or financial.
3. Have you ever been in a similar situation as this person? If so, what was it and how did you react? If not, how do you think you might react?
4. Take a moment to imagine the offender as an infant. Then a young child. If you actually have a photo of the person at these ages, look at it. Consider the negative attributes you associate with this person (incompetent, selfish, lazy, devious, violent, etc.). Was she that way when she was born? Surely, like any infant at birth this person was innocent. If at some point she changed, what may have happened to change her?
5. Write this series of statements in your journal and see if they ring true about the person who hurt you: Just like me, this person wants to avoid pain. Just like me, this person wants to be happy. Just like me, this person has been hurt. Just like me, this person is doing his/her best.

IV. Examining Your Grievance Story

Also based on the work of Dr. Luskin, this exercise requires you to take a hard look at the narrative that you've constructed about a chief complaint in your life.

1. What is your chief grievance or complaint about this topic or person (your parent, your spouse, the colleague you'd love to replace if you could, etc.)?
2. What exactly do you know to be true about that story? (Often we assume why someone behaves the way they do, only to realize that we're relying on our own made-up explanation or interpretation.)
3. Can you do some investigation into this explanation, perhaps even ask the person? If the grievance story is more about a situation than a person, do some thinking outside the box: If you believe you've lost your job because your boss hates you, test the hypothesis. What hard evidence do you have? When you run the situation by people you trust, what do they think about it? Do they share your interpretation or do they raise other possibilities?
4. What might you be taking personally that is actually not personal?

5.   How many other people have suffered a similar painful experience? Are you totally alone, or is this something that has happened to others?
6.   With a recurring complaint or grievance story, we usually continually collect evidence that supports the storyline (such as focusing more on the times lovers have left you than on the times you did the leaving, or on the times your dad forgot to show up to baseball games instead of the times he remembered). What evidence, which experiences and memories and observations, are also true, but don't contribute to your grievance story? When you survey these bits of evidence, what can you conclude?

V. Clearing Away the Past

As you work through these exercises, you will likely have emotions surface that you haven't explored in a long time. You may find yourself agitated and angry. Your resentment may get worse before it gets better. That's normal. Take some time to do this twenty-minute exercise if and when you feel upset, stressed, or unfocused.

1.   Set a timer for twenty minutes.
2.   In a notebook with a pen (preferably not on a computer), write about whatever is on your mind. Don't think, just write. Allow whatever is on your mind to spill out, and don't censor or plan or analyze.
3.   If emotions surface, write about that. If you can't think what to write next, write that. Just don't stop until the timer goes off.
4.   If you do this when upset or agitated, you should feel relieved after twenty minutes. If you don't, if there's still more to dump, write for an additional ten minutes.
5.   When you're finished, take a deep breath. Then think about your intention to forgive, and your larger intentions for your life. Write them down and really let yourself focus on those for a moment before you go about your day.

VI. What Role Did You Play?

Usually, except for in cases of child abuse and other victimization situations which feature a major power differential, we play some sort of role in a hurtful situation (even when we place full blame on the other person).

1.   What was your role, if any, in the hurtful situation you're working on forgiving?
2.   Be honest with yourself. Was there something you did that contributed to the outcome, or something you could have done to avoid the hurtful outcome? Did you ignore some inner knowing, for instance, whether about yourself, the other person, or the situation?
3.   What can you learn from this moving forward?

VII. Practicing Self-Compassion

As you become more aware of your own role in a painful situation or outcome, it's natural to become upset or to blame yourself. It's important to generate your capacity for self-compassion during this time, and as you move ahead.

1. Describe the factors that led to your actions. Circumstances, state of mind, mood, etc.
2. If a close friend had felt, thought, and acted the same way as you did, what would you tell that friend?
3. Remind yourself that you are just as worthy of compassion as anyone else, and that learning requires making mistakes. Taking responsibility for your actions is not the same as feeling bad and ashamed. The first requires courage and honor, the second only makes you small and sad.

VIII. From Victim to Hero

It's much more empowering—and productive—to cast ourselves as the hero of our own story, as opposed to the victim.

1. How have you seen yourself as a victim?
2. How has that made you feel? How has that influenced your behavior?
3. In the situation that you felt the victim, what did you learn from it? Were there any productive results that came out of that situation, painful as it was? Lessons? Positive character traits? New skills or abilities? New knowledge or awareness? How has that painful experience made you who you are today?
4. Rewrite your victim narrative, this time casting yourself as the hero.

IX. Living Well Is the Best Revenge

George Herbert, the English poet generally credited with coining this phrase, was onto something. Instead of wasting valuable time and energy on anger or resentment over something that happened in the past, why not direct it toward building the future that we want?

1. Schedule regular brainstorming sessions about how you want your life to look, and what you want to experience. Sometimes it helps to tackle each life area, including family, love relationship, career, finances, living situation, and health. What would "living well" entail in each of those areas? If you're not already fulfilled in each area, what actions can you take now and in the near future to ensure that you will be?
2. What gives your life meaning and purpose? Family and friends? Helping others? Intellectual or athletic pursuits? If you don't have a clear answer to this question, set aside time each week to brainstorm about it, and then jot down and schedule actions you can take to ensure that you're living a purpose-filled life.

3.   Keep a gratitude list. Daily or weekly, list the things in your life, or in the world at large, for which you are grateful.

X. Seeking Redemption

Our capacity for forgiveness entails seeking it, as well as granting it. And just as granting forgiveness takes practice, so does seeking it.

1.   Think about someone you've hurt or disappointed in the past. Have you apologized? If so, was the apology effective?
2.   Write down what you did (or tell a trusted confidante if you prefer). What was the result of your actions? How did it impact the other person/people? How do you feel about it now?
3.   Write the person a letter of apology, following the guidelines for a true apology in chapter 3. Make sure you include the core four components: acknowledging the offense, giving an authentic explanation (not an excuse), expressing remorse, and providing some sort of reparation. Is there something you can do to make amends, whether physically fixing something, repaying a debt, or providing a service?
4.   Change the hurtful behavior, or at least, as Azim Khamisa counsels in his workshops, stop at least one person from repeating that hurtful act. Get whatever support you need to maintain your promise (counseling, someone to hold you accountable, a recovery program, etc.).

XI. Cultivating Mindfulness

1.   Sit down in a comfortable, private place.
2.   Set an alarm for twenty minutes.
3.   Inhale and exhale deeply, and as you do, feel yourself relax.
4.   Focus on your breath. As thoughts come and go, let them arise and pass by. Refrain from "going with the content" or resisting them. Let them pass as waves in the sea, always returning to your breath.
5.   As you go through your day afterward, practice being mindful and present. This means to focus intensely on the present moment, not the content of your thoughts. When you're eating, fully give your attention to the taste and texture of the food, to the process of chewing. When you're talking with someone, completely focus on that person. Same with your work, or your workout, or anything else. As thoughts arise as possible distractions, just notice them and allow them to pass, then return your focus to the moment.

XII. The Forgiveness Ceremony

Just as the participants and mentors in Colorado Youth at Risk do each year at their retreat, write two letters. In the first, forgive someone. In the second, forgive yourself. If you feel it would be empowering, read your letters to a trusted confidante, or aloud to yourself. Then burn the letters, using a fire-safe bowl or fireplace. Imagine all of the anger, resentment, and pain from the past burning away with the paper.

XIII. Implementing Restorative Practices in Your Community

Restorative circles and conferences can be powerful tools for facilitating the seeking and granting of forgiveness—and brokering consensus—when used in families, schools, and communities. For resources designed for educators or parents interested in using restorative circles in classrooms or family settings, visit the Center for Restorative Process based in Santa Rosa, California (www.centerforrestorativeprocess.com/), and view guides for everything from get-to-know-you circles to conflict-resolution circles (see the "Teaching Restorative Practices with Classroom Circles" guide, available as a PDF, at www.healthiersf.org). Here's a basic restorative script from the International Institute for Restorative Practices (http://store.iirp.edu/restorative-justice-conferencing-real-justice -the-conferencing-handbook/), which can be adapted for various settings. The following example is to be used with an offender who has admitted committing a certain action, and it includes the offender and victim, plus supporters for both:

1. Preamble

"Thank you all for attending. Your presence will help us deal with the matter that has brought us together. This is an opportunity for all of you to be involved in repairing the harm that has been done.

"This conference will focus on an incident which happened. [State the date, place, and nature of offense without elaborating.] It is important to understand that we will focus on what [offender name/s] did and how that behavior has affected others. We are not here to decide whether [offender name/s] is/are good or bad. We want to explore in what way people have been affected and hopefully work toward repairing the harm that has resulted. Does everyone understand this?

"[Offender name/s] has/have admitted his/her/their part in the incident."

Say to offender/s: "I must tell you that you do not have to participate in this conference and are free to leave at any time, as is anyone else. If you do leave, the matter may be referred to court/handled by the school disciplinary policy/handled in another way.

"This matter, however, may be finalized if you participate in a positive manner and comply with the conference agreement."

Say to offender/s: "Do you understand?"

2. Offender/s

"We'll start with (one of offenders' names)."

If there is more than one offender, have each respond to all of the following questions.

- "What happened?"
- "What were you thinking about at the time?"
- "What have you thought about since the incident?"
- "Who do you think has been affected by your actions?"
- "How have they been affected?"

3. Victim/s

If there is more than one victim, have each respond to all of the following questions.

- "What was your reaction at the time of the incident?"
- "How do you feel about what happened?"
- "What has been the hardest thing for you?"
- "How did your family and friends react when they heard about the incident?"

4. Victim Supporters

Have each respond to all of the following questions.

- "What did you think when you heard about the incident?"
- "How do you feel about what happened?"
- "What has been the hardest thing for you?"
- "What do you think are the main issues?"

5. Offender Supporters

To parent/caregiver ask: "This has been difficult for you, hasn't it? Would you like to tell us about it?"
    Have each respond to all of the following questions.

- "What did you think when you heard about the incident?"
- "How do you feel about what happened?"
- "What has been the hardest thing for you?"
- "What do you think are the main issues?"

6. Offender/s

Ask the offender/s: "Is there anything you want to say at this time?"

7. Reaching an Agreement

Ask the victim/s: "What would you like from today's conference?"
    Ask the offender/s to respond.

At this point, the participants discuss what should be in the final agreement. Solicit comments from participants.

It is important that you ask the offender/s to respond to each suggestion before the group moves to the next suggestion, asking, "What do you think about that?" Then determine that the offender/s agree/s before moving on. Allow for negotiation.

As the agreement develops, clarify each item and make the written document as specific as possible, including details, deadlines, and follow-up arrangements.

As you sense that the agreement discussion is drawing to a close, say to the participants: "Before I prepare the written agreement, I'd like to make sure that I have accurately recorded what has been decided."

Read the items in the agreement aloud and look to the participants for acknowledgment. Make any necessary corrections.

8. Closing the Conference

"Before I formally close this conference, I would like to provide everyone with a final opportunity to speak. Is there anything anyone wants to say?"

Allow for participants to respond and when they are done, say:

"Thank you for your contributions in dealing with this difficult matter. Congratulations on the way you have worked through the issues. Please help yourselves to some refreshments while I prepare the agreement."

Allow participants ample time to have refreshments and interact. The informal period after the formal conference is very important.

NOTES

Chapter Two: The Science: Is Forgiveness Natural, and Does It Provide Health Benefits?

35 **Enright's forgiveness model has four parts:** Robert Enright, *The Forgiving Life: A Pathway to Overcoming Resentment and Creating a Legacy of Love* (American Psychological Association, 2012), appendices A, D.

36 **people who forgive more readily have fewer coronary heart problems than those who hold grudges:** Sonja Lyubomirsky, *The How of Happiness: A Scientific Approach to Getting the Life You Want* (New York: Penguin Group, 2007).

37 **concluding in multiple studies that forgiveness elevates mood and increases optimism, while not forgiving is positively correlated with depression, anxiety, and hostility:** Sonja Lyubomirsky, *The How of Happiness: A Scientific Approach to Getting the Life You Want* (New York: Penguin Group, 2007), 173; Felix Neto and Etienne Mullet, "Personality, Self-Esteem, and Self-Construal as Correlates of Forgivingness," *European Journal of Personality* 18 (2004): 15–30, doi: 10.1002/per.500.

42 **a group of primatologists discovered that Japanese macaques that were attacked by a higher-up would leave the aggressor alone but attack one of the offender's younger family members in retaliation:** Michael McCullough, *Beyond Revenge* (San Francisco: Wiley, 2008), 86.

45 **Even nonprimates use such practices to reconcile:** Gabriele Schino, "Beyond the Primates—Expanding the Reconciliation Horizon," in *Natural Conflict Resolution*, ed. Filippo Aureli and Frans de Waal (Berkeley: University of California Press, 2000), 225–242.

45 **several studies on children show they have a conciliatory tendency of around .40 on a scale of 0 to 1, which is similar to chimpanzees:** Michael McCullough, *Beyond Revenge* (San Francisco: Wiley, 2008), 120–121.

47 **the more empathy someone experiences toward a transgressor, the more difficult it is to remain vengeful toward that person:** Michael McCullough, Kenneth Rachal, and Everett Worthington Jr., "Interpersonal Forgiving in Close

Relationships," *Journal of Personality and Social Psychology* 73, no. 2 (1997): 321–336, doi: 10.1037/0022-3514.73.2.321.

47   **children of different ethnicities and social classes are less likely to argue or shun one another when engaged in cooperative projects at school:** Robert Slavin, "Synthesis of Research on Cooperative Learning," *Educational Leadership* 48, no. 5 (1991): 71–81.

47   **peacemaking efforts such as apologies, offers of compensation, and owning up to one's responsibility increase forgiveness:** Michael E. McCullough et al., "Conciliatory Gestures Promote Forgiveness and Reduce Anger in Humans," *Proceedings of the National Academy of Sciences* 111, no. 30 (2014): 11211—11216, doi: 10.1073/pnas.1405072111.

48   **he found that the annual homicide rate in England went from between 4 and 100 homicides per 100,000 people in the Middle Ages to around 0.8 per 100,000 people in the 1950s:** Steven Pinker, *The Better Angels of Our Nature* (New York: Penguin, 2011), 62.

Chapter Three: Making Amends: The Role of Redemption

52   **it's easier to forgive someone who has apologized and made an effort to repair the damage he or she caused:** D. L. Davidson and Gregory Jurkovic, "Forgiveness and Narcissism: Consistency in Experience Across Real and Hypothetical Hurt Situations" (paper presented at the National Convention on Forgiving, Kansas City, Missouri, April 1993); Robert Enright, Maria Santos, and Radhi Al-Mabuk, "The Adolescent as Forgiver," *Journal of Adolescence* 12 (1989): 95–110. doi: 10.1016/0140-1971(89)90092-4; Shih-Tseng Tina Huang, "Cross Cultural and Real-Life Validations of the Theory of Forgiveness in Taiwan, The Republic of China" (PhD diss., University of Wisconsin–Madison, 1990); Bernard Weiner et al., "Public Confession and Forgiveness," *Journal of Personality* 59 (1991): 281–312. doi: 10.1111/j.1467-6494.1991.tb00777.x.

52   **After all, peer-reviewed studies estimate the programs' value:** Lance, Dodes, and Zachary Dodes, "The Pseudo-science of Alcoholics Anonymous: There's a Better Way to Treat Addiction," Salon.com, March 23, 2014, http://www.salon.com/2014/03/23/the_pseudo_science_of_alcoholics_anonymous_theres_a_better_way_to_treat_addiction/.

64   **Remarks such as "I'm sorry you were hurt" made people less inclined to settle than if they received no apology at all:** Jennifer Robbennolt, "Apologies and Settlement Levers," *Journal of Empirical Legal Studies* 3 (2006): 363–64, doi: 10.1111/j.1740-1461.2006.00072.x.

65   **Those who had admitted their mistakes and sought forgiveness from the wronged party were more likely to feel they had the right to forgive themselves:** Thomas Carpenter, Robert Carlisle, and Jo-Ann Tsang, "Tipping the Scales: Conciliatory Behavior and the Morality of Self-Forgiveness," *Journal of Positive Psychology* 9, no. 5 (2014): 389–401. doi: 10.1080/17439760.2014.910823.

65   **chronic self-blame is correlated with high anxiety, depression, and negative self-esteem:** Julie Hall and Frank Fincham, "Self Forgiveness: The Step-Child of Forgiveness Research," *Journal of Social and Clinical Psychology* 24, no. 5 (2005): 621–637; Julie Hall and Frank Fincham, "The Temporal Course of Forgiveness," *Journal of Social and Clinical Psychology* 27, no. 2 (2008): 174–202.

66   **without self-forgiveness, you're at a higher risk of diseases linked to stress-related inflammation, such as cardiovascular disease and Alzheimer's:** Juliana Breines et al., "Self-Compassion as a Predictor of Interleukin-6 Response to Acute Psychosocial Stress," *Brain, Behavior, and Immunity* 37 (2014): 109-114. doi: 10.1016/j.bbi.2013.11.006.

72   **"That was certainly not our intent, and I offer my sincere apology":** Reed Hastings, "An Explanation and Some Reflections," Netflix Blog. September 18, 2011, http://blog.netflix.com/2011/09/explanation-and-some-reflections.html.

73   **"I couldn't say for sure we'd recover. But I was confident that our best odds were to be very steady and focus on improving the service":** James Stewart, "Netflix Looks Back On Its Near-Death Spiral," *New York Times*, April 26, 2013, http://www.nytimes.com/2013/04/27/business/netflix-looks-back-on-its-near-death-spiral.html.

73   **Netflix had surpassed YouTube as the top online video site, 69 percent of subscribers said they were unlikely to leave the service, and its original content, such as *House of Cards*, was drawing additional customers:** Sam Gusting, "4 Reasons to Be Bullish About Netflix," *Fortune*, April 21, 2014, http://fortune.com/2014/04/21/4-reasons-to-be-bullish-about-netflix/.

73   **Who would trust a company that refused to fix a mistake that was killing its customers for more than a decade, and when it finally admitted wrongdoing, continued to hide the truth?:** Matthew Wald et al., "Highlights From House Hearing on G.M. Defects," *The Lede, New York Times* Blog. April 1, 2014, http://thelede.blogs.nytimes.com/2014/04/01/live-updates-from-house-hearing-on-g-m-defects/.

Chapter Four: A Reckoning of Origins: Forgiving Our Parents

86   **getting stuck in those emotions is similar to being unable to grieve properly:**
Dr. Gail Carr Feldman, *From Crisis to Creativity: Creating a Life of Health and Joy at Any Age, In Spite of Everything* (Bloomington, IN: Abbott Press, 2012).

91   **people who reported ruminating more frequently, thinking thoughts such as "Why do I have problems other people don't have?" when feeling sad, were more likely to have elevated symptoms of depression a year later. . . . She also found that ruminators develop major depression four times as often as nonruminators:** Susan Nolen-Hoeksema and Christopher Davis, "'Thanks for Sharing That': Ruminators and Their Social Support Networks," *Journal of Personality and Social Psychology* 77, no. 4 (1999): 801–814. doi: 10.1037/0022-3514.77.4.801.

91   **adolescent girls who reported high rates of rumination were more likely than their less ruminative peers to have depressive episodes, and that those episodes lasted longer:** John Abela and Benjamin Hankin, "Rumination as a Vulnerability Factor to Depression During the Transition from Early to Middle Adolescence: A Multiwave Longitudinal Study," *Journal of Abnormal Psychology* 120, no. 2 (2011): 259–271, doi:10.1037/a0022796.

93   **In 1997, McCullough and a team of researchers had 239 undergraduate students fill out surveys about a situation in which a friend, relative, or romantic partner had hurt or offended them:** Michael McCullough, Everett Worthington Jr., and Kenneth Rachal, "Interpersonal Forgiving In Close Relationships," *Journal of Personality and Social Psychology* 73, no. 2 (1997): 321–336, doi:10.1037/002 2-3514.73.2.321.

93   **In addition to establishing links between empathy and forgiveness, the study confirmed the finding in multiple studies that forgiveness can be increased through clinical intervention:** Radhi Al-Mabuk, Robert Enright, and Paul Cardis, "Forgiving Education with Parentally Deprived Late Adolescents," *Journal of Moral Education* 24 (1995): 427–444, doi: 10.1080/0305724950240405; Suzanne Freedman and Robert Enright, "Forgiveness as an Intervention with Incest Survivors," *Journal of Consulting and Clinical Psychology* 64 (1996): 983–992; John Hebl and Robert Enright, "Forgiveness as a Psychotherapeutic Goal with Elderly Females," *Psychotherapy* 30 (1993): 658–667, doi: 10.1037/0033-3204.30.4.658; Michael McCullough and Everett Worthington Jr., "Promoting Forgiveness: The Comparison of Two Brief Psychoeducational Interventions with a Waiting-List Control," *Counseling and Values* 40 (1995): 55–68, doi: 10.1002/j.2161-007X.1995.tb00387.x.

94   **the forgiveness group reported a higher willingness to forgive, as well as increased hope and self-esteem and decreased anxiety compared to the control group:** Radhi Al-Mabuk, Robert Enright, and Paul Cardis, "Forgiving Education

with Parentally Deprived Late Adolescents," *Journal of Moral Education* 24 (1995): 427–444, doi: 10.1080/0305724950240405.

98   **the ancient Hawaiians believed that an offense created a state of sin, or *hala*, which was represented metaphorically as a cord binding the offender to the offended. To untangle or untie this cord, they would do a series of purification prayers, or *huikala*:** Valerio Valeri, *Kingship and Sacrifice*, 1st ed. (Chicago: University of Chicago Press, 1985), 41; David Malo, *Hawaiian Antiquities (Moolelo Hawaii)*, 1st ed. (Honolulu: The Museum, 1951), 237.

98   **the most complete translation would read, "Loose the cords of mistakes binding us, as we release the strands we hold of others' guilt," or, alternatively, "Detach the fetters of faults that bind us":** Neil Douglas-Klotz, *Prayers of the Cosmos*, 1st ed. (San Francisco: Harper & Row, 1990); Rocco Errico, *Setting a Trap for God*, 1st ed. (Unity Village, Mo.: Unity Books, 1997).

Chapter Five: The Ecology of Trust: Forgiveness in Intimate Relationships

109   **That dovetails with what researcher David Fenell discovered when he interviewed 147 reportedly happy couples married for more than twenty years:** David Fenell, "Characteristics Of Long-Term First Marriages," *Journal of Mental Health Counseling* 51, no. 4 (1993): 446–460.

115   **research shows that couples committed to overcoming infidelity have just as good a chance as other struggling couples to overcome the past . . . they usually start therapy with lower happiness levels than other struggling couples, most finish with just as high a level of relationship satisfaction:** John Gottman, *What Makes Love Last?: How to Build Trust and Avoid Betrayal* (New York: Simon & Schuster 2012), 146–147; David Atkins et al., "Infidelity and Behavioral Couple Therapy: Optimism in the Face of Betrayal," *Journal of Consulting and Clinical Psychology* 73, no. 1 (2005): 144–150, doi:10.1037/0022-006x.73.1.144.

115   **Estimates on infidelity in the United States place males at a higher likelihood of cheating, but women have been catching up in recent decades, reporting having affairs at an increasing rate, most likely because the sexual revolution brought equal opportunity to meet other partners outside of the home:** Emily Brown, *Patterns of Infidelity and Their Treatment*, 1st ed. (New York, N.Y.: Brunner/Mazel, 1991), 1–13.

116   **Cheating is usually the end result of a chain reaction of behavior that erodes trust and closeness:** John Gottman, *What Makes Love Last?: How to Build Trust and Avoid Betrayal* (New York: Simon & Schuster 2012), 43.

117   **cheating happens in around 25 percent of marriages:** Adrian Blow and Kelley Hartnett, "Infidelity in Committed Relationships II: A Substantive Review," *Journal of Marital and Family Therapy* 31 (2005): 217-233, doi: 10.1037/0893-3200.21.2.147; Mark Whisman and Douglas Snyder, "Sexual Infidelity in a National Survey of American Women: Differences in Prevalence and Correlates as a Function of Method of Assessment," *Journal of Family Psychology* 21 (2007): 147–154, doi: 10.1111/j.1752-0606.2005.tb01556.x.

119   **self-compassionate people were described as more accepting and less judgmental, respecting their partners' feelings, opinions, and points of view ... more caring, connected, affectionate, and intimate, as well as more willing to discuss relationship problems:** Kristin Neff, *Self-Compassion* (New York: HarperCollins, 2011), 229.

Chapter Six: A Touch of Grace: Forgiveness as a Spiritual (and Secular) Practice

137   **meditating alters the structure and function of the brain:** Richard Davidson and Antoine Lutz, "Buddha's Brain: Neuroplasticity and Meditation," *IEEE Signal Processing Magazine*, January (2008): 171–174, doi: 10.1109/MSP.2007.910429.

137   **Experienced meditators have more gray matter—and thus more ability—in the parts of the brain important for controlling attention, regulating emotion, and making choices based on all the information available:** Britta Hölzel et al., "Mindfulness Practice Leads to Increases in Regional Brain Gray Matter Density," *Psychiatry Research: Neuroimaging* 191, no. 1 (2011): 36–43, doi: 10.1016/j.pscychresns.2010.08.006.

137   **they have less gray matter in the amygdala, which as the brain's fight-or-flight "alarm system" plays a large role in anxiety, stress, and anger:** Philippe Goldin and James Gross, "Effects of Mindfulness-Based Stress Reduction (MBSR) on Emotion Regulation in Social Anxiety Disorder," *Emotion* 10, no. 1 (2010): 83–91, doi: 10.1037/a0018441.

137   **an eight-week mindfulness meditation course increased electronic activity in the left anterior side of the brain—which is linked to positive affect or mood—a boost still evident four months later:** Richard Davidson et al., "Alterations in Brain and Immune Function Produced by Mindfulness Meditation," *Psychosomatic Medicine* 64 (2003): 564-570, doi: 10.1097/01.PSY.0000077505.67574.E3.

138   **post-meditation brain scans showed more activation in the anterior cingulate cortex, ventromedial prefrontal cortex, and anterior insula, parts of the brain involved in executive function and control of worrying:** Fadel Zeidan et al.,

"Neural Correlates of Mindfulness Meditation-Related Anxiety Relief," *Social Cognitive and Affective Neuroscience* 9, no. 6 (2013):751–759, doi: 10.1093/scan/nst041.

138   **simply noticing and labeling our emotions—the mainstay of mindfulness—turns down the amygdala alarm response that triggers negative feelings and adrenaline-fueled reactions:** Matthew Lieberman, "Putting Feelings Into Words Affect Labeling Disrupts Amygdala Activity in Response to Affective Stimuli," *Psychological Science*, 18, no. 5 (2007): 421-428, doi: 10.1111/j.1467-9280.2007.01916.x.

139   **In people who meditate, this area—considered the seat of empathy in the brain—is substantially thicker than in those who don't:** Sara Lazar et al., "Meditation Experience is Associated with Increased Cortical Thickness," *Neuroreport* 16, no. 17 (2005): 1893-18971, doi: 10.1097/01.wnr.0000186598.66243.19.

148   **After the three-day workshop, all of the women reported higher feelings of goodwill, calm, and the ability to forgive:** Frederic Luskin and Byron Bland, "Stanford-Northern Ireland Hope 1 Project," LearningtoForgive.com, October 2000, http://learningtoforgive.com/research/stanford-northern-ireland-hope-1-project/.

Chapter Eight: Chain Reaction: The Institutional Habits That Spread Forgiveness in Schools and Communities

185   **Recent research on the health and mood impacts of generosity confirms that giving to others is good for your health:** Doug Oman, Carl Thoresen, and Kay McMahon, "Volunteerism and Mortality among the Community-Dwelling Elderly," *Journal of Health Psychology* 4 (1999): 301–313, doi: 10.1177/1359105-39900400301; Stephanie Brown et al. "Caregiving Behavior Is Associated with Decreased Mortality Risk," *Psychological Science* 20, no. 4 (2009): 488-494, doi: 10.1111/j.1467-9280.2009.02323.x.; Rachel Piferi and Kathleen Lawler, "Social Support and Ambulatory Blood Pressure: An Examination of Both Receiving and Giving," *International Journal of Psychophysiology* 62, no. 2 (2006): 328–336, doi: 10.1016/j.ijpsycho.2006.06.002.

192   **found that crime victims who participate in conferences with offenders . . . are 23 times as likely as other crime victims to feel that they've received a sincere apology from their offenders, 4 times less likely to experience lingering desire for revenge, and 2.6 times more likely to report forgiving their offenders:** Lawrence Sherman and Heather Strang, *Restorative Justice: The Evidence* (London: The Smith Institute, 2007), http://www.restorativejustice.org/10fulltext/restorative-justice-the-evidence.

Chapter Nine: Living Peace: How Innovative International Programs
Are Setting the Stage for Forgiveness Between Longtime Adversaries

209   **A 2009 study found that merely guiding people to envision a sequence of positive interactions with a member of another group led to more positive attitudes toward that group:** Richard Crisp and Rhiannon Turner, "Can Imagined Interactions Produce Positive Perceptions?: Reducing Prejudice Through Simulated Social Contact," *American Psychologist* 64, no. 4 (2009): 231–240, doi:10.1037/a0014718.

209   **a 2005 study in Sri Lanka found that when Sinhalese and Tamils spent four days together doing educational activities, their attitudes were still more positive a year later compared to a control group:** Deepak Malhotra, "Long-Term Effects of Peace Workshops In Protracted Conflicts," *Journal of Conflict Resolution* 49, no. 6 (2005): 908–924, doi: 10.1177/0022002705281153.

210   **A 2004 study found that Israelis who studied both sides of the Northern Ireland conflict were better able to see the Palestinian perspective:** Jodi Halpern and Harvey M. Weinstein, "Rehumanizing the Other: Empathy and Reconciliation," *Human Rights Quarterly* 26, no. 3 (2004): 561–583. doi:10.1353/hrq.2004.0036.

210   **Rwandan survivors and perpetrators assessed before and after participating in the Gacaca courts suffered great emotional upset and retriggered trauma symptoms while giving and hearing testimony, but they also showed less negative views about each other afterward:** Patrick Kanyangara et al., "Collective Rituals, Emotional Climate and Intergroup Perception: Participation in 'Gacaca' Tribunals and Assimilation of the Rwandan Genocide," *Journal of Social Issues* 63, no. 2 (2007): 387–403, doi: 10.1111/j.1540-4560.2007.00515.x.

210   **when white South Africans learned through testimonies and education about the inhumane practices of the apartheid government, they developed more conciliatory attitudes toward blacks:** James Gibson, "Does Truth Lead to Reconciliation? Testing the Causal Assumptions of the South African Truth and Reconciliation Process," *American Journal of Political Science* 48, no. 2 (2004): 201–217, doi: 10.2307/1519878.

210   **Jews, for instance, were much more likely to forgive Germans for the Holocaust when presented with historical narratives that identified the Nazis as human beings more than merely as Germans:** Michael Wohl and Nyla Branscombe, "Forgiveness and Collective Guilt Assignment to Historical Perpetrator Groups Depend on Level Of Social Category Inclusiveness," *Journal of Personality and Social Psychology* 88, no. 2 (2005): 288–303, doi:10.1037/0022-3514.88.2.288.

211   **Those who had empathetic reactions to the scene they watched showed increased oxytocin levels while those in the control group remained static, and
also proved more generous during the game:** Jorge Barraza and Paul Zak, "Empathy Toward Strangers Triggers Oxytocin Release And Subsequent Generosity,"
Annals of the New York Academy of Sciences 1167, no. 1 (2009): 182–189,
doi:10.1111/j.1749-6632.2009.04504.x.

211   **just as empathy raises oxytocin levels—and generosity—administering doses
of oxytocin can in turn increase people's empathy and generosity, even toward
people who aren't necessarily part of the family or "tribe":** Paul Zak, Angela
Stanton, and Sheila Ahmadi, "Oxytocin Increases Generosity in Humans," *PLoS
One* 11 (2008): e1128, doi:10.1371/journal.pone.0001128.

INDEX